Experiencing
the
Environment

Experiencing
the
Environment

Edited by

Seymour Wapner, Saul B. Cohen, and Bernard Kaplan

Clark University

PLENUM PRESS · NEW YORK AND LONDON

Library of Congress Cataloging in Publication Data

Main entry under title:

Experiencing the environment.

Papers from a conference held by Clark University at the Warren Center, Ashland, Mass., Jan. 7-8, 1975.
Includes bibliographies and index.
1. Environmental psychology—Congresses.
I. Wapner, Seymour, 1917-   II. Cohen, Saul Bernard, III. Kaplan, Bernard, 1925-
BF353.E9   155.9   75-37839
ISBN 0-306-30873-8

Kenneth H. Craik and the publisher gratefully acknowledge permission to reprint material quoted in Chapter IV, "The Personality Research Paradigm in Environmental Psychology."

"Franklin Jones" (p. 58) from Edgar Lee Masters' *Spoon River Anthology* is reprinted by permission of Ellen C. Masters (Mrs. Edgar Lee Masters) and The Macmillan Company.

The extracts (p. 58) from H. Nicolson's *The Development of English Biography* are reprinted by permission of the author's literary estate and the Hogarth Press.

The extract (p. 66) from I. L. Child's "Problems of personality and some relations to anthropology and sociology," which was published in *Psychology: A Study of Science*, Volume 5, edited by S. Kock, is reprinted by permission of McGraw-Hill Book Company.

The extract (p. 69) from R. G. Barker's *Ecological Psychology: Concepts and Methods for Studying the Environment of Human Behavior* is reprinted by permission of Stanford University Press.

The extract (pp. 69—70) from N. S. Endler's "The person versus the situation—a pseudo issue? A response to Alker," *Journal of Personality* 41, 287–303 (1973), is reprinted by permission of Duke University Press.

©1976 Plenum Press, New York
A Division of Plenum Publishing Corporation
227 West 17th Street, New York, N.Y. 10011

United Kingdom edition published by Plenum Press, London
A Division of Plenum Publishing Company, Ltd.
Davis House (4th Floor), 8 Scrubs Lane, Harlesden, London, NW10 6SE, England

Printed in the United States of America

Contributors

Saul B. Cohen
Clark University
Worcester, Massachusetts

Kenneth H. Craik
University of California
Berkeley, California

Karen A. Franck
The City University of New York
New York, New York

William H. Ittelson
The City University of New York
New York, New York

Bernard Kaplan
Clark University
Worcester, Massachusetts

Robert W. Kates
Clark University
Worcester, Massachusetts

Sandra Kirmeyer
Claremont Graduate School
Claremont, California

Imre Kohn
Pennsylvania State University
University Park, Pennsylvania

Brian R. Little
University of British Columbia
Vancouver, British Columbia

David Lowenthal
University College London
United Kingdom

Albert Mehrabian
University of California
Los Angeles, California

Timothy J. O'Hanlon
The City University of New York
New York, New York

Hugh C. Prince
University College London
United Kingdom

James A. Russell
University of California
Los Angeles, California

Seymour Wapner
Clark University
Worcester, Massachusetts

Allan W. Wicker
Claremont Graduate School
Claremont, California

Joachim F. Wohlwill
Pennsylvania State University
University Park, Pennsylvania

Contents

Introduction

The purpose of this volume is to explore theory, problem formulation, and methodology in "experiencing the environment." In this embryonic field, the writings of a number of individuals already stand out as representative of distinctive viewpoints. In order to facilitate further development of the field, a conference[1] was proposed to gather in one place representatives of a number of major viewpoints with regard to the embryonic field of "environmental psychology." It was hoped that a colloquy among such representatives would facilitate a clarification of the similarities and differences between the various perspectives, and might enable proponents of any given point of view to benefit from the insights of others with different orientations. Hopefully, it might also promote a greater articulation for this emerging field of inquiry. With these ends in mind, the sponsors of the conference asked the various prospective participants to present their theoretical positions and representative research illustrative of those positions.

Some of the perspectives represented at the conference emphasized the point that the construal of phenomena depends heavily on the values and needs of perceivers. Implicit in this kind of position is the thesis that anyone who seeks to describe a complex happening is likely to shape it in terms of presuppositions, biases, etc., that may not be shared by others. With this *caveat* in mind, we present here for the convenience of the reader brief synopses of the positions taken in the papers that are presented in the chapters that follow. These synopses are intended solely as a provisional guide to the body of material presented at the conference. Any of the authors, including ourselves, might take exception to our preliminary summary of what they have written.

The first paper, by James A. Russell and Albert Mehrabian, offers an assessment of the individual's experience of environments in terms of his responsivity to three personally determined aspects of physical environments, viz., pleasantness, arousal quality, and dominance-eliciting quality. In the

[1] This book consists principally of the papers presented at the conference devoted to the theme "Experiencing the Environment." This conference, held under the auspices of Clark University and supported by funds from a NSF Department Science Development Grant to the Psychology Department (GU 03173), took place on January 7–8, 1975, at the Warren Center, Ashland, Massachusetts.

study they report, these qualities of environments are determined by judgments made on rating scales with regard to photographic slides of various physical environments. Their guiding thesis is that environmental settings elicit emotions, describable in terms of the three dimensions, and that these emotions mediate other behaviors, e.g., affiliation with others, exploration behavior, the desire to stay or the desire to leave.

The second paper, by Joachim F. Wohlwill and Imre Kohn, is chiefly concerned with the establishment of functional relationships between attributes of the physical environment and particular aspects of behavior. The main goal guiding their research is the generalization of laws and relationships established under highly controlled, artificial laboratory settings to complex nonlaboratory environmental settings. In the paper, they discuss and illustrate the problems involved in such an attempt at generalization with regard to environmental preferences; the relationship between levels of stimulation, preference, and maximally effective behavioral functioning; and the evaluation of new environments in terms of adaptation level to prior environments.

The next paper by Kenneth H. Craik, focuses on the role of personality variables and dispositional properties of environments in determining the modes of behavior manifested by individuals in different settings. Craik's main thesis seems to be twofold: that a knowledge of personality dispositions enables some degree of prediction as to behavior in everyday environments; and that behavior in everyday environments may serve to advance the understanding of personality dispositions. He proposes an analysis of person–environment interaction in terms of variables constituting three abstractly distinguishable systems, viz., personal system, societal system, and environmental system. In his work, he emphasizes that features constituting the different systems may be viewed now as independent variables and now as dependent variables.

Brian R. Little, in his paper, takes off from the work of personologists such as Craik. His main thesis is that individuals may be categorized in terms of their specialized cognitive, affective, and behavioral relations to the persons and things comprising environments. In his article, he distinguishes thing-specialists, person-specialists, generalists who are oriented to both persons and things, and the nonspecialist who has apparently no developed orientation toward either persons or things. He devotes some attention to the development of specialist orientations, and discusses the application of his typology to students, scientists, schizophrenics, and researchers into environmental psychology.

The paper by the geographers, David Lowenthal and Hugh C. Prince, provides a markedly different perspective for examining environmental experience. They are chiefly concerned with "transcendental modes of experience," with the search for environmental pleasures that go beyond utilitarian satisfactions, pleasures that serve to *enhance* rather than *reflect* ordinary life. In their work, they consider both individual modes of transcendence and forms of projected environments preferred by different national groups. Eschewing survey techniques and other social science instruments, they look at art, music, and literature to provide insights into the search for environmental pleasure, which they take as a fundamental striving of the truly human being.

In his paper, Robert W. Kates considers the implications of the long-range work of a group of geographers on environmental hazards for the problem of experiencing the environment. The principal focus in Kates' paper is on the factors that contribute to the experience of environments as hazardous. He emphasizes the role of the perceiver in determining whether a given environment is to be taken as hazardous or not, and also deals with the attempts of those occupying a hazardous environment to cope with the dangers of such an environment. He examines the measures that are taken by occupants of a hazardous environment to forestall the effects of hazards, to share losses, to modify the events, etc.

The paper by Allan W. Wicker and Sandra Kirmeyer stems from the ecological perspective of Roger Barker. Using both laboratory and field techniques, the authors examine the effects of different conditions of manning in behavioral settings on the subjective experiences, levels of performance, and the character of the verbal interaction of group members. Their work is chiefly directed toward a better understanding of the role of overmanning and undermanning in behavioral settings on inner psychological states and overt behaviors of individuals operating or participating in such settings.

The next paper, by William H. Ittelson, Karen A. Franck, and Timothy J. O'Hanlon, is rooted in the transactional framework and argues that it is specious to separate environmental experience, agent's action, and the environment in itself; the individual is part of the system he experiences. This viewpoint is taken to entail a general methodological standpoint: One cannot generalize from one system to another, but is enjoined to use a variety of different kinds of approaches. The individual in any system is a continuing product of his own active endeavors to create a world for himself in which he can function optimally and achieve his own pattern of satisfaction. Because of the transaction character of experience, it is not possible to come to any definitive picture of environments without considering the needs and actions of individuals engaged in transactions with environments.

In the last article, your editors and their collaborators illustrate the application by psychologists and geographers of the organismic-developmental approach to the issue of experiencing novel environments. We discuss and criticize a number of different methods we have used in a variety of studies, ranging from orthodox investigations of group differences to clinical studies of individual experience. The paper discusses the relationship between these different methods and presents tentative conclusions as to the nature of concrete environmental experience of individuals on the basis of a collocation of the different techniques.

So much for our synopses, our provisional map. . . . We hope that our readers will now turn to each of the papers to derive their own understanding of the different viewpoints presented herein, and to construct their own more refined maps of those sectors of the field of environmental psychology represented in this work.

We wish to acknowledge the efforts of the following institutions and individuals who have made both the conference and this book possible: The National Science Foundation, whose Departmental Science Development grant to the Psychology Department of Clark University supported the conference; Clark University, which served as the host institution for the conference; Patricia Dandonoli, Shinji Ishii, and Steven Schwartz, Clark students who helped with conference organization and preparation; Mary O'Malley of Clark University for her aid in transcribing the proceedings; and Emelia Thamel for her indefatigable managerial efforts in supervising all the work connected with the preconference planning, conduct of the conference, and organization of this book. We are also indebted to Joanne Bennett for her imaginative approach to the preparation of the index.

SEYMOUR WAPNER
SAUL B. COHEN
BERNARD KAPLAN

Some Behavioral Effects of the Physical Environment

JAMES A. RUSSELL and ALBERT MEHRABIAN

Abstract: It was hypothesized that the physical environment elicits an emotional response, which then influences subsequent behaviors. Settings presented by photographic slides were first rated on their pleasantness, arousing quality, and dominance-eliciting quality. A separate sample of subjects was then asked to rate their desire to drink, smoke, affiliate, explore, and stay in those settings. As hypothesized, pleasure due to the setting increased affiliation, exploration, and staying. The familiar inverted-U hypothesis, that these three behaviors are all maximized at moderate levels of arousal, must be modified to include an interaction effect with pleasure: The optimum level of arousal is positively correlated with pleasure. It was found that dominance mediated the effect of the setting on affiliation and that smoking and drinking occurred while in a mood created by having been in undesirable settings. The results confirmed predictions based on a review of studies that used diverse methodologies, and thus indicated that slides provide a valid method of studying the effects of environments on behavior.

The present study investigated the effects of the physical environment on several behaviors, and explored the validity of using photographic slides of environments to assess those effects. A review of the available literature suggested that the effects of the physical environment on behavior are mediated by emotional responses to that environment. Mehrabian and Russell (1974, chap. 2) proposed three independent and bipolar dimensions to summarize the emotional impact of physical settings: pleasure–displeasure, degree of arousal, and dominance–submissiveness.

Analogues of these emotional dimensions were repeatedly identified in

JAMES A. RUSSELL and ALBERT MEHRABIAN • Department of Psychology, University of California, Los Angeles, California.

studies of the semantic differential (Osgood, Suci, and Tannenbaum, 1957; Snider and Osgood, 1969). These studies showed that evaluation, activity, and potency provided a succinct description of human affective responses to varied classes of stimuli such as words, paintings, sonar signals, or facial expressions, thus suggesting that emotional factors are a basic aspect of human response to environments.

Pleasure, arousal, and dominance were identified as basic factors of emotion in studies of verbal descriptions of emotion (Bush, 1973) as well as in studies of nonverbal, facial, vocal, and postural expressions of emotion (Mehrabian, 1972; Mehrabian and Ksionzky, 1974). In addition, investigators found physiological correlates of verbally reported pleasure and arousal (Olds, 1956; Heath and Mickle, 1960, for pleasure; Evans and Day, 1971; Thayer, 1967, 1970, for arousal). Thus, even though pleasure, arousal, and dominance are most readily assessed by verbal self-report, they are nevertheless basic emotional response factors, each consisting of interrelated physiological, behavioral, and verbal report components.

Pleasure–displeasure is a continuum ranging from extreme pain or unhappiness to extreme pleasure or ecstasy at the other end. Arousal ranges from sleep through intermediate states of drowsiness, calm, and then alertness, to frenzied excitement at the opposite extreme. Dominance–submissiveness refers to the extent a person feels powerful *vis-à-vis* the environment (including other persons) that surrounds him. A person feels dominant when he is able to influence or control the situation he is in; he feels submissive when the environment influences him.

Available evidence, as well as new data, suggested that emotional responses to an environment influence, or mediate, other behaviors that occur there (Mehrabian and Russell, 1974, chaps. 6, 7, and 8). A review of the effects of pleasure on various behaviors indicated that the pleasure induced by one aspect of a setting increases the approach toward other aspects of the setting, even though the pleasure is not contingent on the approach (e.g., Griffitt, 1970; Griffitt and Veitch, 1971; Janis, Kaye, and Kirschner, 1965; Maslow and Mintz, 1956; Mehrabian and Russell, 1974, chap. 8; and Razran, 1938, 1940). Approach, versus avoidance, is used here to mean increased preference, liking, evaluation, exploration, motivation at tasks, and desire to affiliate and cooperate.

Berlyne (1960, 1967), Dember and Earl (1957), Fiske and Maddi (1961), and Hebb (1955) proposed that arousal affects approach–avoidance. The proposed relationship was the familiar inverted-U shaped function in which extremes of arousal, high or low, produce avoidance, whereas moderate degrees of arousal produce approach.

Vast amounts of research were interpreted as supporting the inverted-U hypothesis. Nevertheless, this research failed to control for the effects of pleasure; that is, the arousal level elicited was confounded with the degree of pleasure elicited. Typically, the situations labeled extremely high or low in arousal were more unpleasant than the moderately arousing situations. In numerous studies, the highly arousing noise that produced avoidance was also unpleasant, more unpleasant than the no-noise condition. It is therefore incorrect to infer that the observed avoidance reactions in these studies were attributable to extremes of arousal rather than to displeasure.

In three verbal questionnaire studies, Mehrabian and Russell (1974, chap. 8) explored the independent (and interactive) effects of pleasure, arousal, and dominance on approach–avoidance. The results were only partially supportive of the hypothesized inverted-U function. The inverted-U was found between desire to explore and arousal. It was also found for desire to work, but only among pleasant situations; it was found in only one of these studies for desire to affiliate, and again only among pleasant settings. Arousal failed to relate to desire to stay. Additional results helped clarify the inconsistent findings bearing on the inverted-U. These results showed an interaction between pleasure and arousal in determining approach: Among pleasant settings, approach tended to vary directly with arousal; among unpleasant settings, approach tended to vary inversely with arousal.

This interaction effect and a reexamination of the previous literature suggested a modification of the inverted-U hypothesis. Figure 1 summarizes this new pleasure–arousal hypothesis, which incorporates three separate relationships: (1) the positive correlation of approach with pleasure, (2) the inverted-U function of approach with arousal, and (3) the interaction effect in which approach generally increases with arousal when pleasure is experienced, but generally decreases with arousal when displeasure is experienced.

Figure 1 shows the combined effect of these three hypothesized relationships. The inverted-U function between arousal and approach–avoidance is represented by a parabolic curve. The same curve is repeated with shifts upward and to the right to represent increasing degrees of pleasure. This set of curves indicates that pleasure determines the optimum level of arousal, so that the level of arousal producing maximum approach is a direct linear function of pleasure. Of course, the exact shape of these curves, especially over a full range of values of pleasure and arousal, is unknown.

An extrapolation of this set of curves indicates that among extremely pleasant settings approach would be a monotonically increasing function of arousal, and that among extremely unpleasant settings approach would be a monotonically decreasing function of arousal. The pleasure–arousal hypothesis thus predicts that the inverted-U occurs only among situations of intermediate pleasantness–unpleasantness values and thus explains Mehrabian and Russell's (1974) failure to find the inverted-U in most settings.

Figure 1 thus summarizes the hypothesized relationships of approach–

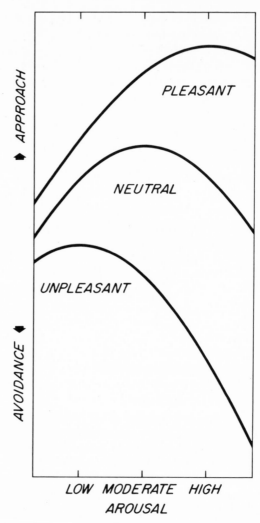

Figure 1. Pleasure–arousal hypothesis, in which pleasure determines the optimum level of arousal.

avoidance with both pleasure and arousal. These relationships were expected to hold for the desire to stay in, and to explore, a setting, but not necessarily for the desire to affiliate there. In the Mehrabian and Russell (1974, chap. 8) studies, even though affiliation was a positive correlate of the other approach variables, it consistently emerged as a separate factor. Furthermore, affiliation was simply found to increase in more pleasant settings, independently of the arousal or dominance levels elicited in those settings.

The present experiment also explored desire to drink alcoholic beverages and the desire to smoke cigarettes as functions of the emotion-eliciting qualities of settings. Some evidence suggested that persons consume more alcohol in unpleasant and unarousing settings (Russell and Mehrabian, 1975; Nathan, O'Brien, and Lowenstein, 1971). Environmental effects on smoking had not been explored previously but were readily included within the present paradigm.

The mode of stimulus presentation in the present experiment differed from that of earlier exploratory efforts by Mehrabian and Russell (1974, chap. 8) to investigate the independent effects of pleasure, arousal, and dominance on various behaviors. Since these earlier experiments employed verbally described stimuli, there was a question whether the obtained results could be generalized to other stimuli, especially to actual environments. The present study sought to answer this question by developing a complementary and extensive set of photographic slides as representations of various environments.

STUDY ONE: A SET OF PHOTOGRAPHIC SLIDES FOR USE AS STIMULI

A set of 240 photographic slides, each of a different physical setting, was obtained. Photographs were taken of as large a diversity of physical settings as possible, including urban, suburban, rural, and wilderness areas. Climatic settings ranged from deserts to snow-covered forests. The slides included scenes from Boston, Los Angeles, New York, San Francisco, and several foreign sites in Africa, Europe, Israel, and Mexico, as well as scenes of interiors and exteriors of buildings. Some scenes showed persons, other scenes did not.

The settings also differed in their emotion-eliciting qualities. Specifically, all possible combinations of pleasantness, arousing quality, and dominance-eliciting quality were sought, together with a wide range of values along each dimension. The scene depicted in each slide in the set of 240 was then rated for its emotion-eliciting quality.

Method

Twelve separate sets of subjects, University of California undergraduates, were selected. Each set rated 20 slides. In a group session, subjects were first informed of the general experimental procedure. Then, with light just sufficient to read by, the first slide was shown on a screen. Written instructions directed each subject to imagine himself actually in the setting shown in the slide, and then to imagine how he would feel there. After 10 seconds the experimenter told the subjects to begin filling out the rating form. This form consisted of Mehrabian and Russell's (1974, Appendix B) scales of pleasure, arousal, and dominance, the items of which were intermixed and presented in a nine-point semantic differential format. When everyone had completed the rating form, the next slide was shown and the procedure repeated. In this manner 20 slides were shown to each group of subjects.

Enough of these sessions were carried out so that a minimum of 16 subjects had rated each slide. Each set of 20 slides was shown in one order to approximately half of the subjects rating the slides and shown in other sessions in the reverse order to the other half of the subjects.

Pleasantness, Arousing Quality, and Dominance-Eliciting Quality Scores

For each slide the mean pleasure, mean arousal, and mean dominance scores were computed across subjects. These means defined the pleasantness, arousing quality, and dominance-eliciting quality, respectively, of each slide. Each dimension was thus scaled with a range of -24 to $+24$ (i.e., a sum of six items each scored -4 to $+4$) and with zero as the neutral point. These values for each setting were then used to assign slides to experimental conditions in the next study reported here, since these mean scores were independent of individual differences in response to the settings.

To estimate the reliability of these mean scores, a technique given by Winer (1962, p. 131, Equation 4′) was used. Data from 28 subjects who had all rated the same 20 slides were arbitrarily selected from all the obtained data and were analyzed. Reliability coefficients of 0.97 for pleasantness, 0.92 for arousing quality, and 0.78 for dominance-eliciting quality were obtained. Each reliability coefficient is interpreted as an estimate of the correlation of mean scores (for example, the pleasantness scores) across these 20 slides that would be obtained from two different groups of subjects.

STUDY TWO: BEHAVIORAL EFFECTS OF SETTINGS

Method

Subjects

A sample of 44 University of California undergraduates served as subjects as part of a course requirement.

Materials

From the set of 240 photographic slides scaled in Study One, 60 slides were selected, irrespective of content, to form 12 cells of a factorial design in which two levels of pleasantness, three levels of arousing quality, and two levels of dominance-eliciting quality were completely crossed. There were thus five slides per cell, which were selected to have similar emotion-eliciting qualities; e.g., each of the five scenes in one cell had been rated high on pleasantness, low on arousing quality, and low on dominance-eliciting quality.

Mean pleasantness, arousing quality, and dominance-eliciting quality within each cell were computed across the five slides. The six cells for pleasant settings—that is, in which pleasantness was uniformly high but arousing quality and dominance-eliciting quality varied—had a range of mean pleasantness scores of 7.0 to 7.9 and an overall mean of 7.6. Among the cells for unpleasant settings, pleasantness averaged −2.4 and ranged from −2.9 to −2.0. Among the four cells for moderately arousing settings, arousing quality averaged 5.2 and ranged from 4.7 to 5.4. Among the cells for slightly arousing settings, arousing quality averaged 0.9 and ranged from 0.6 to 1.1. Among the cells for unarousing settings, arousing quality averaged −3.0 and ranged from −4.0 to −2.5. Among the six cells for moderate dominance-eliciting settings, dominance-eliciting quality averaged 2.4 and ranged from 2.0 to 3.0. Among the cells for submissiveness-eliciting (low dominance-eliciting) settings, dominance-eliciting quality averaged −3.5 and ranged from −4.0 to −2.9. The ranges of mean values given above within each set of cells show that pleasantness, arousing quality, and dominance-eliciting quality varied independently across cells; that is, without one factor being confounded by another.

Procedure

In a group session, written instructions informed each of the 44 subjects that he would see a set of five photographic slides. He was to imagine himself in each of the five different settings and imagine that he had been in no other place for a couple of hours. The instructions continued, "Try to imagine the kind of mood or emotional state that you are in, having spent all that time in these situations . . . The important thing is that you place yourself in those settings and views and recreate for yourself the feelings that you would have after the total of those five experiences."

The strategy of asking subjects to consider their emotional state after five different settings was used to minimize the effects of particular physical attributes of the settings and thus to better focus on their emotion-eliciting qualities.

The lights were dimmed and the first set of five slides was shown for 10 seconds per slide, and then the set was shown again for another 10 seconds per slide. The experimenter then asked the subjects to answer 11 written questions, which were the dependent measures of the study. The point in time for the answers to the questions was "just after the five experiences . . . while you are still in the mood created there."

The desire-to-affiliate items were:

(+)   To what extent is this a time you would feel friendly and talkative to a stranger who happens to be near you?

(−)   Is this a time when you might try to avoid other people, avoid having to talk to them? (0 = no avoidance)

The desire-to-explore items were:

(+)   How much would you enjoy going back to these settings and exploring around?

(−)   How much would you try to avoid going back to look around or to explore these settings? (0 = no avoidance)

The desire-to-stay items were:

(+)   How much time would you like to spend once you're back in these settings?

(+)   How much do you like the way you are feeling at this time (that is, *just after* the five experiences)?

(−)   How hard would you try to avoid ever having to return?

The desire-to-smoke items were:

(+)   At this time would you feel like smoking a cigarette?

(−)   Would you refuse an offer of a cigarette to smoke?

The desire-to-drink items were:

(+)   Would you feel like having a drink (something alcoholic)?

(−)   Do you think that "It's just *not* the right time to have an alcoholic drink"?

On the actual rating form, the plus and minus scoring keys of the 11 items were omitted as were the labels of the five variables. Items were answered on a nine-point scale ranging from "not at all" to "extremely so," except the desire to stay item concerned with amount of time, which was answered on a nine-point scale: none, a few minutes, half an hour, one hour, a few hours, a day, a few days, many days, many months.

When everyone had completed the rating forms, subjects were told that this procedure would be repeated again exactly as before, except that a totally new set of situations would be shown and they could therefore forget about the previous set. In this manner 13 sets of five slides were shown. The initial set shown (data for which were not analyzed) was an anchor of intermediate values on pleasure, arousal, and dominance, to familiarize the subjects with the procedure. The remaining 12 sets were presented in random order.

Results and Discussion

Dependent Measures

The reliability of each dependent measure was assessed by computing the intercorrelations of responses to the items within each measure. Desire-to-stay consisted of three items. The negatively worded item correlated -0.59 with each of the two positively worded items. The positively worded items intercorrelated 0.72. The two desire-to-explore items intercorrelated -0.71. The two desire-to-affiliate items intercorrelated -0.54. The two desire-to-smoke items intercorrelated -0.68. The two desire-to-drink items intercorrelated -0.60. Responses to items within each of the five measures were thus simply summed, after reversing signs where appropriate, to form the dependent measures for the remainder of the analysis.

The intercorrelations among the five dependent measures were computed across subjects and conditions. Since not all subjects smoked or drank, the correlations involving desire-to-smoke or desire-to-drink were based on only the data from those 16 subjects who smoked and drank. The other correlations were based on the 44 subjects. The results are given in Table 1. Desire-to-stay and desire-to-explore were a single approach–avoidance factor. As anticipated, desire-for-affiliation was positively, but only moderately, related to exploration and staying. In contrast, both smoking and drinking were negatively related to approach; that is, they both involved an avoidance of the situation, at least to a slight degree. Interestingly, drinking was positively related to affiliation.

Analysis of Variance

Analysis of variance was used to explore each of the five dependent measures as functions of two levels (low and high) of the pleasure, three levels

Table 1. Intercorrelations of Dependent Variables*

Dependent variable	2	3	4	5
1. Desire-to-stay	.88	.37	−.19	−.16
2. Desire-to-explore		.36	−.17	−.19
3. Desire-to-affiliate			.08	.27
4. Desire-to-smoke				.41
5. Desire-to-drink				

* Correlations involving desire-to-smoke or desire-to-drink are based on 192 observations (16 subjects) and are significant ($p < .05$) when in excess of 0.14. Other correlations are based on 528 observations (44 subjects) and are significant ($p < .05$) when in excess of 0.09.

Table 2. Analysis of Variance Results†

Dependent variable	Source	F	df	Mean square error	Cell means
Desire-to-stay	Pleasure	224.3**	1/42	24.29	Pleasure: low / high → 0.87 / 7.29
	Arousal	7.0**	2/84	9.37	Arousal: low slight moderate → 3.40 ↔ 4.26 / 4.59
	Dominance	47.6**	1/42	12.48	Dominance: low / moderate → 5.14 / 3.02
	Pleasure × arousal	24.8**	2/84	9.02	Arousal: low slight moderate / Pleasure: high 5.56 ↔ 7.34 ↔ 8.99 / low 1.25 1.17 ↔ 0.19
Desire-to-explore	Pleasure	317.9**	1/42	10.11	Pleasure: low / high → −1.75 / 3.19
	Arousal	9.7**	2/84	7.75	Arousal: low slight moderate → −0.02 ↔ 0.95 / 1.23
	Dominance	47.5**	1/42	8.47	Dominance: low / moderate → 1.59 / −0.15
	Pleasure × arousal	33.4**	2/84	6.98	Arousal: low slight moderate / Pleasure: high 1.32 ↔ 3.39 ↔ 4.86 / low −1.35 −1.48 ↔ −2.41
Desire-to-affiliate	Pleasure	28.3**	1/42	12.74	Pleasure: low / high → 0.57 / 2.22
	Pleasure × arousal	3.4*	2/84	3.69	Arousal: low slight moderate / Pleasure: high 2.28 1.74 ↔ 2.64 / ↕ ↕ ↕ / low 0.60 0.64 0.47
	Pleasure × dominance	27.2**	1/42	10.05	Dominance: low moderate / Pleasure: high 1.47 ←——→ 2.97 / ↕ / low 1.26 ←——→ −0.12
	Pleasure × arousal × dominance	N.S.			Arousal: low slight moderate / Dominance: moderate / Pleasure: high 2.66 2.39 ↔ 3.86 / ↕ ↕ ↕ / low −0.25 0.07 −0.18 / Dominance: low / Pleasure: high 1.91 1.09 1.41 / low 1.45 1.20 1.11

Table 2. (Continued)

Dependent variable	Source	F	df	Mean square error	Cell means		
Desire-to-smoke	Pleasure	6.5*	1/14	21.52	Pleasure:	low 0.62	high −1.08
	Pleasure × Arousal	5.2*	2/28	7.51	Arousal: Pleasure:	low	slight moderate
					high	0.03 ↔ −1.84	−1.43
					low	−0.06 0.84	1.09
Desire-to-drink	Pleasure	5.9*	1/14	12.50	Pleasure:	low 0.18	high −1.06
	Arousal	4.8*	2/28	6.89	Arousal:	low slight 0.30↔−1.14	moderate −0.48

* $p < .05$.
** $p < .01$.
† Based on t-tests, cell means connected by arrows differ significantly at the 0.05 level.

(low, slight, and moderate) of the arousal, and two levels (low and moderate) of the dominance elicited by the settings. The results achieving significance and corresponding cell means are given in Table 2. Since a repeated measures design was used, the 44 subjects contributed a total of 528 observations over the 12 cells for each dependent measure item, except the items for desire-to-smoke and desire-to-drink, data for which were based on 192 observations from 16 subjects.

The results in Table 2 for desire-to-stay were identical to those for desire-to-explore, as would be expected from the 0.88 correlation between these variables already reported in Table 1. Pleasure produced the most powerful effect. Somewhat unexpectedly, dominance had a negative effect: A more dominant feeling decreased the desire to stay and to explore. One interpretation is that dominance-eliciting situations often require responsibility and work rather than more carefree activities. Among the college student sample, such responsibility was shunned.

The arousal and pleasure × arousal effects were both significant. These results can be interpreted in terms of the pleasure–arousal hypothesis of Figure 1. Since the mean level of pleasure was above neutral over all the 12 conditions, the main enhancing effect of arousal on approach was as expected. More important, in the highly pleasant settings, exploration and desire-to-stay were very strong direct functions of arousal. In contrast, in unpleasant settings arousal was inversely related to approach. This was exactly as predicted by the pleasure–arousal hypothesis for the intermediate range of arousal levels employed in this study. These results thus showed that pleasure determined the desired level of arousal, a result not predicted by the simple inverted-U relation of arousal with approach. The curvilinear relationship of approach with arousal is expected to be found only when a broader range of arousal is studied.

To clarify the somewhat more complicated results for desire-to-affiliate, the cell means for all levels of pleasure, arousal, and dominance are given in Table 2, along with several relevant t-tests, even though the triple interaction effect was nonsignificant. The expected main effect due to pleasure was obtained but must be qualified by the pleasure × dominance interaction. The cell means for that interaction showed that the main effect of pleasure was actually significant only in the moderate dominance conditions and not in the low dominance ones. Indeed, the cell means for the triple interaction show that the means in all six cells for low dominance (i.e., regardless of pleasure or arousal) were similar; no significant differences based on t-tests were found. When a person felt submissive, the pleasure- and arousal-eliciting qualities of the setting did not significantly affect his desire-for-affiliation.

In contrast, in dominance-eliciting settings, pleasure and arousal did affect affiliation. Specifically, the main effect of pleasure was quite strong in the moderate dominance condition. The pleasure × arousal interaction was also evident only in the moderate dominance condition, as can be seen in the triple interaction cell means. Arousal increased the desire-to-affiliate, but only in pleasant (and dominance-eliciting) settings. Desire-for-affiliation was thus greatest in dominance-eliciting, pleasant, and arousing settings. Altogether the results showed that the main effect of pleasure and pleasure × arousal interaction were actually significant only in dominance-eliciting settings. The feeling of dominance, in other words, allows a person to express strong preferences regarding where he wants to affiliate. Such preferences are not found when he feels submissive.

The results in Table 2 for desire-to-affiliate differed from those for desire-to-stay and desire-to-explore. Settings desired for affiliation were not always the same as those desired for staying and exploring. This difference helps explain the rather low correlations reported in Table 1 between desire-to-affiliate and desire-to-stay and desire-to-explore (.37 and .36 respectively). Approach toward the setting itself is therefore a separate factor from interpersonal approach, or the desire to affiliate.

The negative correlation of smoking with the desire-to-stay and desire-to-explore measures suggested that the desire-to-smoke increases after having been in undesirable settings. The analysis of variance results strongly supported that view. Desire-to-smoke yielded results that were the inverse of those obtained for the desire-to-explore and desire-to-stay variables. In other words, smoking occurred after exposure to undesirable settings. One interpretation is that smoking provided a diversion from an undesirable mood, at least for the smokers who provided these data.

The results for drinking were as expected and were similar to those for smoking. The obtained main effects in Table 2 simply showed that drinking occurred after being in situations that were unpleasant or unarousing; that is, boring or depressing settings.

Conclusion

The results were highly significant and as predicted, thus demonstrating the power of the physical environment, even when communicated in a single modality, to influence human feelings. These results strongly supported our basic thesis that settings elicit emotions, which, in turn, systematically influence other behaviors. The results specifically supported the experimental findings of Mehrabian and Russell (1974, chap. 8), despite the use of different stimuli and, more important, the use of slides rather than verbal descriptions of settings. The complementarity of the present results with earlier ones using verbally described settings and with various studies using actual settings are reassuring for the validity of representing environments by means of slides; that is, these results provided empirical evidence for the generalizability of data based on slides.

The present results also supported an important reinterpretation of the familiar inverted-U-shaped relation of arousal and approach–avoidance. Future experimental work on the inverted-U would only be valuable if it were to consider the independent effects of pleasure.

ACKNOWLEDGMENT

This study was supported by grant AA1874 from the National Institute on Alcohol Abuse and Alcoholism to Albert Mehrabian.

REFERENCES

Berlyne, D. E. *Conflict, arousal, and curiosity.* New York: McGraw-Hill, 1960.

Berlyne, D. E. Arousal and reinforcement. In D. Levine (Ed.), *Nebraska symposium on motivation.* Lincoln, Nebraska: University of Nebraska Press, 1967. Pp. 1–110.

Bush, L. E., II. Individual differences multidimensional scaling of adjectives denoting feelings. *Journal of Personality and Social Psychology,* 1973, *25*, 50–57.

Dember, W. N., and Earl, R. W. Analysis of exploratory, manipulatory and curiosity behaviors. *Psychological Review,* 1957, *64*, 91–96.

Evans, D. R., and Day, H. I. The factorial structure of responses to perceptual complexity. *Psychonomic Science,* 1971, *22*, 357–359.

Fiske, D. W., and Maddi, S. R. *Functions of varied experience.* Homewood, Illinois: Dorsey, 1961.

Griffitt, W. Environmental effects on interpersonal affective behavior: Ambient effective temperature and attraction. *Journal of Personality and Social Psychology,* 1970, *15,* 240–244.

Griffitt, W., and Veitch, R. Hot and crowded: Influences of population density and temperature on interpersonal affective behavior. *Journal of Personality and Social Psychology,* 1971, *17,* 92–98.

Heath, R. G., and Mickle, W. A. Evaluation of seven years' experience with depth electrode studies in human patients. In E. R. Ramey and D. S. O'Doherty (Eds.), *Electrical studies on the unanesthetized brain.* New York: Hoeber, 1960. Pp. 214–247.

Hebb, D. O. Drives and the C.N.S. (conceptual nervous system). *Psychological Review,* 1955, *62,* 243–254.

Janis, I. L., Kaye, D., and Kirschner, P. Facilitating effects of "eating-while-reading" on responsiveness to persuasive communications. *Journal of Personality and Social Psychology,* 1965, *1,* 181–186.

Maslow, A. H., and Mintz, N. L. Effects of esthetic surroundings: I. Initial effects of three esthetic conditions upon perceiving "energy" and "well-being" in faces. *Journal of Psychology,* 1956, *41,* 247–254.

Mehrabian, A. *Nonverbal communication.* Chicago, Illinois: Aldine-Atherton, 1972.

Mehrabian, A., and Ksionzky, S. *A theory of affiliation.* Lexington, Massachusetts: D. C. Heath, 1974.

Mehrabian, A., and Russell, J. A. *An approach to environmental psychology.* Cambridge, Massachusetts: M.I.T. Press, 1974.

Nathan, P. E., O'Brien, J. S., and Lowenstein, L. M. Operant studies of chronic alcoholism: Interaction of alcohol and alcoholics. In M. K. Roach, W. M. McIsaac, and P. J. Creaven (Eds.), *Biological aspects of alcohol.* Austin, Texas: University of Texas Press, 1971.

Olds, J. Pleasure centers in the brain. *Scientific American,* 1956, *195* (4), 105–116.

Osgood, C. E., Suci, G. J., and Tannenbaum, P. H. *The measurement of meaning.* Urbana, Illinois: University of Illinois Press, 1957.

Razran, G. H. S. Conditioning away social bias by the luncheon technique. *Psychological Bulletin,* 1938, *35,* 693.

Razran, G. H. S. Conditional response changes in rating and appraising sociopolitical slogans. *Psychological Bulletin,* 1940, *37,* 481.

Russell, J. A., and Mehrabian, A. The mediating role of emotions in alcohol use. *Journal of Studies on Alcohol,* 1975.

Snider, J. G., and Osgood, C. E. (Eds.) *Semantic differential technique.* Chicago, Illinois: Aldine, 1969.

Thayer, R. E. Measurement of activation through self-report. *Psychological Reports,* 1967, *20,* 663–678.

Thayer, R. E. Activation states as assessed by verbal report and four psychophysiological variables. *Psychophysiology,* 1970, *7,* 86–94.

Winer, B. J. *Statistical principles in experimental design.* New York: McGraw-Hill, 1962.

III

Dimensionalizing the Environmental Manifold

JOACHIM F. WOHLWILL and IMRE KOHN

Abstract: This paper presents an analysis of selected problems in environmental psychology. It starts from a focus on independently defined dimensions of the environment and examines the functional relationships between these and given behavioral variables, by recourse to a variety of constructs derived from theory and research in the realms of exploratory behavior, experimental aesthetics, arousal and levels of stimulation, and adaptation level. The approach is illustrated with respect to three particular problem areas: the stimulus correlates of environmental preference, the optimal-level-of-stimulation problem, and the role of frame of reference, i.e., adaptation level, in environmental assessment. The treatment of these problems dwells on diverse, theoretical, and methodological problems involved in the isolation and specification of pertinent environmental variables, as well as in the handling of individual differences, and of variables relating to the person, in the context of the proposed approach built on the postulate of an objectively definable environment. An investigation of the evaluation of environments by migrants who have moved from communities of differing sizes to New York City is presented in some detail to illustrate the applicability of the adaptation-level framework to judgments of diverse environmental attributes.

Like the concept of "the person," that of "*the* environment" represents one of those abstractions that is probably overly broad and unfocused to prove particularly useful. Despite the proliferation of books, courses, programs, institutes, conferences, etc., on the theme of man and his environment, the fact is that there is clearly no such thing. Rather, there are environments—of all varieties and descriptions. There are diverse ways of analyzing environmental properties

JOACHIM F. WOHLWILL and IMRE KOHN • Pennsylvania State University, University Park, Pennsylvania. Mr. Kohn is currently affiliated with the Institute for Community Design Analysis, New York City.

(e.g., Ittelson, 1973, pp. 1–19; Moss, 1973; Sells, 1963, pp. 3–15); the one we have chosen contrasts with that of Ittelson, for instance, in focusing on environments, not as a metaphorical sheath *surrounding* the individual, but rather as a source of diverse kinds of stimulation impinging on him or her. More specifically, we intend to abstract from the unorganized, unclassified hash that we choose to label "environment" certain *dimensional* variables that have been demonstrated to be functionally relevant to behavior.

This is the crux of the position we wish to develop in this paper. As environmental psychologists, we see our task to be one of specifying functional relationships between given attributes of the physical environment and relevant aspects of behavior. We believe that this task can most effectively be carried out—at least for purposes of a first approximation—by abstracting from the environmental manifold selected dimensions of stimulation that on both theoretical and empirical grounds can be shown to be of significance in the study of such functional relationships.

Where are we to look for such variables? There are several different sources available to the environmental psychologist, for when we view the field in this manner, it becomes apparent that psychologists of diverse interests and persuasions have been the precursors of environmental psychology, in the sense that they have considered and uncovered functional relationships between given dimensions of the stimulus environment and particular aspects of behavior. Among those whose work appears the most directly relevant for us may be mentioned James Gibson, from the side of perception (e.g., Gibson, 1950; 1966; 1973), Daniel Berlyne, from the side of motivation and psychological aesthetics (e.g., Berlyne, 1960; 1971), Fiske and Maddi (1961, pp. 11–56), and others who have dealt with the concept of levels of stimulation in relation to arousal; and Hebb (1949) and his followers—notably White (1971) at the human level—in terms of conceptions of the role of stimulus experience in the behavioral development of the individual. To this list, finally, we must add the name of Harry Helson (1964), whose work, while cutting across the various substantive concerns of the individual theorists just cited, has given us the concept of adaptation level as a modulator of the effects of particular levels of a stimulus on behavior (whether perceptual, affective, or overt behavior).

Some may consider this juxtaposition of assorted psychologists and psychological theories hopelessly eclectic, and unlikely to lead to significant advances at a conceptual level. If we recognize, however, that our task is not to build a new theory of behavior, but rather to arrive at as complete an account as possible of the varied forms of environmental–behavioral interrelationships, then such a synthetic strategy appears defensible. We see the main problem as one of generalizing the laws and relationships uncovered under highly controlled, artificial laboratory settings with regard to the role of individual stimulus variables to the effects of corresponding environmental variables on behavior. This generalization task involves (a) a shift from molecular to molar units of analysis in the definition and measurement of independent variables; (b) a shift from artifactual stimuli constructed to allow specific operationally defined variables to be manipulated, singly or in combinations of two or three properties, to ready-made environmental locales whose status with regard to the variables of interest must be assessed in *ex post facto* fashion, and typically without recourse to objective measurement; (c) a corresponding shift from experimental methodology and research design to multivariate correlational models; and (d) a confrontation of the problem of sampling *environments*, which turns out to be vastly more difficult to resolve than that of the sampling of subjects in traditional laboratory research.

Let us illustrate the nature of our approach by reference to three general problems, each couched in terms of a postulate; in the process of elaborating on each, we will have occasion as well to illustrate and explain the four methodological points just cited.

THE ENVIRONMENTAL PREFERENCE PROBLEM

Postulate 1. Environmental preference is, in general, an inverse function of the uncertainty or conflict generated by a given environment.

Theoretical Basis

This particular postulate (in contrast to the two to follow) is still searching for a sound theoretical underpinning, and even its empirical basis is far from firmly established at present. Thus, it is offered here only in a tentative manner, and mainly with the aim of highlighting a number of interesting substantive and methodological issues. Indeed, it might appear to fly in the face of the positive role that has been assigned to the so-called collative variables (complexity, novelty, incongruity, surprise) by Berlyne (1960), as determinants of attention and exploratory activity. It goes counter, furthermore, to the assertions of a variety of commentators and critics of the man-made environment, from Jane Jacobs (1961), with her emphasis on the values of diversity in the urban landscape (though more in a functional than in a perceptual sense), to Venturi (1966) (cf. also Venturi, Brown, and Izenour, 1972), who have built an environmental aesthetic on the exploitation of complexity, incongruity, and conflict. To these we may add Rapoport and Kantor (1967) and Rapoport and Hawkes (1970), who have similarly stressed the positive value of complexity and ambiguity in our environment, based on their reading of Berlyne and other psychologists, along with diverse art and architectural historians, planners, etc.

Upon closer examination, however, it appears that this commonly held view lacks a firm basis in either psychological theory or empirical fact. While it is true that such variables as complexity or diversity have frequently been found to be positively correlated with extent of voluntary exploration of a stimulus, or ratings of interestingness, there is a substantial body of literature pointing to the importance of differentiating between these response variables and measures of preference, ratings of pleasingness or liking, and similar affective responses (Berlyne, 1971, pp. 213 ff.; Berlyne, 1974, chaps. 2, 4, and 5; Wohlwill, 1968; in press).[1]

This work, along with much other research on preference and affect (cf. Berlyne and Madsen, 1973), discloses a vastly more complex and intricate pattern of relationships to manipulated stimulus dimensions such as complexity, suggesting that an adequate account of preference for different types of environmental scenes or locales is still a most uncertain prospect at the present. A brief review of some of the pertinent evidence may aid in correcting some of the prevalent misconceptions in regard to the role played by complexity and diversity in environmental preference, and, equally important, in bringing out some of the major methodological problems to be faced in research on this question.

Empirical Support

An early study of the senior author's (Wohlwill, 1968), relating preference to rated complexity for sets of photographically portrayed environmental scenes, yielded generally irregular functions, which were noteworthy mainly for the contrast between it and the function obtained for amount of voluntary exploration. Subsequent research (Wohlwill, in press) with children at different ages resulted in a preference function that conformed more clearly to the inverted-U shaped function that had previously been obtained in a variety of research with artificially constructed stimuli varying in complexity, both visual and auditory. Kaplan, Kaplan, and Wendt (1972) correctly pointed, however,

---

[1] The distinction between these two varieties of response variables is related, though not equivalent to that which Berlyne has drawn between two modes of responding to stimuli; i.e., specific vs. diversive exploration (e.g., Berlyne, 1971, p. 100). The former represents activity directed at reducing uncertainty or conflict elicited by a stimulus, and may be plausibly operationalized by measures of voluntary exploration times. The latter, on the other hand, represents activity directed at achieving an optimal state of arousal and is at best very indirectly related to, and certainly not identifiable with measures of preference or liking.

to the apparent confounding between the complexity dimension and the differentiation between the natural and the man-made world, since the low-complexity stimuli consisted of pure natural scenes, while those at the high end were predominantly man-made scenes. Kaplan and Wendt's own data brought out the importance of the natural versus man-made distinction, indicating a strong overall bias in favor of natural scenes, which was confirmed in subsequent research of the senior author's (Wohlwill, 1973).

The true basis for this bias remains as yet unclear. We will return to it, as well as to certain additional points arising in connection with the studies just cited, in the methodological section that follows. At this point we wish rather to dwell on certain additional findings by both S. Kaplan (1973) and Wohlwill (1973), which appear to provide support for our postulate. Both of these investigators found a number of variables of a quasi-Gestaltist nature that play an important role as determinants of preference in the environment (at least as simulated through photographic slides). They include Kaplan's "identifiability" and "coherence" as well as congruence between the natural and the man-made environment (in Wohlwill's research), the results indicating that preference is directly related to clarity and congruity, rather than their opposites. It is interesting to note the similar conclusion with specific reference to the attribute of "balance," which appears closely akin to harmony, in experimental-aesthetics research by Ertel (1973, pp. 115–132).[2]

Finally, a further variable similarly related positively to environmental preference is of interest, since it was manifest in both S. Kaplan's (1973) and Wohlwill's (1973) data. This is the variable of depth of view, or spaciousness. At first blush this variable does not seem to fit the postulate enunciated above; indeed one might suggest that the more expansive the view, the greater the diversity (i.e., complexity) contained within it, and thus the greater the uncertainty (at least in the technical sense) engendered by it. In fact, this variable proved to be uncorrelated with diversity. Furthermore, one could argue that expansiveness of view reduces uncertainty, in the sense that a wider field is accessible to direct inspection, without interference from vertical surfaces (be they walls, trees, or hillsides) blocking the view. Thus, the finding that Ss on the average prefer views characterized by depth and expansiveness may in fact be consonant with our initial postulate.

---

[2] In seeming conflict with the stress being placed on perceptual clarity or lack of ambiguity as factors positively related to preference is R. Kaplan's (1973) finding of a positive correlation between preference and the degree of "mystery" contained in a scene. This attribute was primarily related, however, to sources of uncertainty in the environment along directions in the third dimension, such as a road "vanishing" around a bend; in fact, the "mystery" ratings were obtained by asking subjects to rate "the promise of further information . . . if you could walk deeper into the scene." Thus, it is possible that the depth factor was confounded with this variable. But even if that should not turn out to be the explanation, it is apparent that this "mystery" factor does not represent a *generalized* preference for ambiguity or uncertainty.

Methodological Problems

The research cited above illustrates a variety of problems intrinsic to environmental-perception research that warrant more detailed discussion. These will be seen to be closely related to the four general problems in the generalization of laboratory-based principles to the environmental realm that were cited above.

Isolating and Defining Relevant Stimulus Dimensions. As already mentioned, we have not as yet succeeded in getting an effective handle on the basis for the preference for the natural versus the man-made domain. One plausible assumption might be that this bias has an essentially associational foundation; i.e., the natural world, particularly to contemporary college-age youth, has a connotation of "goodness" and positive value, in contrast to the man-made. Such a bias could well result from a reaction against the problems created by our man-made inventions, whether considered in interpersonal, social, or environmental terms. An alternative approach may be suggested, however, that would entail the isolation of particular stimulus attributes that in an ecological sense differentiate the natural from the man-made domain, along the lines of Gibson's (1973) ecological approach to perception. Thus, one may speculate that such attributes as curvilinear as opposed to rectilinear forms, gradual change versus sharp contrasts (e.g., in texture and color), and more typically expansive as opposed to compressed or blocked fields of view serve to differentiate the natural from the man-made domain. One of the problems here is clearly that of ensuring a reasonably complete description of environments in terms of pertinent dimensions or attributes, so that those relevant to the bias in preference under consideration will in fact be recognized.[3]

Assessing the Relevant Variables in Natura. Even if we may trust our intuitions, reinforced by judicious observation and geographically or ecologically sophisticated analysis, to uncover the relevant dimensions, we still need to find adequate ways of assessing particular environmental locales with respect to them on an *a posteriori* basis, since it is manifestly impossible to rely on experimental manipulation of such dimensions when dealing with real environments. Here the most commonly followed procedure is to obtain ratings from trained judges. To the extent that variables are defined in terms of quasi-objective topographical characteristics [e.g., the "factors of recognition" and "compositional types" that Litton (1973) has proposed for landscape assessment], a reasonable approach to reliability and determinacy of the resulting measurements may be hoped for, in comparison to the assessment of such more elusive

---

[3] In support of the stimulus-based interpretation of the bias in favor of natural scenes (as opposed to an associational one), one might cite R. Kaplan's (1973) data, which show that this bias is magnified when stimuli are presented under brief exposure-time conditions. Conceivably certain characteristics differentiating natural from man-made environments (e.g., color contrast) become dominant under brief exposure.

attributes as the aesthetic criteria of unity, vividness, and variety proposed by Litton. At the same time, in certain cases more objective methods may in fact be utilized; e.g., in the assessment of amount of brightness contrast in a photograph. With regard to the aforementioned Gestaltist-flavored attributes of coherence and balance, on the other hand, one will need to settle for either indirect methods (e.g., ease of recognition; degree of univocality of interpretation, as measures of "legibility"), or sheer interjudge agreement, to ensure some reasonable amount of consensus for attributes defined in purely phenomenal, impressionistic terms.

Teasing Out the Respective Roles of Different Variables. Considerable reliance must necessarily be placed on such techniques of analysis as partial and multiple correlation, in contrast to models such as analysis of variance favored by the laboratory experimentalist. This point was nicely illustrated in a study carried out by the senior author, in collaboration with several graduate students at Pennsylvania State University (cf. Wohlwill, 1973). We had originally attempted to create series of stimuli to represent the domain of natural scenes, that of man-made scenes, and that involving a mixture of the two, while varying level of complexity (i.e., diversity) independently of these categories. But the attempt to make up sets of slides that would allow one to assess the role of these two variables independently proved unsuccessful, as we failed in our efforts to locate representative scenes of the natural and mixed domains equivalent in degree of complexity to the upper levels of complexity encountered in the man-made domain. There is, in other words, an intrinsic association between these two dimensions of the physical environment, which corresponds to our intuitive association of the world of nature as relatively simple, and that of civilization as complex. Thus, any attempt to force the two into an orthogonal analysis-of-variance design would at best result in a highly biased selection of environmental stimuli, and at worst be foredoomed to failure. This experience suggests that investigators in this realm will need to shift from the hypothesis-testing model to one of determining relative amounts of variance accounted for by different environmental attributes, both individually and in combination, i.e., through partial and multiple correlation methodology.

The Problem of Sampling of Environments. It is apparent that in the study of environmental perception and preference we need to adopt a more satisfactory basis for selecting our stimuli than the haphazardous, expedient approach that has been typical in this area of research. Here Brunswik's (1956) plea for "representative sampling" of stimuli is clearly to the point, but even Brunswik, beyond exhorting us to avoid the artificial restriction built into stimuli constructed or devised according to the principles of laboratory control, is not of much help in suggesting how such representative sampling may be achieved. It appears that there are two major alternative strategies, which are equivalent to the random and stratified sampling techniques utilized in the selection of subjects. Random sampling of stimuli is hardly a feasible method for any but fairly narrowly circumscribed environments, such as that of a single city, as in Milgram's (1972) selection of locales to represent the several boroughs of New York City, in which a random sampling approach was in fact employed. The equivalent of the stratified sampling method presupposes, on the other hand, that the task of a comprehensive ecological description of environments in terms of the specification of relevant attributes, along with their statistical distribution has been carried out. The dimensions of the problem are effectively brought out by considering it in the context of the study of differential responses to man-made versus natural stimuli. What, indeed, is a "representative sample" of either of these two domains? Consider merely the tremendous diversity of human settlements over the globe, *qua* perceptual stimuli; and consider similarly the fully comparable diversity of natural settings, not only in terms of their topographical characteristics, but in terms of their commonness or uniqueness, or their variation from the drab to the spectacular. At the moment, no fully satisfactory mode of resolving these problems appears in sight. Probably the most realistic suggestion is to aim at stratified sampling, but sampling from a more narrowly restricted set of environments, even if at the sacrifice of some generalizability.

THE OPTIMIZATION PRINCIPLE

Postulate 2. Effects of differential levels of stimulation, and of intensity of stimulation in particular, are subject to a pervasive optimization principle, with intermediate levels being maximally preferred, or leading to maximally effective behavioral functioning.

Theoretical Basis

In a variety of contexts, variants of the optimization principle just enunciated have been fixtures in psychology for many years. They range from the realm of aesthetics, where Wundt proposed a function relating pleasantness or hedonic tone to stimulus intensity that rises to a maximum in the low-intensity range, to more general theories of arousal such as Berlyne's (1967), Fiske and Maddi's (1961) conception of the role of stimulus variation, Leuba's (1955; 1962) analysis of learning and development, and a variety of theories of performance as related to levels of motivation, tension, or stress (e.g., Welford, 1973). The principle has similarly been applied to the function relating preferential choice to stimulus properties such as complexity, or informational content (e.g., Vitz, 1966a,b). The issues to be resolved in this regard concern (a) the range of dimensions of stimulation to which the principle should be extended (e.g., is it limited to variables of intensity, or does it include such qualitative variables as pitch and hue, redundancy of pattern, novelty, and incongruity, etc.?), (b) the basis for the operation of the principle, and (c) its extension to cover the role of levels of stimulation in development. While each of these questions is in part theoretical, they are best examined in the context of the empirical information available regarding them.

Empirical Evidence

No attempt to review the extensive experimental literature relating to this question would be appropriate here; suffice it to refer to Berlyne's (1967) theoretical paper, which summarizes much of the data available up to that date, and to point to further demonstrations of similar inverted-U shaped relationships to preference with respect to auditory frequency and amplitude by Vitz (1972) and Schoenpflug (1971), along with a variety of further recent experimental aesthetics data summarized by Berlyne (1971, pp. 210 ff.). These studies do appear to have established the validity of the principle for other than intensity dimensions, including most of those cited above. Of particular interest for us is the finding that environmental stimuli scaled for complexity, including both experimentally constructed ones (Schwarz and Werbik, 1971) and actual scenes from the physical environment (Wohlwill, 1968; 1973; in press) have provided evidence for the applicability of the optimization principle in this realm.

What is the actual basis for this ubiquitous tendency for intermediate values along the most diverse stimulus dimensions to be maximally preferred, or to lead to optimal performance? Two possibilities may be suggested. One would postulate an intrinsic homeostatic process governing response to stimulus dimensions, having the effect of an avoidance or aversive response to any stimulus that, by virtue of its degree of deviation from some assumed neutral point, results in a disturbance of the organism's equilibrium. Responses to extremes of temperature represent a clear instance of such a process, which is similarly plausible for aversive reactions to high-intensity stimuli, whether visual, auditory, or olfactory, particularly where these approach the threshold of pain or discomfort.

Can such a model be extended to the low-intensity end of continua, or to stimulus dimensions such as complexity, where it is more difficult to invoke a physiologically based homeostatic mechanism? In order to do so, one would need to postulate a rather more general process, directed at the maintenance of an optimal level of arousal or activation (e.g., Fiske and Maddi, 1961), and involving perhaps some modal rate of information-processing, as well as optimal levels with respect to intensity variables. The fact that measures of cortical activity, along with those of autonomic activity of the central nervous system, have each in their different way been shown to be correlated with dimensions such as complexity and other collative properties (cf. Berlyne, 1967), along with the more obvious physiological correlates of stimulus-intensity, renders such a general mechanism rather plausible.

A second alternative must, however, be considered, not necessarily in competition with the first, but at the least complementing it and being moderated by it. This is the role of the individual's adaptation level established with respect to a particular dimension. The inverted-U shaped function may in fact be in part based on differential responses to stimuli as a function of their deviation from such ALs; that is, we may postulate that response is optimal for levels of stimuli within a certain range of the adaptation level, falling off to either side. This interpretation derives special cogency from two sets of findings. First, research on preference for visual complexity, by Vitz (1966*b*) and Dorfman and McKenna (1966) has disclosed that such data are subject to very large individual differences, so that the modal inverted-U shaped form emerging from the averaged data represents in fact a composite of individual sets of curves that vary from approximately linear, positive monotonic functions of complexity through inverted-V shaped to negative monotonic functions. Although no direct evidence exists that would allow us to ascribe these individual differences to differences in adaptation levels, this appears to be a reasonable interpretation for them.

The argument is further strengthened by considering an interesting finding of Vitz (1972), who reports preference functions for loudness (of tones) and for pitch individually by subject ($N = 16$). The loudness functions reveal a high degree of inconsistency across individuals, while those for pitch are much more uniform. Since loudness is subject to the individual's control to a considerable extent, particularly for musical stimuli (simply by adjusting the volume control on radio, hi-fi, or TV set), one would expect it to show much greater variation in adaptation levels than would be the case for tonal pitch, for which different individuals' experience (in our culture) would be fairly constant.

Finally, we may consider briefly the applicability of the optimal-level concept to the realm of behavioral development. This question has most recently been discussed at some length in another paper by the senior author (Wohlwill, 1974*a*), and thus will only be given rather summary treatment here. Psychologists who have concerned themselves with the role of early experience, whether at the animal level (e.g., Hebb) or at the human level, have been inclined to work from a basically linear model, in which cognitive development, as well as behavioral development in a more general sense, is regarded as monotonically related to sheer amount of perceptual and cognitive stimulation.

In the paper just referred to, evidence is cited from a variety of sources to indicate the inadequacy of such a linear hypothesis. The evidence derives in part from research on development in infancy by Wachs and his associates (Wachs, Uzgiris, and Hunt, 1971; Wachs, 1973), which points to conditions of *over*stimulation as indeed detrimental to development. This syndrome includes such conditions as high noise levels in the home, high incidents of interaction with visitors and neighbors, and lack of privacy—a syndrome that is suggestive in its resemblance to the typical environmental conditions faced by a child growing up in an inner city slum. To further counteract the assumption that optimal development requires a maximum of stimulus experience, data can be cited from children growing up under relatively isolated conditions in northern Norway (Haggard, 1973, pp. 99–144; Hollos and Cowan, 1973). These show a highly selective pattern of relatively minor impairment, on particular measures of verbal and intellectual development (e.g., verbal subtests of the Wechsler Intelligence Scale for Children [WISC]; role-taking measures), suggestive of a process of adaptation to the requirements of a given environment more than of any generalized type of developmental retardation, such as found, for instance, in some studies of institutionalized children. The upshot of this evidence, then, is that the behavioral development of children appears also to be subject to a principle of optimal–levels of stimulation; at the same time, as argued more fully in the abovementioned papers, qualitative aspects of the stimulus environment, and in particular the extent to which it may interfere with selective attention to relevant features of the environment, need to be taken into account to complement the role of stimulation level.

Methodological Issues

Three important methodological points derive from the research discussed above. First of all, to the extent that curvilinear relationships hold between levels of stimulation and behavioral responses, it clearly becomes imperative to obtain adequately scaled measures of a given environmental variable, at the very least at an ordinal, and preferably an equal-interval level, and to sample the dimension of interest over a sufficiently wide range of the variable to detect any possible curvilinearity in the function. Indeed, Berlyne (1967) suggests that in a number of instances where the expected inverted-U pattern has not been encountered, this may be the result of a failure to include a sufficiently extended range of the stimulus continuum. Thus the resort to dichotomous classification of stimuli, practiced by Berlyne himself with regard to the collative variables he has studied, and by all too many other investigators, emerges as highly unsatisfactory. A particular instance of interest for us comes from the work of Sonnenfeld (1967, pp. 42–59) on preference for terrains of differing topography, where such variables as amount of relief, water, and vegetation in the terrain, along with the variable of temperature, were all represented in dichotomous form in a study of the relationship between preference and the individual's adaptation to a particular type of environment. While the refined degree of scaling required to demonstrate the validity of the bimodal "butterfly" curve relating preference to discrepancy from adaptation level may be difficult to achieve with respect to such variables, it does seem possible to strive for at least an ordinally scaled set of stimuli that would give a more complete picture of different groups' response to such stimuli.

A second, closely related point is that the application of linear-correlation methods, including in particular factor-analysis, to such data is necessarily suspect. For instance, Mehrabian and Russell's (1974) selection of arousal and pleasantness as independent dimensions, based on their emergence as orthogonal factors in their factor-analytic data, ignores the considerable amount of evidence amassed that points to a curvilinear relationship between the two, as in fact suggested by the optimization principle. We are very much in need in this area of multivariate techniques applicable to sets of variables that are not related in linear fashion to one another.

Finally, the compelling evidence provided by Vitz (1966b) and by Dorfman and McKenna (1966) of marked individual differences in the shapes of preference functions shows the need for caution in relying on group data to derive such functions, which may result in a serious loss of information, and indeed outright distortion of the true state of affairs. More positively, it points to the desirability of obtaining relevant information concerning the individual, to aid in the interpretation of individual differences encountered with respect to such functions. Determination of the subject's pre-existing adaptation level with respect to the dimension under study should prove particularly valuable. Indeed Schoenpflug (1971) was able to demonstrate that maxima for preference functions in response to tones varying in frequency may be systematically displaced through experimentally induced changes in adaptation–levels resulting from prior extended exposure to a particular tone. This reference to adaptation levels as possible parameters governing the shape of the preference function leads us directly into the third problem area of our paper.

THE ROLE OF ADAPTATION LEVEL IN RESPONSE TO ENVIRONMENTS

Postulate 3.   The individual evaluates an environment on a given dimension in terms of a frame of reference established through prior experience in previous environments. This frame of reference determines the adaptation level to which magnitudes on such dimensions are referred.

The theoretical basis for this postulate is, of course, to be found in the adaptation-level theory of Harry Helson (1964); it represents, in fact, little more than a direct application of that theory to the realm of judgment of environmental attributes. While the empirical support for that theory in a general sense is abundant, very little prior research has attempted to apply it to the environmental area. The previously mentioned study by Sonnenfeld (1967) represents a partial exception in this regard, but is limited by the dichotomized form in which the various stimulus attributes included in the study were presented.

The pilot study we carried out (Wohlwill and Kohn, 1973) served to impress us with the potential value of this theoretical framework when applied to an individual's evaluation of his environment. It involved a comparison of ratings of a middle-sized community (that of Harrisburg, Pennsylvania), along a number of dimensions of the physical and social environment, on the part of persons who had recently moved to that area from two contrasting types of prior environments; i.e., large metropolitan areas, as opposed to small-town or rural residences. On a number of different dimensions, we found significant differences in the assessment of Harrisburg that were as predicted from adaptation-level theory; i.e., the city was judged more noisy, crowded, polluted, etc., by migrants from small-town environments than from those who had come from metropolitan areas.

This study is largely superseded by the junior author's recently completed dissertation, which warrants presentation in some detail, to illustrate not only the different ways in which the adaptation-level framework can be applied to the problem of environmental assessment, but the limits on its applicability, and the methodological issues that arise in using this approach.

ADAPTATION LEVELS AND ENVIRONMENTAL ASSESSMENT: AN ILLUSTRATIVE STUDY[4]

The rationale of this study was derived from experiments on the effects of internalized anchors on judgment of stimulus magnitude (cf. Guilford, 1954; Sherif and Hovland, 1961; Helson, 1964; Appley, 1971). These investigations offered empirical verification of propositions concerning the effects of anchor values and past experiences on the prevailing adaptation level. They provided

[4] The assistance of Mr. Harold Donohue and of The New York City Board of Election in the conduct of this research is gratefully acknowledged. The research was supported in part by a Doctoral Dissertation Support Grant from the National Science Foundation.

fairly consistent evidence, both with readily quantifiable physical stimuli and with more complex stimulus materials, that internalized frames of reference function as anchors in judgment and, of particular importance for the present study, such frames shift with a change in the level of stimulation.

In the present study, the judgments were made in terms of a set of rating scales referring to diverse aspects of the environment that could reasonably be assumed to be related to community size. Thus a subject's adaptation level with respect to these attributes may be assumed to be proportional to the size (i.e., population) of the community in which he has been living.

Four major hypotheses have been formulated in relation to four separate research objectives. The first objective is to apply adaptation-level theory principles to a comparative study of responses to an environment located at the extreme of the size dimension (New York City), on the part of persons migrating from communities of three different sizes. The hypothesis is that newcomers from smaller communities will evaluate New York as higher on dimensions assumed to be directly related to size, such as noise, crowding, incidence of crime, and pace of life, and lower on dimensions assumed to be inversely related to size, such as friendliness and safety, in comparison with newcomers from larger communities.

The second research objective is to study the effect of a change in environments on the individual's assessment of his former community. This problem is of interest in regard to the question (heretofore unexplored) of whether adaptation level phenomena work backward in time; i.e., whether the memory of an earlier experienced environment is affected by a subsequently experienced one. An extension of adaptation-level theory to such retrospective judgments leads to the hypothesis that migrants from a given community size will judge their former community to be higher on dimensions negatively related to size and lower on those related positively compared to the current (control group) residents.

The third objective is to show that differences in the individual's adaptation level produce differences in the functions relating perceived levels of stimulation to the variable of community size. The stimuli used for this phase of the investigation are communities of varying size portrayed by sets of photographs.

Here, the hypothesis is that for any given level of size of a community that is the object of judgment, individuals residing in or having migrated from larger communities will assess the community being evaluated as higher on dimensions related negatively to size and lower on those related positively, compared with individuals from smaller communities.

The final research objective is to study the effects of a change in environment on the individual's assessment of the photographically represented communities. Thus, the comparison is between the migrant and control groups, and the hypothesis is that for any given level of size of the judged community, individuals who have recently migrated to New York City will assess the community being evaluated as higher on dimensions related negatively to size and lower on those related positively, compared to the control-group judges residing in communities comparable to the newcomer's place of origin in size.

Method

The migrant groups, consisting of 117 residents of Manhattan, were obtained in part through newspaper advertisements and in part from rolls of newly registered voters. These groups are defined in terms of the size of their former communities. Thus, the large-urban group is composed of individuals who came from urban areas whose metropolitan populations exceeded 1.1 million (N = 43). The middle-sized-city group is made up of individuals who came from cities whose metropolitan area was greater than 100,000 and less than 750,000 persons (N = 45). The small-town group consists of individuals who have lived in communities of 25,000 persons or less (N = 29).

All newcomers had to be married, have moved to Manhattan for the first time during the previous year, and have lived in their former community, or communities of equivalent size, for at least five years prior to moving to New York.

All participants in the study were interviewed at their homes.

The migrant groups were found to be fairly comparable: The age range within each group was from the mid-twenties to the mid-thirties; all had some education beyond high school (in fact, the majority had college degrees); the size of each household was small, ranging from two to four persons; and most families lived in four-room apartments. Perhaps the most important criterion is the length of time the newcomers had been in New York at the time of the interview. Again, the groups were found to be comparable, each having moved to New York City about eight months previously, on the average.

Once the migrant sample was completed, an attempt was made to locate control large-urban, middle-sized-city, and small-town groups that would have comparable distributions with respect to age, education, income, and family size. One hundred and eighteen control subjects were obtained from three large urban cities (N = 46), four middle-sized cities (N = 41), and five small towns (N = 31). However, the control sample as a whole differed from the migrant sample in certain respects: The control group subjects were on the average two years older, had a lower income, two years less education, one more child in the family, and lived in homes with more indoor and outdoor space.

Table 1. Mean Ratings of New York City for 15 Dimensions for Each Place-of-Origin Group

Question	Label of penultimate categories	Migrant group			
		Large urban $N = 43$	Middle-sized $N = 45$	Small town $N = 49$	p^*
1. How friendly would you say the people are here?	Very friendly (8) Very unfriendly (2)	5.36	5.22	5.18	NS
2. How much environmental noise would you say there is around town?	A great deal (8) Very little (2)	8.00	7.83	7.86	NS
3. How would you characterize the pace of life here?	Very rushed (8) Very relaxed (2)	7.47	7.36	7.50	NS
4. How large would you say New York is?	Very large (8) Very small (2)	8.86	8.49	8.79	NS
5. How safe are women alone at night?	Very safe (8) Very unsafe (2)	3.73	3.15	3.25	NS
6. How badly polluted would you say the air is?	Very much (8) Very little (2)	7.21	7.67	7.89	NS
7. How frequently would you say that incidents of major crimes occur?	Very frequently (8) Very rarely (2)	6.79	7.36	7.04	NS

Question	Anchors				
8. How would you characterize this place in terms of general crowding and congestion?	A great deal (8) Very little (2)	7.43	7.87	7.61	NS
9. How crowded were the stores where you do most of your shopping?	A great deal (8) Very little (2)	6.47	6.78	6.85	NS
10. How much greenery would you say there is around town?	A great deal (8) Very little (2)	2.79	3.28	3.00	NS
11. How would you describe the choice of goods available to you?	Very good (8) Very bad (2)	8.17	8.31	8.46	NS
12. How would you rate the opportunities for recreation?	Very good (8) Very bad (2)	5.82	7.29	6.65	$< .01$
13. How safe do you feel going from place to place?	Very safe (8) Very unsafe (2)	6.39	6.04	5.85	NS
14. How difficult would you say it is getting around?	Very difficult (8) Very easy (2)	4.46	4.50	4.14	NS
15. How do you find the service you get in stores and other places of business?	Very good (8) Very bad (2)	5.20	4.69	4.04	$< .05$

* Significance levels of differences among migrant groups, based on univariate ANOVAS.

Table 2. Mean Ratings of the Migrant Groups' Former Communities and the Control Groups' Current Communities

Scale	Group	Large urban $N = 46, 43^*$	Middle-sized $N = 41, 45^*$	Small town $N = 31, 29^*$	p
1. Friendliness	Control	6.12	5.99	6.97	$< .05$ CS[a]
	Migrant	5.88	6.53	6.38	NS M-C[b]
2. Noise level	Control	6.19	5.02	3.64	$< .01$ CS
	Migrant	4.81	3.37	2.57	$< .01$ M-C
3. Pace of life	Control	5.43	5.15	3.93	$< .01$ CS
	Migrant	4.88	3.91	2.96	$< .01$ M-C
4. Size of community	Control	5.68	4.97	3.00	$< .01$ CS
	Migrant	5.87	4.47	2.96	NS M-C
5. Safety of women	Control	4.21	4.97	7.09	$< .01$ CS
	Migrant	5.18	6.07	7.20	$< .01$ M-C
6. Air pollution	Control	6.27	5.31	3.38	$< .01$ CS
	Migrant	5.83	4.27	2.08	$< .01$ M-C

7. Crime	Control	6.58	4.33	2.14	<.01 CS
	Migrant	5.67	4.30	2.73	NS M-C
8. Crowding and congestion	Control	5.34	4.80	2.49	<.01 CS
	Migrant	4.62	3.54	2.55	<.01 M-C
9. Crowding in stores	Control	5.50	4.97	3.90	<.01 CS
	Migrant	4.96	4.20	3.77	<.01 M-C
10. Greenery	Control	5.89	6.46	7.64	<.01 CS
	Migrant	6.88	7.67	8.41	<.01 M-C
11. Choice of goods	Control	6.50	5.68	5.10	<.01 CS
	Migrant	5.95	5.18	4.06	<.01 M-C
12. Recreation opportunities	Control	6.42	6.12	6.15	<.05 CS
	Migrant	6.66	5.73	5.21	NS M-C
13. Sense of personal safety	Control	6.85	6.70	7.34	<.01 CS
	Migrant	6.90	7.58	8.10	<.01 M-C
14. Difficulty in getting around	Control	4.76	3.90	2.49	<.01 CS
	Migrant	4.53	3.50	2.97	NS M-C
15. Service received in stores	Control	5.82	5.84	6.39	<.05 CS
	Migrant	5.85	6.28	6.47	NS M-C

* First listed N is for control group, second for migrant group.
a CS = Significance level of the analysis-of-variance test for community-size differences.
b M-C = Significance level for migrant control group differences.

Results

Evaluation of Present and Former Communities

A set of 15 9-point rating scales was employed to determine the subjects' evaluation of their former and present communities. (The scales used are shown in Table 1.)

The results are based on both multivariate and univariate analysis-of-variance tests, since the responses to the individual scales were significantly intercorrelated. In regard to the first hypothesis, the multivariate test of the New York City ratings by the migrant groups showed significant overall place-of-origin group differences (approximately $F = 1.73$ for 30/192 df: $p < .05$).

The univariate tests showed significant differences as hypothesized for only one of the 15 scales: judgments of service received in stores. The newcomers from larger communities assessed the city as higher on the service dimension compared to the newcomers from smaller communities ($p < .05$). A second scale, opportunities for recreation, showed a significant group difference that went counter to the hypothesis ($F = 6.37$, $p < .01$). The mean rating of the middle-sized-city group (7.29), was *higher* than the mean of the small-town group (6.65).

Thus, the prior environments of the newcomers, and the adaptation levels established in those environments, appear to have been largely ineffectual in their influence on the evaluations of New York City. The meaning of this finding may emerge more clearly after we have considered the results from the control groups.

Let us turn now to the test of the second hypothesis, which concerns the ratings of the migrants' former communities, compared to those of the control groups' current communities (see Table 2). The multivariate test of these ratings revealed very significant differences between the migrant and control groups (approximately $F = 5.98$, 15/209 df; $p < .01$), as well as differences across the three community-size categories within the migrant and control groups ($F = 10.40$, 30/418 df; $p < .01$).

The univariate tests showed that the newcomers judged their former communities, which were equivalent in size to the control groups' current communities, as being lower on the dimensions of noise level, air pollution, pace of life, general crowding and congestion, choice of goods, and as being higher on the dimensions of amount of greenery, sense of personal safety and safety of women alone at night, in comparison with the control group ratings ($p < .01$).

While the analysis-of-variance data concerning the community-size variable do not bear on the second hypothesis directly, these data are important for two reasons. First, significant differences were found among the group means for all 15 scales; 10 of these differences were significant beyond the .01 level.

These differences were all in accordance with the assumed direct relationship between the perceived environmental dimensions and the population levels. The scales that were less highly correlated with community size—friendliness, sense of personal safety, service received in stores, recreation opportunities, and difficulty in getting around—generally refer to the more subjective aspects of the social environment, and it is plausible that they would be less strongly determined by population magnitude alone.

The second reason why the community-size variable is of importance for us relates to differences between the evaluations of the large urban communities and those of New York City. With the exception of the five scales mentioned above, the three means for the New York environment are sharply differentiated from the mean of the large-urban group ratings of both the former and current metropolitan areas; i.e., cities with more than one million in population. It thus appears that for the New York migrants, the city is experienced as being extreme with respect to nearly all of the environmental attributes.

Evaluation of Photographically Represented Communities

The ratings obtained for the seven dimensions of the photographically portrayed communities that bear on our third and fourth hypotheses will now be considered. Before discussing these results, we should explain the manner in which communities were represented through sets of photographs and the procedure employed for this phase of the study.

More than 700 color slides were taken of 24 towns and cities in Pennsylvania, New Jersey, Connecticut, and Massachusetts. Within each community, a diversity of geographic locations were photographed. These places approximated populations of 400, 4000, 40,000, 400,000, and 4,000,000. (The choice of such a geometric progression seemed reasonable, both in terms of what we know about the perception of incremental changes in such variables as brightness and loudness, and in view of Helson's formulation of adaptation level as the geometric mean of a set of stimuli.)

These photographs were combined in sets of nine, each set representing a single community. Seven different series of such sets were constructed. Each series consisted of five different communities, representing the five population levels. The order of presentation of the communities was randomized.

Each subject was given the seven environmental scales and asked to apply each in turn to one of the seven series of photographic sets. The order of presentation of the scales was rotated, with the exception of the community-size scale, which was administered last, so as not to draw the subject's attention directly to population size as an independent variable.

The main results are shown in Figures 1 and 2. They reveal fairly consistent differences between the large-urban, middle-sized-city, and small-

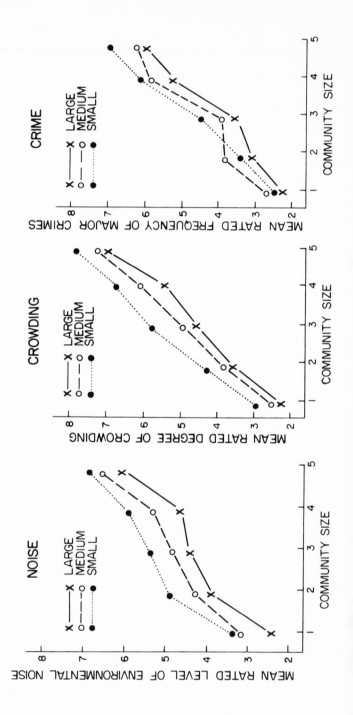

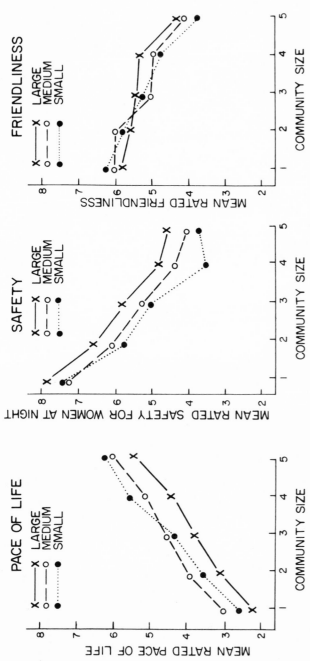

Figure 1. Ratings of photographically portrayed communities varying in size on six environmental attributes. (The levels of the size variable represent communities of metropolitan areas of about 400, 4000, 40,000, 400,000, and 4,000,000 population for levels 1 through 5, respectively.) Only the ratings of the three control groups are shown.

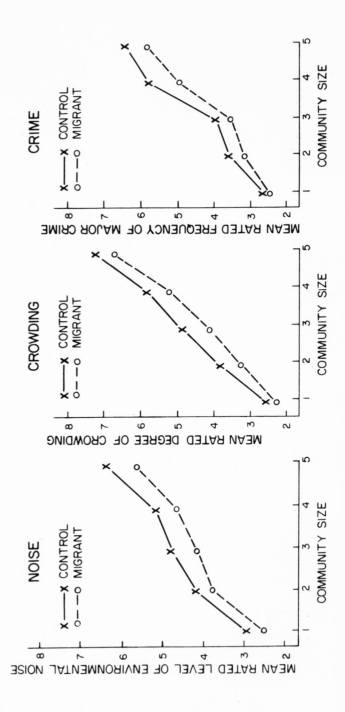

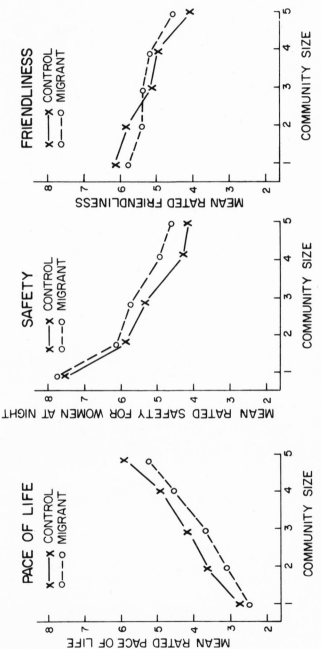

Figure 2. Ratings of the migrant and control group of photographically portrayed communities varying in size on six environmental attributes.

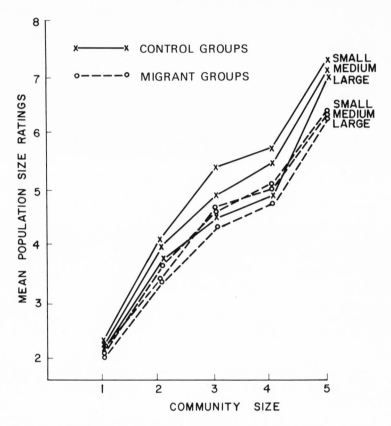

Figure 3. Population-size ratings of photographically portrayed communities varying in size.

town groups (Figure 1)[5] and between the migrant and control groups (Figure 2), which were statistically significant beyond the .01 level for all of the dimensions except friendliness, where no group differences were found at all. Furthermore, almost without exception, these group differences are in the direction predicted from adaptation-level theory; i.e., for communities of a given size, the small town group gave higher ratings for noise, crowding, crime, and pace of life, and lower ratings for safety, in accordance with the third hypothesis. Similarly, the migrant group ratings were lower than those of the control group

[5] The values plotted here are limited to the data for the control group, since this group provided a more direct test of the role of adaptation level, based on differences in the size of their respective communities, than the migrant group, whose adaptation levels would have been contaminated by their more recent experience in New York City. In actual fact, however, the results for the migrant group exhibited very similar group differences, though to an attenuated degree, as would be expected.

for noise, crowding, crime, and pace of life, and higher for safety, as predicted according to the fourth hypothesis.

In a more general vein, it is worth pointing out the demonstrated effectiveness of these sets of photographs in conveying a sense of differentiable communities that could serve as a basis for far-reaching inferences about the attributes of these environments. More particularly, the results portrayed in Figures 1 and 2 give testimony to the high degree of relationship, in the minds of our respondents, between the various attributes on which the communities were rated and the size of these communities. Only the friendliness dimension proved an exception, showing but a weak association with the size variable. It might be noted that many of the respondents found it difficult to make this particular rating, with the result that many of them failed to discriminate among the communities on this dimension.

Finally, we may draw attention to the ratings for the community-size dimension shown in Figure 3, which demonstrates that these photographic sets did indeed elicit highly consistent judgments as to size that were directly related to the actual size of these communities.[6] At the same time, we see here again evidence of adaptation-level effects in the separation between the migrant- and control-group functions, and to a lesser extent in the differences associated with the size of the respondent's community of origin.

Discussion

What, then, do these results indicate in regard to the role played by a newcomer's frame of reference or adaptation level in his evaluation of both his new and his former environments?

In regard to the ratings of New York City by the three migrant groups, the data are hardly supportive, with only one of the 15 scales showing group differences as hypothesized. The failure of adaptation-level effects to operate in this setting may well be related to the extremity of the stimulus environment that was the object of judgment. As noted above, the earlier study (Wohlwill and Kohn, 1973) of migrants' evaluation of a middle-size community, Harrisburg, Pennsylvania, did reveal group differences on a number of dimensions that were in accordance with adaptation-level theory. Similarly, in the present study, judgments of intermediate-sized communities, such as those at levels 2,

---

[6] Subjects were also asked for estimates of *absolute* (i.e., population) size of the portrayed communities. These, interestingly enough, revealed relatively accurate perceptions for those communities that corresponded to the size of the respondents' own former home towns (or current ones, in the case of the control group). This accuracy tended to fall off, however, in proportion to the discrepancy between the size of that home town and that of the photographically portrayed community.

3, and 4 of the photographic sets, were found to be systematically related to the respondent's adaptation level, inferred from the size of his home community.

Furthermore, if we consider the migrants' ratings of the photographed communities and of their own former communities, as compared to the control groups' ratings of the same photographed communities and their own communities, we find strong support for the conclusion that perceptions of an earlier experienced environment are affected by subsequently experienced ones in a manner consistent with adaptation-level theory. These findings suggest that as our adaptation levels shift toward a new level of stimulation, previously experienced levels cease to be experienced as neutral. As a result, should any of the migrants decide to return to their former communities, they may well experience them as being noisier and more crowded, as well as less safe than they remembered, even though the communities in question may not have changed much. In other words, after their "homecoming" their evaluation of their communities may be made not so much in direct comparison with the levels of stimulation experienced in New York, but in comparison with their memory of their old communities, which has been changed by the experience of adapting to New York.

CONCLUSION

In this concluding section we propose to take up briefly two broader theoretical issues that are not only raised by our treatment of environment–behavior relations but appear to cut across the major varieties of research in this area. The first concerns the approach to be taken in isolating and defining environmental variables. The second, closely related to the first, concerns the way in which the individual should be incorporated into the $B = f(E)$ equation.

The Objectivity Issue in the Definition of Environmental Variables

Workers in the field of environmental perception have stressed the importance of studying the environment as perceived or experienced, *rather than* as defined and measured in objective, physical terms. For a number of reasons we wish to oppose ourselves to this view. First of all, this subjectivist bias will inevitably lead to an environmental psychology built on quicksand, given the difficulty, not to say impossibility, of studying in any systematic fashion functional relationships between phenomenally or experientially defined variables and behavioral variables. What, in fact, tends to occur under the influence of such a view is that the establishment of such relationships is sidestepped altogether, and replaced by a sterile mode of essentially descriptive research, best exemplified by the profusion of factor-analytic studies of semantic-differential ratings and, more recently, personal-construct analyses that have filled the pages of environment-and-behavior publications.

Furthermore, if we replace objective by phenomenal or experiential measures of environmental variables the result is that one of the central questions for an environmental psychologist is immediately begged out of existence—i.e., what are the objective determinants or correlates of our experiential world? Rather than short-circuiting this question by attempting a direct linkage between phenomenal experience and response variables such as preference, for instance, we would suggest that factors relating to the perceiver—e.g., selective attention, limited information-processing capacity, preferential response to particular cues, as well as motivational and value-related factors of a more individual nature—be studied as intervening variables modulating environment-behavior relations.

The case for objective definition of environmental dimensions emerges most sharply with reference to the first of the postulates discussed in our paper. Indeed, that discussion was intended as much to delineate the research strategy that appears to us to be indicated in the study of environmental preference—as well as the problems involved in specifying and isolating the stimulus determinants of such preference—as to provide support for the postulate in a substantive sense; as we saw, the empirical foundation for the proposition in question remains somewhat shaky at present.

Even in the case of this research, however, the issue may seem to be substantially clouded by the fact that in environmental research the assessment of stimulus variables must typically be carried out by recourse to ratings by independent judges, rather than by strictly objective measurement. Variables such as "complexity," "incongruity," "unity," and the like are difficult to specify in strictly physical terms. The approach we are advocating would, however, attempt to come as close as possible to the model of objective measurement by providing judges with concrete referents for the attributes to be judged, and treating them as sensors of environmental variation with respect to these attributes. Thus, complexity may be defined in terms of diversity with respect to specified stimulus dimensions such as color and texture. The degree of consensus for the resulting judgments serves, furthermore, as a validating criterion in this procedure.

Turning to the second postulate, the argument remains basically the same, though the problem of specifying the particular dimensions that would be expected to conform to the optimization principle was dealt with only on an illustrative basis. At the same time the very specification of a curvilinear relationship is itself a strong argument for the importance of objective, quantifiable measures; indeed, the substitution of phenomenal for objective measures may well prevent the postulated relationships from emerging. For instance, when preference is related to phenomenal complexity, it is conceivable that the U-shaped relationship fails to emerge, because high objective levels of complexity may be experienced as random, unanalyzable, and unstructurable stimulus fields, and thus as relatively lacking in complexity (cf. Heckhausen, 1964). This is not an argument against the use of objective measures, but rather for monitoring the relationship between objectively defined and phenomenally experienced quantities, as one possible clue to the interpretation of optimization-type functions.

Finally, in the case of the third postulate, the seeming neatness of the observed functions shown in Figures 1 and 2 actually belies the fact that the responses were necessarily mediated by a series of inferential steps, linking the stimulus series (the five photographically portrayed communities) to the variables being judged; that is, the respondents presumably picked up unspecified cues from these stimuli that suggested the relative size of the portrayed communities to them. Further, we must assume that they operated on the basis of inferences concerning the relationships between community size and the dimensions to be rated—inferences that, in the case of some of these dimensions (such as pace of life and incidence of crime) could bear little if any relation to identifiable stimulus attributes of these environments. Admittedly, then, our focus on objectively defined measures of environmental variables remains largely implicit in the case of this study. Yet, the fact remains that these functions demonstrate the individual's readiness to respond to the most diverse environments in dimensional terms, and in a highly consistent fashion.[7]

It would be valuable, in further research on this problem, to subject both of these presumed inferential steps to closer scrutiny. For instance, the particular cues that are possible carriers of the information with respect to community size—density of buildings; amount of traffic; amount of greenery; diversity of buildings and other structures; prevalence of commercial establishments—could be investigated more specifically by suitable selection of stimuli to represent a given environment. On the other hand, the assumed relationship between community size and the several environmental attributes that have been found to covary with it might be validated, e.g., by presenting individuals with a series of verbally described communities, defined in terms of both size

---

[7] In principle, the most direct application of the adaptation-level framework to this situation would have entailed the presentation of the environmental variables explicitly, scaled in terms of some objective criteria. For instance, for the noise variable, recordings taken from various areas within communities at each of the five levels of size could have been utilized. Clearly this would have been impossible for such dimensions as pace of life and frequency of crime, however. Furthermore, the work was predicated to begin with on the existence of a substantial relationship between community size and adaptation level with respect to each of these dimensions, without which the rationale for the comparison among our three groups of origin would obviously have been invalid.

and other characteristics (e.g., "a largely residential suburb of 20,000 people, at the outskirts of a large metropolitan area in the Midwest"). In this manner, one could determine more directly the extent of the relationship between not only size but other social and geographical characteristics of communities to the rated environmental traits, and perhaps probe the bases on which such inferences are made.

The Role of the Individual in the Study of Environment–Behavior Relationships

The predilection for phenomenological or response-inferred modes of defining environmental variables in the field of environmental perception has not only diverted attention away from the description and specification of environmental properties and their relations to behavioral variables, but has, in our view, resulted in an exaggerated stress on the relativity of environmental experience to the personal perspective of a particular individual. This stress has, somewhat paradoxically, characterized much of the research and theorizing on the part of architects and geographers on problems of environmental perception. On the other hand, it has also been the object of criticism from diverse quarters (e.g., Carr and Schissler, 1969; Gump, 1971; Michelson, 1970, pp. 28 ff; Zannaras, in press), as being both unjustifiable on empirical grounds and unsatisfactory as a foundation on which to build the study of man–environment problems.

Such criticism need not by any means imply the acceptance of a simplistic environmental determinism, or of a black-box approach to the analysis of behavior. The work of Berlyne, for one, presents an excellent demonstration that a systematic study of stimulus parameters of behavior can be effectively incorporated into a theoretical framework that is directed at the internal processes mediating the role of stimulation in behavior (cf. his discussion of arousal [Berlyne, 1967]). Nor need it be incompatible with a proper recognition and treatment of individual differences in environmental–behavioral functions. For instance, it is apparent, in reference to the work considered under the first postulate, that preferential choices and other evaluative responses must inevitably be a *joint* function of stimulus parameters and variables relating to the individual respondent, whether considered in terms of the meaning he or she ascribes to a given environmental stimulus, to his or her background of experience, attitudes, and values, etc. We would maintain nevertheless that such factors should in general be regarded as modulating the expression of the environmental variables; thus, their role cannot be adequately ascertained prior to or independently of the sort of analysis of the stimulus environment that we have advocated.

Similarly, in regard to the second postulate, we did in fact point to the incontrovertible evidence of dramatic individual differences in the location of the postulated optimal levels, and indeed of the very shape of the function relating stimulus levels to responses. These facts forced us to suggest a reinterpretation of the basis and meaning of the optimal-level principle, without however detracting from the validity of our dimensional model of response to environmental stimulation. If we attribute the observed individual differences to differences in the adaptation levels that had been established through prior experience with the dimension of stimulation in question, it becomes possible to treat them as parameters that enter into the determination of the optimization function for a particular individual.

The need to recognize the interaction of stimulus variables with factors related to the individual emerges in more specific and concrete form when we consider the data from Kohn's dissertation, presented in relation to the third postulate. If we examine the curves in Figures 1 and 2, obtained from the photographic ratings, it becomes apparent that the individual's frame of reference for making these judgments, established through his prior and current experiences, acted to modulate the shape of the functions in a highly predictable fashion.

We would not claim that this formulation represents a complete account of the complex process of adaptation to a new environment, however. In fact, we have some evidence that the utility of our adaptation-level perspective is enhanced by complementing it with further information concerning the individual's mode of response to a new environment. Thus, in both the Harrisburg and New York studies we endeavored to obtain an indication of the respondents's level of environmental awareness and his use of resources, not so much for the purpose of arriving at definitive answers to these questions, but to provide cues for further investigation relating environmental perception to the process of learning to live in one's community effectively.

For instance, Harrisburg respondents were asked to locate places and buildings in and around the city. We found that the newcomers from cities larger than Harrisburg had formed a more accurate and more fully articulated cognitive map of their new environment compared to the newcomers from smaller communities. In the New York City study, another approach was employed: The respondents were asked to list the variety of places in the city they had used for all types of shopping and recreation (not a difficult task, as the respondents had only been there a few months.) These results showed that the large-urban newcomers, compared with the other two groups, sampled a larger variety of establishments and traveled a larger distance from home. Thus, there is some evidence that persons from other large cities search and consult appropriate channels of information more intensively, and presumably make better use of available resources.

The role of the information available to the person, and of the overt activity in his or her exploration of or accommodation to a new environment is not necessarily inconsistent with the adaptation-level view, but may be looked at as essential data in the allocation of a proper value to the focal, residual, and contextual stimuli that enter into adaptation-level effects, according to Helson. For instance, through overt exploratory activity (as well as with the aid of requisite knowledge) the individual may in fact succeed, in an objective sense, in reducing the actual disparity between his present and his former environments, possibly to the extent that assimilation processes replace the contrast phenomena that the classical adaptation-level effect presupposes; i.e., the actual differences are diminished, rather than exaggerated.

These considerations suggest that research on adaptation to a new environment would profit from an attempt to monitor the migrant's behavior, as well as his or her information, expectations, motivations for moving, etc. Such an approach would in fact bring the investigation of this problem closer to that which a transactionalist might favor, as represented by an actual study of newcomers' response to a new environment carried out within this theoretical framework, by Franck, Unseld, and Wentworth (1974). We would only reiterate our conviction, in this regard, that the role of these factors based in the individual should be formulated in such a way as to allow them to be incorporated into the adaptation-level formula, as modulators of the relationships predicted according to that framework. More generally, we would argue that proper attention to such factors should not and need not detract from a proper concern for the description of the actual environment within which the individual's experience is contained.

REFERENCES

Appley, M. (Ed.). *Adaptation-level theory: A symposium.* New York: Academic Press, 1971.

Berlyne, D. E. *Conflict, arousal and curiosity.* New York: McGraw-Hill, 1960.

Berlyne, D. E. Arousal and reinforcement. *Nebraska Symposium on Motivation,* 1967, *15,* 1–110.

Berlyne, D. E. *Aesthetics and psychobiology.* New York: Appleton-Century, 1971.

Berlyne, D. E. (Ed.). *Studies in the new experimental aesthetics.* New York: Wiley, 1974.

Berlyne, D. E., and Madsen, K. B. (Eds.). *Pleasure, reward, preference: Their nature, determinants, and role in behavior.* New York: Academic Press, 1973.

Brunswik, E. *Perception and the representative design of psychological experiments.* Berkeley, California: University of California Press, 1956.

Carr, S., & Schissler, D. The city as a trip; Perceptual selection and memory in the view from the road. *Environment and Behavior,* 1969, *1,* 7–36.

Dorfman, D. D. and McKenna, H. Pattern preference as a function of pattern uncertainty. *Canadian Journal of Psychology,* 1966, *20,* 143–153.

Ertel, S. Exploratory choice and verbal judgment. In D. E. Berlyne and K. B. Madsen (Eds.), *Pleasure, reward, preference.* New York: Academic Press, 1973.

Fiske, D. W. and Maddi, S. R. A conceptual framework. In D. W. Fiske and S. R. Maddi (Eds.), *Functions of varied experience.* Homewood, Illinois: Dorsey Press, 1961.

Franck, K. A., Unseld, C. T., & Wentworth, W. R. Adaptation of the newcomer: A process of construction. Unpublished manuscript, 1974.

Gibson, J. J. *The perception of the visual world.* Boston, Massachusetts: Houghton-Mifflin, 1950.

Gibson, J. J. *The senses considered as perceptual systems.* Boston, Massachusetts: Houghton-Mifflin, 1966.

Gibson, J. J. An ecological approach to visual perception. Manuscript in preparation, 1973.

Guilford, J. P. *Psychometric methods* (2nd ed.) New York: McGraw-Hill, 1954.

Gump, P. V. The behavior setting: A promising unit for environmental designers. *Landscape Architecture,* 1971, *61,* 130–134.

Haggard, E. A. Some effects of geographic and social isolation in natural settings. In J. Rasmussen (Ed.), *Man in isolation and confinement.* Chicago, Illinois: Aldine, 1973.

Hebb, D. O. *The organization of behavior.* New York: Wiley, 1949.

Heckhausen, H. Complexity in perception: phenomenal criteria and information theoretic calculus—a note on D. E. Berlyne's "Complexity Effects." *Canadian Journal of Psychology,* 1964, *18,* 168–173.

Helson, H. *Adaptation-level theory.* New York: Harper & Row, 1964.

Hollos, M. C. & Cowan, F. A. Social isolation and cognitive development: Logical operations and role-taking abilities in three Norwegian social settings. *Child Development,* 1973, *44,* 630–641.

Ittelson, W. H. Environmental perception and contemporary perceptual theory. In W. H. Ittelson (Ed.), *Environment and cognition.* New York: Seminar Press, 1973.

Jacobs, J. *The death and life of great American cities.* New York: Vintage, 1961.

Kaplan, R. Prediction of preference in the outdoor environment. Paper presented at meetings of American Psychological Association, Montreal, 1973.

Kaplan, S. Some functional aspects of environmental preference. Paper presented at meetings of American Psychological Association, Montreal, 1973.

Kaplan, S., Kaplan, R., and Wendt, J. S. Rated preference and complexity for natural and urban visual material. *Perception & Psychophysics,* 1972, *12,* 334–356.

Leuba, C. J. Toward some integration of learning theories: The concept of optimal stimulation. *Psychological Reports,* 1955, *1,* 27–33.

Leuba, C. J. Relation of stimulation intensities to learning and development. *Psychological Reports,* 1962, *11,* 55–65.

Litton, R. B. Jr. Aesthetic dimensions of the landscape. In J. V. Krutilla (Ed.), *Natural environments: Studies in theoretical and applied analysis.* Baltimore, Maryland. Johns Hopkins Press, 1973.

Lynch, K. *The image of the city.* Cambridge, Massachusetts: MIT Press, 1960.

Michelson, W. *Man and his urban environment: A sociological approach.* Reading, Massachusetts: Addison-Wesley, 1970.

Mehrabian, A., and Russell, J. A. *An approach to environmental psychology.* Cambridge, Massachusetts: MIT Press, 1974.

Milgram, S. A psychological map of New York City. *American Scientist,* 1972, *60,* 181–194.

Moos, R, H. Conceptualizations of human environments. *American Psychologist,* 1973, *28,* 652–665.

Rapoport, A., and Hawkes, R. The perception of urban complexity. *Journal of the American Institute of Planners,* 1970, *36,* 106–111.

Rapoport, A., and Kantor, R. E. Complexity and ambiguity in environmental design. *Journal of the American Institute of Planners,* 1967, *33,* 210–222.

Schoenpflug, W. *Adaptation, Aktiviertheit und Valenz.* Meisenheim, Glan, Germany: Anton Hain, 1971.

Schwarz, H., and Werbik, H. Eine experimentelle Untersuchung über den Einfluss der syntaktischen information der Anordnung von Baukorpern entlang einer Strasse auf Stimmungen des Betrachters. *Zeitschrift fur experimentelle und angewandte Psychologie,* 1971, *18,* 499–511.

Sells, S. B. Dimensions of stimulus situations which account for behavior variance. In S. B. Sells (Ed.), *Stimulus determinants of behavior.* New York: Ronald Press, 1963.

Sherif, M., and Hovland, C. I. *Social judgment.* New Haven, Connecticut: Yale University Press, 1961.

Sonnenfeld, J. Environmental perception and adaptation level in the Arctic. In D. Lowenthal (Ed.), Environmental Perception and Behavior. Chicago, Illinois: University of Chicago, (Department of Geography, *Research Paper #*109), 1967.

Venturi, R. *Complexity and contradiction in architecture.* New York: Museum of Modern Art, 1966.

Venturi, R., Brown, D. S., and Izenour, S. *Learning from Las Vegas.* Cambridge, Massachusetts: MIT Press, 1972.

Vitz, P. C. Affect as a function of stimulus variation. *Journal of Experimental Psychology,* 1966, *71,* 74–79. (a)

Vitz, P. C. Preference for different amounts of visual complexity. *Behavioral Science,* 1966, *11,* 105–114. (b)

Vitz, P. C. Preference for tones as a function of frequency (hertz) and intensity (decibels). *Perception and Psychophysics,* 1972, *11,* 84–88.

Wachs, T. D. Utilization of Piagetian approach in the investigation of early experience effects: A research strategy and some illustrative data. Paper presented at meetings of American Psychological Association, Montreal, 1973.

Wachs, T. D., Uzgiris, I. C., Hunt, J. McV. Cognitive development in infants of different age levels and from different environmental backgrounds: An explanatory investigation. *Merrill-Palmer Quarterly of Behavior and Development,* 1971, *17,* 283–317.

Wapner, S., Kaplan, B., and Cohen, S. B. An organismic-developmental perspective for understanding transactions of men in environments. *Environment and Behavior,* 1973, *5,* 255–290.

Welford, A. T. Stress and performance. *Ergonomics,* 1973, *16,* 567–580.

White, B. L. *Human infants: Experience and psychological development.* Englewood Cliffs, New Jersey: Prentice-Hall, 1971.

Wohlwill, J. F. Amount of stimulus exploration and preference as differential functions of stimulus complexity. *Perception & Psychophysics,* 1968, *4,* 307–312.

Wohlwill, J. F. Factors in the differential response to the natural and the man-made environment. Paper presented at meetings of American Psychological Association, Montreal, August, 1973.

Wohlwill, J. F. Environmental stimulation and the development of the child: How much, and what kind? Paper presented at Conference on the Environment and Cognitive Development, Arad, Israel, 1974. (a)

Wohlwill, J. F. The place of aesthetics in studies of the environment. Paper presented at meetings of International Congress of Applied Psychology, Montreal, 1974. (b)

Wohlwill, J. F. Children's response to meaningful pictures varying in diversity: Exploration time vs. preference. *Journal of Experimental Child Psychology.* In press.

Wohlwill, J. F., & Kohn, I. The environment as experienced by the migrant: An adaptation-level view. *Representative Research in Social Psychology,* 1973, *4,* 135–164.

Zannaras, G. The relation between cognitive structure and urban form: The use of maps and models. In G. Moore & R. Golledge (Eds.), *Environmental knowing.* Stroudsburg, Pennsylvania: Dowden, Hutchinson & Ross. In press.

IV

The Personality Research Paradigm in Environmental Psychology

KENNETH H. CRAIK

Abstract: The personality research paradigm, one of several strands of normal science that have been usefully engaged by the challenge of man–environment relations, is briefly described in this paper. Two extensions of the scope of personality research are reviewed: (1) the development of new techniques for assessing environmental dispositions, and (2) the use of personality assessment in predicting a range of environmental behaviors and outcomes. Application of the personality paradigm in environmental psychology may facilitate the paradigm's further articulation and refinement. Two illustrations of this possibility are discussed: (1) analyses of the concept of personal disposition, and (2) investigations of the interplay between persons and environments.

Over the last decade, the study of man–environment relations has been invigorated by the active intellectual engagement of several disciplines, including geography, environmental design and planning, psychology, natural resources management, anthropology, sociology, and political science. In the development of environmental psychology, several discrete research paradigms currently viable within scientific psychology have discovered engaging puzzles within the man-environment context. Indeed, these relatively autonomous strands of normal science undertakings largely make up the current fabric of environmental psychology (Craik, 1976). Consequently, the structure of the field can be most readily discerned by seeking to understand each psychological research

KENNETH H. CRAIK • University of California, Berkeley, California.

paradigm and how it has been extended for the purposes of studying man–environment relations.

This presentation of the role of personality research in environmental psychology will seek to convey the general spirit and scientific intentions of the paradigm, to illustrate the more or less straightforward extensions of its basic research model to the man–environment domain, and to suggest ways in which these applications of the personality research paradigm may contribute fundamentally to its further articulation and refinement. The emphasis will be upon conceptual issues and relations; illustrations of empirical findings can be found in a companion piece in this conference (Little, Chapter V).

PERSONS AND PLACES

The personality research paradigm takes *the person* as the basic unit of analysis and pays attention to the organization of each individual's total pattern of behavior (Murray, 1938). In contrast, many psychological research paradigms are organized around given classes of behavior, such as perception, cognition, motivation, and learning, seeking the determinants and conditions affecting such behaviors and the formulation of general organismic laws that hold across individuals. Personality psychologists, or personologists, offer the reminder that cognitive representations of the large-scale environment, beliefs about natural hazards, proxemic behaviors, environmental preferences, and landscape tastes are the behavioral properties of individual organisms. While a variety of psychological processes are involved in man–environment relations, the personological perspective focuses upon the person as a dynamically organized entity with its own temporal course and spatial mobility.

One can look at Midwest and see an organization of behavior settings (Barker and Wright, 1955), or one can follow the fate of persons as they individually move from one behavior setting to another and, over a longer period of observation, as they move through the life cycle. It is noteworthy that Barker and his associates initially devoted the resources of the Midwest Psychological Field Station to unobtrusive observations of the stream of behavior of persons (Barker and Wright, 1951). However, this commitment eventually shifted from person-centered observations to the study of behavior settings, a unit of analysis deemed to account more fully for overt behavior. We will return later to this scientific choice point.

DESCRIBING PERSONS

The field of personality is the scientific caretaker for the age-old problem of how best to describe a person. The task is one also encountered in everyday life and its reflective treatment has a scholarly history that is far more extensive than that of psychology. The rendering of descriptions of persons is ubiquitous in social life, often taking quite spontaneous and fleeting forms. Even the more formal personological efforts vary in their occasions, intents, formats, and audiences, as Table 1 indicates.

Many personality sketches are rendered for commemorative purposes, to celebrate the dead. The audience for a eulogy is usually a group of relatives and acquaintances, who "knew him well." The task of the eulogist is to evoke the personality of the deceased, to sum up as well as summon, and to praise or at least to appreciate. (I often begin my personality assessment course with a reading from Edward Everett's eulogy of Daniel Webster.) The audience for epitaphs tend to be strangers; epitaphs are written for the long haul of

Table 1. Occasions, Intents, and Audiences of Personality Assessments

Occasion and intent	Type of assessment	Audience

Commemorative
  To celebrate the
  dead
	Eulogies
	Epitaphs
		Friends
		Strangers

Didactic
  To provide models
  and exemplars
	"Lives" of the saints, of the
	  Caesars
	Early biographies
	"Campaign" biographies
	Case studies
		The young
		The non-elite (e.g., voters)
		The aspiring

Intrinsic or instru-
  mental
  To portray accu-
  rately
	"Pure" or objective
	  biographies
	Reports of Renaissance
	  diplomats
		Ideal standards of truth
		  and objectivity
		The government

Communicative
  To convey an impres-
  sion of a person to
  another
	Letters of introduction
	Letters of recommenda-
	  tion
		Common acquaintances
		Decision-makers

Scientific
  To specify standards
  and create methods
  for portraying others
  accurately in order
  to understand them
	Personality assessment
	  techniques
		Scientists

Applied
  To employ accurate
  assessments of persons in
  order to select and
  assign them to societal
  positions and to predict
  their performances
	Personality assessment
	  techniques
		Institutional managers and
		  decision-makers

centuries. William Butler Yeats' famous epitaph for his own gravestone in Sligo, Ireland has the lines:

> Cast a cold eye
> On life, on death.
> Horseman, pass by!

In his *Spoon River Anthology,* Edgar Lee Masters used the format of the epitaph to depict in vivid summaries the key sentiments, insights, and events in the lives of former inhabitants of a small mid-American agricultural town, perhaps not unlike Midwest itself. Here is Franklin Jones:

> If I could have lived another year
> I could have finished my flying machine
> And become rich and famous.
> Hence it is fitting the workmen
> Who tried to chisel a dove for me
> Made it look more like a chicken.
> For what is it all but being hatched,
> And running about the yard,
> To the day of the block?
> Save a man has an angel's brain
> And sees the ax from the first!
> (Masters, 1916, p. 84)

Collectively, the epitaphs of Spoon River convey the rich diversity of persons to be found in any community or social unit.

Another occasion for rendering descriptions of persons is to accomplish didactic aims, by providing models and exemplars for the young, the aspiring and the non-elite. Thus we have the "lives" of the Caesars and the saints, the biographies of heroes and other estimable persons and, for contemporary voters, the campaign biographies of political candidates. In psychiatry and clinical psychology, case studies are developed to show novices and apprentices what certain kinds of infrequently encountered persons are like. In didactic personality descriptions, the highlighting of virtues, vices, and psychological impairments overrides any inclination toward detached portrayal. Indeed, many historians of the biographical form readily accept the intent to praise heroes and blame villains. Johnston, for example, observes:

> However wide of the mark many biographies may actually be, with few exceptions the intent has doubtless been to memorialize the best that has been known as to the springs of human conduct and accomplishment—to explain why the man has stood out from the crowd and to gratify the world's deep desire to honor its heroes. (Johnston, 1927, p. 86)

The eminent biographical scholar, Harold Nicolson, has stressed the need to balance empathy and esteem with realism. In delineating the salient and unifying themes of character in his lives of the Caesars, Plutarch noted that "sometimes a matter of less moment, an expression or a jest, informs us better of their characters and inclinations than the most famous sieges, the greatest armaments, or the bloodiest battles whatsoever." Nevertheless, it was Suetonius, in his lives of the Caesars, who came closer to this goal through his more detached curiosity, his keener eye for significant detail, and his greater readiness to debunk and tell all (and there was a lot to tell about some of the Caesars). To convey his ideal of the "pure" biography, free of commemorative and didactic biases, Nicolson points to Chaucer:

> . . . Chaucer, the greatest of English realists, a man who possessed all the energies and all the faculties of the supreme biographer: curiosity, acute psychological observation, humour, sympathy, immense synthetic force, a genius for selection— such were the gifts which Chaucer, had he wished, could have brought to biography. (Nicolson, 1928, p. 25)

However, in continuing this thought, Nicolson brings to mind the ever-present and vexing issue of validity:

> What lives could Chaucer have written of his acquaintance Petrarch or his patron John of Gaunt—inaccurate perhaps, obscene possibly, but overwhelmingly vivid and convincing! (Nicolson, 1928, p. 25)

Nicolson is well known for his advocacy of "pure" or objective biographies, foreseeing the involvement of psychology in these efforts and anticipating such modern works as Edel's biography of Henry James (Edel, 1953–1972). The intent of intrinsic and instrumental personality descriptions thereby shifts to the goal of accurate portrayal. In intrinsic personality descriptions, the audience is difficult to identify; perhaps it is the ideal standards of truth and objectivity. The scientific field of personality assessment continues this intrinsic orientation, seeking to specify standards and methods for portraying others accurately in order to understand persons. In instrumental assessments, the audience may well be the government or other institutions. Someone (I believe David Riesman) traces the interview as a formal social encounter to the Renaissance diplomats who would be sent to one of the Italian states with the main goals of gaining an audience with the prince, sizing him up as a person, and conveying as accurately as possible in his dispatches the character and dispositions of the foreign prince. Machiavelli was one of the diplomats who often waited for months through long frustrating efforts to gain such an interview with the local prince (Chabod, 1958).

In other instances, the occasions for personality descriptions may be primarily communicative, yielding surrogates for direct acquaintance with the person. In previous centuries, when persons traveled to foreign lands, they commonly carried letters of introduction to individuals encountered there, written by mutual acquaintances. The present-day letter of recommendation serves a similar function and can stand as a prototype of the use of personality descriptions within the modern social system for selecting individuals for various positions within it. These communicative and instrumental uses of personality assessment techniques are clearly a cultural product, reflecting contemporary trends of individual mobility, urbanization, occupational specialization, and complex social structures.

EXTENDING THE PERSONALITY PARADIGM IN ENVIRONMENTAL PSYCHOLOGY

The scientific study of personality begins with the recognition that persons are extraordinarily complex and multidimensional entities. Indeed, personality assessors delight in the diversity of persons and they are connoisseurs of individuality. In this respect, personality assessment is somewhat akin to aesthetic criticism, which asks, "How can a work of art be appreciated and appraised?" and "Along what dimensions can two or more works of art be compared?" Personality assessment addresses itself to the same questions but asks them about persons. At the same time, these appreciative and analytic impulses are joined to a sterner effort to attain objective descriptions and a comprehensive taxonomy of persons, thus displaying a kinship with botany and zoology. Once the means are available to measure personality dimensions objectively, research can be undertaken to monitor the interrelationships among the attributes of persons, and to gauge the utility of using personal attributes to predict significant behavioral and social outcomes. The predominance of this attribute model in personality research has been noted by McReynolds (1971).

Assessing Dimensions of Personality

As Table 2 indicates, there are presently in use a variety of well-understood instruments and techniques for assessing such facets of personality as intrapsychic functioning, interpersonal traits, personal values, cognitive capacities and styles, vocational interests, social attitude orientations, and psychopathological propensities. But despite the advances yielded by over five decades of research, the descriptive task truly remains unfinished. The search for important dimensions of personality and the development of techniques for measuring individual variations in them continue apace.

Environmental psychology is extending the scope of personality research by contributing new techniques for assessing environmental dispositions, a heretofore neglected array of personal attributes. While some personality dimensions refer to the way a person relates to himself (for example, intrapsychic traits such as self-accepting and self-punishing) or to his characteristic manner in relating to other persons (such as dominant, nurturant, or hostile), environmental dispositions denote individual variations in fairly enduring styles of relating to the everyday physical environment (Craik, 1966; 1970a; 1970b).

The Environmental Response Inventory (McKechnie, 1972; 1974a; 1975a) is a 184-item inventory designed to assess an array of eight environmental dispositions: pastoralism, urbanism, environmental adaptation, stimulus seeking, environmental trust, antiquarianism, need for privacy, and mechanical orientation. Little (1968; 1972a,b; Sewell and Little, 1973) has developed measures of thing–person orientations, yielding a fourfold typology: thing specialists, person specialists, generalists, and nonspecialists. The Environmental Personality Inventory (Sonnenfeld, 1969) is directed toward four environmental dispositions: sensitivity to the environment, control over the environment, mobility, and environmental risk-taking. Marshall (1970; 1972) has devised a set of scales assessing orientations toward privacy; while several approaches have been made to assess sensation-seeking and arousal-seeking tendencies (McCarroll, Mitchell, Carpenter, and Anderson, 1967; Mehrabian and Russell, 1974; Zuckerman, 1971).

The psychological import and worth of personality assessment techniques accrue from their content and mode of development; from independent descriptions of persons who score high or low on the measures; from their correlation with other established indices; and from their relationship to significant real-life behaviors and outcomes (Gough, 1965). We must await the findings of extensive research before coming to certain appraisals of the psychological meaning and value of the new techniques for assessing environmental dispositions. The manual of the Environmental Response Inventory (McKechnie, 1974a) provides an exemplary presentation of this range of interpretative information.

Uses of Personality Assessments

Table 2 indicates the range of scientific applications of personality assessment. In the context of exploration and discovery, the case study remains a valuable exercise. Balint (1955), for example, has contributed two insightful environmental case studies. One describes what he terms an "ocnophil," an individual with strong affective, clinging ties to personal settings and objects, and the other, a "philobat," a restless thrill-seeker, the sort of person who should score high on measures of sensation-seeking.

At another level of scientific research, comprehensive objective and quantified personality assessments of strategically selected samples of individuals are conducted for descriptive, comparative, and predictive purposes. Descriptively, this research can delineate the modal, or typical, personality characteristics of selected groups of environmental agents, decision-makers and users, whose views and actions influence the total adjustment of a society to its physical environment. Here, the question is: If you were to meet a large number of water resources managers, for example, then systematically described them, what kind of persons would you find them to be? In what ways, if at all, would they

Table 2. Personality Paradigm

Assessing dimensions of personality	Uses of personality assessment
Development of assessment techniques	Case studies
Establishing the meaning of persono-	Modal personalities of groups
logical scores and indices	
Traditional domains of personality	Group comparisons
Intrapsychic dynamics	Change studies
Interpersonal traits	Developmental
Personal values	Experimental
Cognitive capacities and styles	Predictive
Vocational interest patterns	Nonenvironmental criteria, e.g.:
Social attitude orientations	Capacity for leadership
Psychopathological propensities	Managerial style
Environmental dispositions, e.g.:	Job satisfaction
Pastoralism	Marital adjustment
Urbanism	Liberalism-conservatism
Environmental adaptation	Extent of participation in
Stimulus seeking	community life
Environmental trust	Violation of laws and social
Antiquarianism	norms
Need privacy	Drinking behavior
Mechanical orientation	Environmental criteria, e.g.:
Thing–person orientation	Adjustment to migration
Sensitivity to environment	Judgments of environmental quality
Mobility	Extent of home area and personal
Control over environment	orbit
Environmental risk-taking	Outdoor recreational activities
Orientations toward privacy	Environmental policy orientation
Intimacy	Adjustment to natural hazards
Not neighboring	Housing choices
Seclusion	Conceptions of distance and of
Solitude	urban structure
Anonymity	Proxemic behavior patterns
Reserve vs. self-disclosure	Environmental delinquency

differ from persons in general? The same questions can be asked of architects, drought plain farmers, Sierra Club members, hunters, etc.

For this purpose, the living-in assessment program is the method of choice. In these programs, groups of approximately 10 persons are studied at a time, over several days, by a staff of personologists in a quasi-social setting, with a wide range of techniques and procedures, including standard inventories and tests, interviews, projective techniques, and situational tests (such as leaderless group discussions and charades). From these diverse vantage points the method provides an assessment of the person's social impact (recorded by staff observers on adjective checklists and other formats), personality traits, early life history factors, patterns of career development, environmental dispositions, intellectual styles, interest patterns, social attitude orientations, and personal values (Barron, 1965; MacKinnon, 1967). Of course, more focused and abbreviated studies can select from this repertory of techniques. Either way, descriptive assessments take on more substantive import when key comparisons can be made, for example, between more or less creative architects (MacKinnon, 1962; Hall and MacKinnon, 1969), between drought plain farmers and flood plain farmers, between water resources managers and public health officers who both have a responsibility and jurisdiction over water quality (Sewell, 1971), or between hunters and birdwatchers.

Descriptive personality assessments can play a role in developmental research, where they are employed in tracing change in environmental orientations over the life cycle. In addition, when planned interventions in environmental behavior are undertaken, as in the rapidly expanding field of environmental education, standard assessment techniques can gauge the impact of educational and training programs on enduring styles of relating to the physical environment.

The application of personality assessment to the task of forecasting significant behaviors and outcomes is the final element in the research approach (Table 2). Personality measures (e.g., of values, interest patterns, interpersonal traits) have traditionally been used in attempts to predict individual differences in such behaviors and personal outcomes as job satisfaction, marital adjustment, participation in community life, alcoholism, norm violations, and effectiveness in various occupational roles and positions.

Environmental psychology is extending the scope of personality research by focusing upon criterion behaviors and outcomes having significant implications and consequences for the use and form of the everyday physical environment. Environmental criterion behaviors possessing theoretical and practical importance include: decisions to migrate and adjustments to migration, geographical preferences, judgments of environmental quality, extent of home area and personal orbit, outdoor recreational activities, environmental policy orientations, adjustment to natural hazards, conceptions of distance and of urban structure, proxemic behavior patterns, environmental delinquency, neighborhood and housing choices, and participation in environmental decision-making in various civic and professional roles.

The distinctive contribution of personality research is to consider this entire array of environmental criterion behaviors and outcomes within the context of the person as a whole. The hypothetical case of Samuel Mendon can be cited on this point (see box). As Mr. Mendon makes his choices and takes actions relevant to the everyday physical environment, we can readily begin to construct a partial, but fairly coherent picture of the sort of person he is.

In addition, personality research can study environmental behaviors and outcomes that are also being analyzed by other research traditions and can readily complement those efforts. Consider, as one example, the topic of spatial

---

The Case of Samuel Mendon

Mr. Samuel Mendon is a district manager for a nationwide corporation who has recently been reassigned to a branch office in a moderately large American city. He had been offered a choice of offices in several geographical settings and elected the northeastern section of the country. In resettling, did Mr. Mendon and his family decide to live well out into the countryside or in the suburban outskirts or within the older central district? Did they seek a purely residential neighborhood with single-family homes, and a large shopping center nearby, or perhaps a neighborhood with assorted dwellings, grocery store, post office, drugstore, physician, churches, elementary schools all located within it? Among the dwelling units on the market within their price range, what physical features attracted them to their ultimate choice? Did they design their living room in contemporary or traditional decor? What recreational use does Mr. Mendon make of the outdoor environment? If his weekend avocation is nautical, does he purchase a motorboat (or sailboat or cabin cruiser or a Monterey fishing boat)? Does he sail along highly used and developed waterfronts with diverse facilities or on remote pastoral lakes? If at vacation time he is a wilderness user, does he stay on the periphery or does he backpack in? What disagreements does he have with the management policies of the wilderness areas he frequents? How are his children learning to use, appreciate, and understand the physical environment, and how does that learning reflect family activities and values? On weekdays, does Samuel Mendon use his lunch time to explore the city, stroll its streets, sample its restaurants, and browse in its shops, or does he remain in his building at the local cafeteria? At the weekly businessmen's luncheon, does he spontaneously express approval or disapproval of the design and plans for two new office buildings being constructed nearby? Does the layout of his own office complex accommodate his style of social interaction and contact with his staff, and if it does not, what does he do about it? How does he describe his new office to his family? Does Mr. Mendon use his influence to protest against or to lobby for the routing of a new highway (or expansion of an airport) in the region? Does he join local conservation organizations and those dedicated to improving the quality of the urban environment? If his building is located within an urban flood plain, what steps does Mr. Mendon take to cope with this natural hazard? Does he vote for or against increased taxation for pollution abatement? Does he oppose use of the region's water supply reservoirs for outdoor recreational activities? Is he familiar with the National Environmental Policy Act of 1969? A year after his arrival in his new habitat, has Mr. Mendon adjusted with ease or difficulty to his move? Would he be willing to shift to another branch office in the near future? (Adapted from Craik, 1972*b*, p. 102)

---

behavior in the urban environment, which has gained the attention of urban geographers, sociologists, and environmental psychologists, including Lee (1968), Chapin (1968), Buttimer (1972), Boal (1969; 1971) and Everitt and Cadwallader (1972). Among the behavioral variables involved in these investigations are (1) the extent of the residents' concept of home area, that local region in which they feel "at home," (2) the frequency and diversity of out-of-the-house activities (the shut-in versus gadabout dimension), (3) the magnitude of the behavioral range, or orbit, of the residents (based upon time and distance attributes of their out-of-the-house activities), and (4) the residents' satisfaction with their current behavioral range. Each of these indices displays impressive variation among individuals and each constitutes a substantively interesting environmental criterion behavior. Hopefully, research will soon begin to determine what aspects of personality are implicated in such stylistic differences in spatial behavior.

Research on man–environment relations operates within a societal context, of course, and has tended to become organized around the somewhat discrete interests of a number of scientific and professional disciplines, and the often urgent needs of a variety of sponsoring agencies and units. It is conceivable, though admittedly unlikely, that Mr. Mendon could find himself serving as a member of three research samples being studied by independent scientists unacquainted with each other's endeavors and investigating respectively outdoor recreation, housing choice, and adjustment to natural hazards. Such a rare event, nevertheless, might usefully turn the focus of attention upon Mr. Mendon himself, not as an occasional doer of environmental deeds but as a single enduring organism, a distinctive personological entity, a system with its own structure, dynamics, and behavioral order.

CURRENT CONCEPTUAL AND EMPIRICAL ISSUES

The normal science activities engendered by a viable research paradigm, in Kuhn's view, include extending its application to new areas and increasing the scope and precision of its observations (Kuhn, 1970). As we have seen, the personality research paradigm is demonstrating this capacity in its development of new techniques for assessing environmental dispositions and in its evident potential for forecasting a wide range of environmental criterion behaviors and outcomes.

Normal science undertakings also encompass the further articulation of a scientific paradigm through clarifications and reformulations of its conceptual framework (Kuhn, 1970). The period of the early nineteen-seventies finds the personality research tradition emerging from three decades of heavy emphasis on maximizing precision in measurement and gauging the unilateral predictive power of personality dispositions. These endeavors have yielded a remarkable range of measurement instruments and techniques (Goldberg, 1971) and an even more impressive repertory of self-critical concepts, indices, and standards, including incremental validity, base rates, experience tables, response sets, and multitrait–multimethod analysis (Wiggins, 1973).

A highly critical appraisal of the entire personality research paradigm, questioning the value of its accomplishments and challenging its viability, was issued by Mischel in 1968, thereby heralding and in important ways instigating the current period of valuable stocktaking (Alker, 1972; Argyle and Little, 1972; Bem, 1972; Craik, 1969; Dahlstrom, 1970; Wachtel, 1973). In particular, the central concept of personal disposition is being re-examined in light of present scientific knowledge and philosophical analysis (Averill, 1973; Wiggins, 1974). Following the appearance of Mischel's volume, the importance of analyzing the interaction of person and environment has also received prominent analytic and empirical attention (Bowers, 1973; Cronbach, 1974; Endler, 1973). These interrelated efforts to clarify and reformulate the concept of personal disposition and to study person × environment interactions constitute important articulations of the personality paradigm, which may be advanced and facilitated by its extension into environmental psychology.

The Concept of Personal Disposition

At the heart of the personality research paradigm is the concept of personal disposition, the tendency to behave in certain ways; for example, to be self-pitying regarding oneself, to be dominant in relation to others, and to display a sensation-seeking orientation toward one's everyday physical environment. As Wiggins observes: "If persons are not more or less prone to behave in certain ways on certain occasions, then the psychometric approach is out of business at the outset; as are all approaches to personality study" (Wiggins, 1974). The degree of personal consistency that should be expected from occasion to occasion and from situation to situation has been treated with a rather easygoing ambiguity in the personality paradigm. Child, for example, acknowledged:

> Most attempts at theoretical understanding of human behavior would lead one to expect some intermediate degree of consistency in personality—neither complete determination by variables in the momentary situation nor complete absence of determination by them. The student of personality, then, may regard as a part of his task the assessment of the degree of consistency actually found. (Child, 1963, p. 599)

However, when Mischel examined the empirical evidence and concluded that the best estimates of consistency hovered around +.30, he appraised them as not large enough to support the scientific utility of the personality paradigm (Mischel, 1968, p. 43). Certainly, morale would be justifiably jolted if the concept of disposition led necessarily to expectations of cross-situational correlations of +1.00; that is, a person disposed to be dominant would invariably be socially ascendant, in all situations (Bem, 1972). However, careful philosophical analysis reveals that situational constraints and specifications are intrinsically entailed in the concept of personal disposition.

Two alternative formulations of personal disposition have been championed in recent philosophical discourse (Wiggins, 1974). Ryle (1949) considers personal dispositions to be hypothetical propositions, somewhat like dispositional statements in physics. Thus, the assertion that "Mary is dominant" is akin to the assertion that "The glass is brittle"; each takes the form: it is likely, or a good bet, that the entity will respond in certain ways (x, y, z) to certain circumstances (a, b, c). Verification of the dispositional assertion in the case of objects is relatively clear-cut, requiring specification of the conditions (e.g., being struck with a stone), the ways of responding (e.g., shattering), and sufficient tests to estimate a probability level for the assertion. Both the conditions and the ways of responding that constitute appropriate tests are, in the assertion of dominance, less readily specified and probably constitute broader classes than in the case of brittleness.

In a somewhat different analysis, by Hampshire (1971), the concept of personal disposition is considered to be a summarizing statement, taking the form: "So far, the term 'dominant' is the right word to summarize the general trend of Mary's conduct." We also employ such statements, instead of hypothetical propositions, to summarize the general character of physical things, particularly, as Hampshire notes, when compelled by our ignorance of causal laws, as in: "The New England climate is changeable." In this view, the emphasis is not on the likelihood of a person manifesting a certain behavior in a particular circumstance, but on the general trend of behaviors over prolonged periods of observation. Verification or justification of a dispositional assertion, according to Hampshire, requires that: "(a) one has had occasion for prolonged and continuous study of the conduct and calculations of the person in question," and "(b) . . . one can quote many incidents in which the disposition manifested itself and can quote virtually no incidents which would count as instances of a contrary disposition" (Hampshire, 1971, p. 35). The stress is upon acts of commission, rather than omission, across many occasions, and Hampshire notes that in exercises of justifying dispositional assertions: "The incidents which may count as manifestations of human dispositions—of intelligence, ambition, generosity, honesty—are essentially various, and these words are essentially vague, summary, interpretative, and indeterminate" (Hampshire, 1971, p. 38).

The two formulations of personal disposition appear to have different implications for the scientific personality paradigm.[1] The Ryle viewpoint seems to

[1] Wiggins (1974) favors Hampshire's analysis of dispositions because, in addition to being less burdened metaphysically, it appears closer to ordinary usage. Ordinary usage and the research findings on how ordinary persons comprehend other persons have begun to play an important role in recent discourse about personality, and have added an intriguing degree of reflexivity to efforts toward the further articulation of the personality paradigm (e.g., Little, 1972b). The relationship between how persons comprehend other persons and how scientists might best do so deserves fuller treatment than it has received. Should the tendency of persons performing an act not to have recourse to dispositional notions in accounting for their behavior (while observers do so) (Jones and Nisbett, 1971) somehow count against the personality paradigm? Should the findings that the use of dispositional concepts is positively related to higher cognitive-developmental levels (Peevers and Secord, 1973; Flapan, 1968; Hardy, 1974) somehow count for it? Probably not, in either case. But beyond mutual heuristic benefits, what implications lurk in the relations between person-perception research and the personality paradigm?

call for more precise specifications of the appropriate test conditions for a given dispositional assertion, in order to generate more elegant "if . . . then" propositions. The Hampshire viewpoint, by stressing observations over a long period, raises the issue of representative sampling of observed situations and life conditions; single, isolated tests of the dispositional status of persons are held to be inadequate and inappropriate.

Both notions of personal disposition highlight the need to devote greater attention to specification of the kinds of acts or qualities of acts that will "count" as manifestations of given dispositions (Wiggins, 1974). The complexity of behavior and the subtlety of observation required is illustrated in a study by Megargee (1969). Pairs of individuals were placed in a situation calling for them to perform a task requiring a leader and a follower. The dyad, rather than the investigator, decided upon the assignment of each person to the two roles. Participants were asserted to be dominant or not dominant (on the basis of scores on the dominance scale of the California Psychological Inventory [CPI]), and samples of four kinds of dyads were studied: (1) dominant male; nondominant male, (2) dominant female; nondominant female, (3) dominant male; nondominant female, and (4) dominant female; nondominant male. The dominant person tended to occupy the leadership position significantly more often in all instances except the fourth type of dyad (i.e., dominant female; nondominant male). Megargee marshaled the notion of sex-role expectations to account for the latter findings, but also examined tape recordings of the very brief discussions between members of each dyad that led to the assignments. Independent judgments of which member of the dyad made the decision showed that in the fourth type, the dominant female tended to make the decision, although her decision frequently was to assign the nondominant male to the leadership position.

Thus, for dispositional assertions regarding dominance, attaining a leadership position, and deciding on such assignments might each constitute a telling incident for Hampshire or be included in the set of criterion responses for Ryle's verification procedure. Hampshire's notion of disposition is especially compatible with the shift from single-act–single-situation criteria to multiple-act–multiple-situation criteria (Fishbein and Ajzen, 1974). Thus, Jaccard (1974) has shown that assertions of dominance (based on the CPI dominance scale) yield an average correlation of $+.20$ with single acts of dominance, but $+.58$ with a multiple-act criterion (indexing the number of different acts of dominance, out of 40 listed, that the person had displayed). Two limitations of the Jaccard study are readily apparent: (1) the multiple-act criterion was based on self-reports rather than direct observation over a prolonged period; and (2) the list of 40 "dominant" acts was compiled from panel nominations rather than drawn from sensitive and comprehensive observations of the multifarious manifestations of dominance occurring in behavior across everyday situations.

These analyses of the concept of personal disposition warrant careful examination in current efforts to articulate and refine the conceptual framework and methods of the personality paradigm. Without doubt, their implications clearly direct personologists out into the "field"—to the study of behavior in the everyday environment, to sensitive, fine-grained analyses of the style of acts and deeds, to the development of taxonomies for, and representative sampling from, everyday situations, and to the direct but unobtrusive observation of persons in context. Indeed, the person-centered observational strategies pioneered at the Midwest Psychological Field Station (Barker, 1963) hold considerable promise for the current phase of personality investigation, although what is needed is not *One Boy's Day* (Barker and Wright, 1951), but, for example, *One Dominant Boy's Day*. The failure of personologists to have studied unobtrusively the stream of behavior of persons assessed or reputed to be, e.g., highly dominant, constitutes a remarkable oversight. Such detailed behavior specimen records, properly analyzed, would offer opportunities to develop criteria for assessing the qualities of acts (Wiggins, 1974) and to examine the manifestations of personal dispositions *in situ*.

The Interplay of Persons and Environments

For a personologist to advocate a return to the investigative strategies illustrated in *One Boy's Day* may seem decidedly (even "characteristically") wrong-headed and stubborn; for it was disillusionment with this person-centered approach that led to the development of ecological psychology, with its crucial substitution of the behavior setting for the person as the primary unit of analysis. In *Ecological Psychology*, Barker recalls:

> When, early in our work at the Field Station, we made long records of children's behavior in real-life settings in accordance with a traditional person-centered approach, we found that some attributes of behavior varied less across children within settings than across settings within the days of children . . . It was this experience that led us to look at the real-life environment in which behavior occurs, with the methodological and theoretical consequences that are reported in this book. (Barker, 1968, p. 4)

Thus, the decision was made that situational variables, properly conceptualized and identified, offered greater promise than personality variables in accounting for behavior.

Of course, discourse on personality and environmental variables can readily dwell on the pseudo-issue, Which of the two is more important in accounting for behavior? Endler correctly maintains:

> Asking whether behavioral variance is due to either situations *or* persons, or how much variation is contributed by persons and how much by situations (an additive approach) is analogous to asking whether air *or* blood is more essential to life or

asking one to define the area of a rectangle in terms of length *or* width. The more sensible question is "*How* do individual differences and situations interact in evoking behavior?" (Endler, 1973, p. 289)

Research designs and statistical analyses can now monitor some of the interplay between persons and environments.

In a study of sixteen psychiatric patients and six psychiatric ward settings (i.e., intake interview, individual therapy, group therapy, community meeting, lunch, and free time), Moos (1969) analyzed the percentage of behavioral variance accounted for by differences among persons and among settings, and by interactions between them. As Table 3 shows, some activities were relatively strongly tied to the setting (e.g., talking, nodding yes) or to persons (e.g., smiling, smoking) but in most cases, the particular combination of person and setting played an important role (i.e., the P × S interaction).

The available evidence documents the existence of important person × environment interactions and tends to show that the interactions account for more of the variance than either personal or environmental variables (Bowers, 1973; Argyle and Little, 1972; Endler, 1973). Review of this research also suggests several highly desirable features for interactional studies: (1) assessed attributes of persons, (2) assessed attributes of environments, (3) behavioral responses observed *in situ*, and (4) representative types and ranges of persons and environments.

The Moos (1969) study has the advantage of directly observed dependent variables but lacks a taxonomy of persons and settings. Recent research by Mehrabian and Russell (1974) illustrates the application of personality assessment and environmental assessment to interaction studies. A set of 65 briefly described situations were independently rated on their arousal quality; then a

Table 3. Percentages of Variance Accounted for by Different Sources of Variance in Behavior Categories—Second Observations[a]

	Source			
Category	Persons	Settings	P × S	Within
Hand and arm movement	17.2	13.8	29.6	39.3
Foot and leg movement	27.3	13.0	31.2	28.6
Scratch, pick, rub	26.3	18.2	27.6	27.9
General movement and shifting	23.1	4.4	48.2	24.3
Nod yes	4.6	56.5	21.3	18.5
Smile	33.4	8.3	36.1	22.3
Talk	7.4	60.1	19.9	12.5
Smoke	36.5	12.2	10.2	41.1

[a] From Moos, 1969, p. 409.

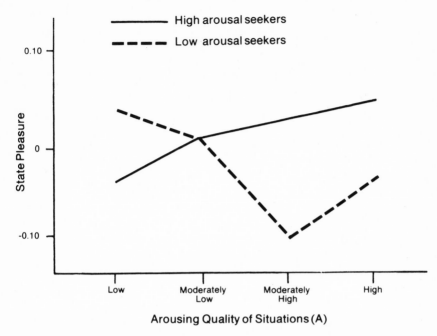

Figure 1. The effect of the arousal quality of situation × arousal-seeking tendency interaction on ratings of pleasurable states. (These are adjusted cell means, with the effect of assessed pleasantness of situations partialed out.) (From Mehrabian and Russell, 1974, p. 181.)

sample of 214 persons whose arousal-seeking dispositions had been assessed by a personality scale rated six of the situations on the amount of pleasure they would experience if they found themselves in each situation. Figure 1 depicts the interactions between the arousal qualities of the situations, and the arousal–seeking propensities of persons. In this instance, pleasurable reactions were only slightly affected by the arousal quality of the situations, across persons, and by the arousal-seeking disposition of persons, across situations, but are strikingly affected by the combination of the two: High-arousal seekers report more pleasure in high-arousal situations while low-arousal seekers derive more pleasure from low-arousal situations. However, like the earlier studies by Endler and Hunt (1966; 1968; 1969), the Mehrabian and Russell studies are limited to self-reports of responses to hypothetical situations.

With the use of somewhat more realistic dependent variables, Domino (1968; 1971) has studied the interaction between achievement orientations of students and educational atmospheres of introductory psychology classes. Two achievement orientations were assessed by the CPI scales for achievement via independence (Ai) and achievement via conformance (Ac) (Gough, 1957;

1968); two types of educational atmospheres, autonomous and structured, were assessed by nine criteria, including type of student participation, type of examination and grading practice, aims of the course, and relation of reading assignments to class material. Dependent variables included class performance (examination, grade) and satisfaction (ratings of teacher effectiveness, course evaluation). In both naturally occurring and experimentally established educational atmospheres, evidence for an interaction was obtained; e.g., Ai students performed better when matched with an autonomous instructional context, while Ac students did better in a structured setting.

Note the range of environmental variables that can be examined in interactional studies, ranging from physical–social settings to the stimulation–arousal quality of situations to educational atmosphere. The latter can be linked to analyses of social atmospheres and organizational climates (Stern, 1970; Tagiuri and Litwin, 1968; Gerst and Moos, 1972; Moos and Houts, 1970). The development of comprehensive environmental assessment techniques (Craik, 1971; Moos, 1973) is a critical prerequisite to progress in understanding person by environment interactions.

In the meantime, it is reasonable to consider the interaction between persons and environments as part of the full articulation of the personality paradigm; that is, its domain encompasses the main effects of personality variables and the interaction effects. Similarly, situational analysis, as conducted by social ecologists, ecological psychologists, and others dedicated to environmental assessment (Craik, 1971), would encompass the main effects of environmental variables and the interaction effects. Thus, man–environment relations are manifested not only in various forms of independent–dependent relations but also in interactive influences.

Person × environment research will inevitably yield joint efforts by personology and ecological psychology. Both fields have developed somewhat apart from and in tension with the mainstream of academic psychology (Barker, 1968; Sanford, 1963) but also in notable isolation from each other. The two paradigms have quite distinct internal structures and scientific agendas; nevertheless, there exist a number of unexplored but potentially important relations between them. This topic cannot be fully explored here but some observations can be offered. First, the person × environment interactional research design can, of course, include the study of behavior settings. The recent taxonomic endeavors in ecological psychology (Price, 1974) will facilitate these investigations. Second, behavior-setting variables (Barker, 1968, pp. 46–90) can constitute criterion variables for traditional personality research. For example: (1) personal dispositions may be manifested in the selective occupancy of, and relative occupancy times in, types of behavior settings[2] (e.g., for recrea-

---

[2] In this regard, Wachtel (1973) has called attention to the manifestation of dispositions in the ways persons select, interpret, and create the more ephemeral but still meaningful encounters that, combined with relatively stable behavior settings, comprise everyday social life.

tion action patterns, see McKechnie, 1974*b*; 1974*c*; 1975*b*); (2) personal dispositions may be manifested in the degree of penetration of behavior settings (i.e., from onlooker to leader); and (3) dispositions may be manifested in the styles of participation in behavior settings (any participant observer of a "classic" behavior setting, e.g., the soda-jerk in a neighborhood drugstore, comes to appreciate the diversity of nuance and expressiveness that embellishes the enactment of standing patterns of behavior).

The Interplay among Personal, Societal, and Environmental Systems

Personal dispositions, according to the general consensus regarding the personality paradigm, are best understood as elements forming an adaptive and developing system (Block, 1971; Emmerich, 1968; Sanford, 1963). The conceptualization of systems, system boundaries, and system relations offers a usefully broad perspective upon man–environment relations and upon the direction of research in this area (Craik, 1972*a*). Although it does not represent sequential relations, Figure 2 will serve as a guide for discussion of the interplay between personal, societal, and environmental systems. The personality system refers to

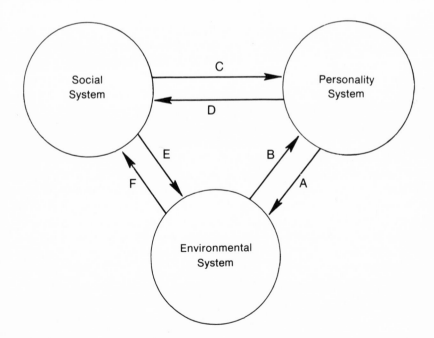

Figure 2. The interplay of personal, societal, and environmental systems.

the skills, cognitive capacities, values, and psychodynamics of the individual agent, while the social system comprises the institutional structures, regulatory principles, technological capacities, and adjustment mechanisms of a society (Smelser and Smelser, 1970).[3] Despite the emphasis of current research in man–environment relations upon the relatively stable structural properties of buildings and objects and the geomorphological attributes of land surfaces, the environmental system must be recognized as a dynamic linked network of physical, chemical, and biological subsystems (Hertz, 1970).

The attributes of each system can function in research as independent variables in studying the attributes of another system, which serve as dependent variables. The environmental dispositions of environmental decision-makers may influence policy (e.g., dam construction versus zoning in flood-plain management) which has impact upon the environmental system (Relationship A). Environmental transformations (e.g., the design of planned residential communities) may influence the self-concept and social behaviors of user-clients (Relationship B). Much of recent research in man–environment relations has focused on Relationships A and B (Craik, 1973). Social-system variables may serve as antecedents to the environmental behaviors of decision-makers and lay persons, via professional training programs and environmental socialization agents such as the family, school, and mass media (Relationship C). The development and organization of behavior settings—that is, the large-scale dynamic issues of ecological psychology—can perhaps best be considered within a social-systems framework (Smith, 1974). The impact of environmental activists upon environmental norms, legal structures, and administration illustrates Relationship D. Relationships C and D require interdisciplinary research between psychology and anthropology (Hsu, 1961) and between psychology and sociology (Smelser and Smelser, 1970). The comparative study of social systems in their relationship to the environment (Relationships E and F) entail cross-cultural and trans-national research that has been the province of the ecological approach in cultural anthropology (Vayda, 1969).

Obviously, Figure 2 does not capture the full complexity of man–environment relations, failing, for example, to depict the joint effect of independent variables from two systems upon a dependent variable of a third, as well as other possible interactions among them of the sort described previously. Figure 2 also lacks representation of the differing temporal scales of the systems. For example, relationships between persons and environments may be stable and

[3] The current challenges to the Parsonian social-system constructs (e.g., Gouldner, 1970) cannot be treated adequately here. However, their parallels with the recent critiques of the personality paradigm are noteworthy. In both instances, the case is argued that: (1) the system constructs presume greater structure and stability than the empirical evidence warrants; (2) structure and stability in persons and societies derive largely from nonveridical attributions that represent common misconceptions in person perception and social perception; and (3) these theoretical constructs tend to resist or thwart adaptive change and are philosophically or ideologically unappetizing (Gouldner, 1970; Mischel, 1968, 1973; Jones and Nisbett, 1971).

replicable over relatively short time spans, but then shift as a consequence of slower paced changes in social-systems variables (e.g., related to family structure, legal codes). Similarly, gradual changes in the environmental system (e.g., in certain nonreplaceable resources; in irreversible shifts in environmental quality indices) may upset well-founded and moderately stable relations between personal- and social-system variables (e.g., links between the agents and aims of environmental socialization and individual environmental preferences).

Indeed, the intricacy of person × environment interactions and the temporal phasing of personal- and social-system processes has led Cronbach (1974), in an important recent appraisal, to some refreshingly modest aspirations for the scope of generalization in the social and behavioral sciences. Clearly, his emphasis on the contextual boundedness of social science and behavioral science findings is very much in keeping with current orientations in the field of man–environment relations.

CONCLUDING OBSERVATIONS

The personality research paradigm has emerged from concerted scientific attention during the middle decades of the twentieth century to the age-old question of how best to describe a person. Considerable inventiveness has been displayed in the development of techniques for assessing dimensions of personality; perhaps even more ingenuity has been shown in devising self-critical methods for appraising the reliability, validity, and utility of personality measurements.

The domain of man–environment relations offers diverse, feasible, and important opportunities for the application of the contemporary personality-research paradigm. Of course, it does so for other research traditions as well. Indeed, present-day students of man–environment relations have tended to bring their research traditions with them from early training in their own disciplines. Some consider this tendency an asset, providing an effective readiness to identify interesting puzzles and the conceptual and methodological equipment for attempting to solve them. Others deem the carry-over a liability, leading to cognitive and strategic rigidity and thwarting efforts to view man–environment phenomena in new and appropriate ways.

In the case of the personality research paradigm, the field of man–environment relations not only engages its most technically refined components but also affords a milieu for its conceptual growing edge. Thus, in addition to straightforward applications, fundamental questions must be addressed with creativeness and fresh insights, including: What is the nature of personal dispositions? How do persons and places, individuals and situations, interact? What degree of stability and generality exists in relations among personality, societal, and environmental systems?

ACKNOWLEDGMENT

This paper was prepared while the author served as a visiting scientist in the Institute for Man and Environment and the Department of Psychology, University of Massachusetts, Amherst, 1974–75. Preparation was supported in part by NSF Grant No. SOC73-05706 A02.

REFERENCES

Alker, H. A. Is personality situationally specific or intrapsychically consistent? *Journal of Personality*, 1972, *40*, 1–16.
Argyle, M., and Little, B. R. Do personality traits apply to social behavior? *Journal for the Theory of Social Behavior*, 1972, *2*, 1–35.
Averill, J. R. The dis-position of psychological dispositions. *Journal of Experimental Research in Personality*, 1973, *6*, 275–282.
Balint, M. Friendly expanses—horrid empty spaces. *International Journal of Psychoanalysis*, 1955, *36*, 225–241.
Barker, R. G. (Ed.). *The stream of behavior*. New York: Appleton-Century-Crofts, 1963.
Barker, R. G. *Ecological psychology: Concepts and methods for studying the environment of human behavior*. Stanford, California: Stanford University Press, 1968.
Barker, R. G., and Wright, H. F. *One boy's day*. New York: Harper & Row, 1951.
Barker, R. G., and Wright, H. F. *Midwest and its children*. New York: Harper & Row, 1955.
Barron, F. The psychology of creativity. In Barron, F., *et al.*, *New Directions in Psychology II*. New York: Holt, Rinehart and Winston, 1965.
Bem, D. J. Constructing cross-situational consistencies in behavior: Some thoughts on Alker's critique of Mischel. *Journal of Personality*, 1972, *40*, 17–27.
Block, J. *Lives through time*. Berkeley, California: Bancroft Books, 1971.
Boal, F. W. Territoriality on the Shankill-Falls Divide, Belfast. *Irish Geography*, 1969, *6*, 30–50.
Boal, F. W. Territoriality and class: A study of two residential areas in Belfast. *Irish Geography*, 1971, *8*, 229–248.
Bowers, K. B. Situationism in psychology: An analysis and critique. *Psychological Review*, 1973, *80*, 307–336.
Buttimer, A. Social space and the planning of residential areas. *Environment and Behavior*, 1972, *4*, 267–278.
Chabod, F. *Machiavelli and the Renaissance*. London: Bowes and Bowes, 1958.
Chapin, F. S., Jr. Activity systems and urban structure: A working schema. *Journal of the American Institute of Planners*, 1968, *34*, 11–18.
Child, I. L. Problems of personality and some relations to anthropology and sociology. In S. Kock (Ed.), *Psychology: A study of science* (Vol. 5). New York: McGraw-Hill, 1963.
Craik, K. H. The prospects for an environmental psychology. *IPAR Research Bulletin*. Berkeley, California: University of California, 1966.
Craik, K. H. Personality unvanquished. (Review of Walter Mischel: *Personality and assessment*. New York: Wiley, 1968). *Contemporary Psychology*, 1969, *14*, 147–148.

Craik, K. H. Environmental psychology. In K. H. Craik, *et al.*, *New directions in psychology 4.* New York: Holt, Rinehart and Winston, 1970. (a)

Craik, K. H. The environmental dispositions of environmental decision-makers. *Annals of the American Academy of Political and Social Science,* 1970, *389,* 87–94. (b)

Craik, K. H. The assessment of places. In P. McReynolds (Ed.), *Advances in psychological assessment* (Vol. 2). Palo Alto, California: Science and Behavior Books, 1971.

Craik, K. H. An ecological perspective on environmental decision-making. *Human Ecology,* 1972, *1,* 69–80. (a)

Craik, K. H. The individual and the physical environment: Assessment strategies in environmental psychology. In W. M. Smith (Ed.), *Behavior, design and policy: Aspects of human habitats.* Green Bay, Wisconsin: University of Wisconsin, 1972. (b)

Craik, K. H. Environmental psychology. In P. H. Mussen, and M. R. Rosenzweig (Eds.), *Annual Review of Psychology* (Vol. 24). Palo Alto, California: Annual Reviews, Inc., 1973.

Craik, K. H. Environmental psychology: A multi-paradigm venture. Berkeley, California: University of California, unpublished report, 1976.

Cronbach, L. J. Beyond the two disciplines of scientific psychology. *American Psychologist,* 1975, *30,* 116–129.

Dahlstrom, W. G. Personality. In P. H. Mussen, and M. R. Rosenzweig (Eds.), *Annual Review of Psychology* (Vol. 21). Palo Alto, California: Annual Reviews, Inc., 1970.

Domino, G. Differential prediction of academic achievement in conforming and independent settings. *Journal of Educational Psychology,* 1968, *59,* 256–260.

Domino, G. Interactive effects of achievement orientation and teaching style on academic achievement. *Journal of Educational Psychology,* 1971, *62,* 427–431.

Edel, L. *Henry James* (5 vols.). Philadelphia, Pennsylvania; Lippincott, 1953–1972.

Emmerich, W. Personality development and concepts of structure. *Child Development,* 1968, *39,* 671–690.

Endler, N. S. The person versus the situation—a pseudo issue? A response to Alker. *Journal of Personality,* 1973, *41,* 287–303.

Endler, N. S., and Hunt, J. McV. Sources of behavioral variance as measured by the S-R Inventory of Anxiousness. *Psychological Bulletin,* 1966, *65,* 336–346.

Endler, N. S., and Hunt, J. McV. S-R Inventories of hostility and comparisons of the proportions of variance from persons, responses, and situations for hostility and anxiousness. *Journal of Personality and Social Psychology,* 1968, *9,* 309–315.

Endler, N. S., and Hunt, J. McV. Generalizability of contributions from sources of variance in S-R Inventories of Anxiousness. *Journal of Personality,* 1969, *37,* 1–24.

Everitt, J., and Cadwallader, M. The home area concept in urban analysis. In W. J. Mitchell (Ed.), *Environmental design: Research and practice.* (*Proceedings of the EDRA 3/AR 8 Conference*). Los Angeles, University of California, 1972. Pp. 1-2-1 to 1-2-10.

Fishbein, M., and Ajzen, I. Attitudes toward objects as predictors of single and multiple behavioral criteria. *Psychological Review,* 1974, *81,* 59–74.

Flapan, D. *Children's understanding of social interaction.* New York: Teachers College Press of Columbia University, 1968.

Gerst, M. S., and Moos, R. H. The social ecology of university student residences. *Journal of Educational Psychology,* 1972, *63,* 513–525.

Goldberg, L. R. The proliferation of personality scales and inventories: An historical analysis. In P. McReynolds (Ed.), *Advances in psychological assessment* (Vol. 2). Palo Alto, California: Science and Behavior Books, 1971.

Gough, H. G. *Manual for the California Psychological Inventory.* Palo Alto, California: Consulting Psychologists Press, 1957. (Rev'd, 1964).

Gough, H. G. Conceptual analysis of psychological test scores and other diagnostic variables. *Journal of Abnormal Psychology,* 1965, *70,* 294–302.

Gough, H. G. An interpreter's syllabus for the California Psychological Inventory. In P. McReynolds (Ed.), *Advances in psychological assessment* (Vol. 1). Palo Alto, California: Science and Behavior Books, 1968.

Gouldner, A. W. *The coming crisis of Western sociology.* New York: Basic Books, 1970.

Hall, W. B., and MacKinnon, D. W. Personality inventory correlates of creativity among architects. *Journal of Applied Psychology,* 1969, *53,* 322–326.

Hampshire, S. Dispositions. In S. Hampshire, *Freedom of mind and other essays.* Princeton, New Jersey: Princeton University Press, 1971.

Hardy, R. R. Construct differences in children as generated by a Kelley Repertory Test. Unpublished senior honors thesis, University of California, Berkeley, 1974.

Hertz, D. B. The technological imperative—social implications of professional technology. *Annals of the American Academy of Political and Social Science,* 1970, *389,* 95–106.

Hsu, F. L. K. (Ed.). *Psychological anthropology: Approaches to culture and personality.* Homewood, Illinois: Dorsey Press, 1961.

Jaccard, J. J. Predicting social behavior from personality traits. *Journal of Research in Personality,* 1974, *7,* 358–367.

Johnston, James C. *Biography: The literature of personality.* New York: Century, 1927.

Jones, E. E., and Nisbett, R. E. *The actor and the observer: Divergent perceptions of the causes of behavior.* Morristown, New Jersey: General Learning Press, 1971.

Kuhn, T. S. *The structure of scientific revolutions.* Chicago, Illinois: University of Chicago Press, 1962.

Lee, T. Urban neighborhood as a socio-spatial schema. *Human Relations,* 1968, *21,* 241–268.

Little, B. R. Psychospecialization: Functions of differential interest in persons and things. *Bulletin of the British Psychological Society,* 1968, *21,* 113.

Little, B. R. *Person-thing orientation: A provisional manual for the T-P Scale.* Department of Experimental Psychology, Oxford University, 1972. (a)

Little, B. R. Psychological man as scientist, humanist and specialist. *Journal of Experimental Research in Personality,* 1972, *6,* 95–118. (b)

McCarroll, J. R., Mitchell, K. M., Carpenter, R. J., & Anderson, J. P. Analysis of three stimulation-seeking scales. *Psychological Reports,* 1967, *21,* 853–856.

McKechnie, G. E. A study of environmental life styles. Unpublished Ph.D. dissertation, University of California, Berkeley, 1972.

McKechnie, G. E. *Manual for the Environmental Response Inventory.* Palo Alto, California: Consulting Psychologists Press, 1974. (a)

McKechnie, G. E. Psychological foundations of leisure counseling: An empirical strategy. *Therapeutic Recreation Journal,* 1974, *8,* 1, 4–16. (b)

McKechnie, G. E. The psychological structure of leisure: Past Behavior. *Journal of Leisure Research,* 1974, *6,* 27–45. (c)

McKechnie, G. E. Explorations in environmental dispositions: Notes for extending a paradigm. Berkeley, California: University of California. In preparation.

McKechnie, G. E. *Manual for the Leisure Activities Blank.* Palo Alto, California: Consulting Psychologists Press. In press. (b)

MacKinnon, D. W. The nature and nurture of creative talent. *American Psychologist,* 1962, *17,* 484–495.

MacKinnon, D. W. Assessing creative persons. *Journal of Creative Behavior,* 1967, *1,* 291–304.

McReynolds, P. Introduction. In P. McReynolds (Ed.), *Advances in psychological assessment* (Vol. 2). Palo Alto, California: Science and Behavior Books, 1971.

Marshall, N. J. Orientations toward privacy: Environmental and personality components. Unpublished Ph.D. dissertation, University of California, Berkeley, 1970.

Marshall, N. J. Privacy and environment. *Human Ecology,* 1972, *1,* 93–110.

Masters, E. L. *Spoon River anthology*. New York: Macmillan, 1916.

Mehrabian, A., and Russell, J. A. *An approach to environmental psychology*. Cambridge, Massachusetts: MIT Press, 1974.

Megargee, E. I. Influence of sex roles on the manifestation of leadership. *Journal of Applied Psychology*, 1969, *53*, 377–382.

Mischel, W. *Personality and assessment*. New York: Wiley, 1968.

Mischel, W. Toward a cognitive social learning reconceptualization of personality. *Psychological Review*, 1973, *80*, 252–283.

Moos, R. H. Sources of variance in responses to questionnaires and in behavior. *Journal of Abnormal Psychology*, 1969, *74*, 405–412.

Moos, R. H. Conceptualizations of human environments. *American Psychologist*, 1973, *28*, 652–665.

Moos, R. H., and Houts, P. S. Differential effects of the social atmospheres of psychiatric wards. *Human Relations*, 1970, *23*, 47–60.

Murray, H. A. *Explorations in personality*. New York: Oxford University Press, 1938.

Nicolson, H. *The development of English biography*. London: Hogarth Press, 1928.

Peevers, B. H., and Secord, P. F. Developmental changes in attribution of descriptive concepts to persons. *Journal of Personality and Social Psychology*, 1973, *27*, 120–128.

Plutarch. *Lives of the noble Grecians and Romans*. (J. Dryden, trans.). New York: Dell, 1968.

Price, R. H. The taxonomic classifications of behaviors and situations and the problem of behavior-environment congruence. *Human Relations*, 1974, *27*, 567–585.

Ryle, G. *The concept of mind*. New York: Barnes & Noble, 1949.

Sanford, N. Personality: Its place in psychology. In S. Koch (Ed.), *Psychology: A study of a science* (Vol. 5). New York: McGraw-Hill, 1963.

Sewell, W. R. D. Environmental perceptions and attitudes of engineers and public health officials. *Environment and Behavior*, 1971, *3*, 23–59.

Sewell, W. R. D., and Little, B. R. Specialists, laymen and the process of environmental appraisal. *Regional Studies*, 1973, *7*, 82–101.

Smelser, N. J., and Smelser, W. T. (Eds.). *Personality and social systems* (2nd ed.). New York: Wiley, 1970.

Smith, M. B. Psychology in two small towns (Review of Barker, R. G., and Schoggen, P. *Qualities of community life*. San Francisco, California: Jossey-Bass, 1973). *Science*, 1974, *184*, 671–673.

Sonnenfeld, J. Personality and behavior in environment. *Proceedings of the Association of American Geographers*, 1969, *1*, 136–140.

Stern, G. G. *People in context: The measurement of environmental interaction in school and society*. New York: Wiley, 1970.

Suetonious. *The twelve Caesars*. (R. Graves, trans.) Harmondsworth, Middlesex, England: Penguin Books, 1957.

Tagiuri, R., and Litwin, G. H. (Eds.). *Organizational climate: explorations of a concept*. Boston, Massachusetts: Harvard Business School, 1968.

Vayda, A. P. (Ed.). *Environment and cultural behavior: Ecological studies in cultural anthropology*. Garden City, New York: Natural History Press (Doubleday & Co.), 1969.

Wachtel, P. L. Psychodynamics, behavior therapy, and the implacable experimenter: An inquiry into the consistency of personality. *Journal of Abnormal Psychology*, 1973, *82*, 324–334.

Wiggins, J. S. *Personality and prediction: Principles of personality assessment*. Reading, Massachusetts: Addison-Wesley, 1973.

Wiggins, J. S. In defense of traits. Vancouver, B. C.: University of British Columbia. Unpublished report, 1974.

Zuckerman, M. Dimensions of sensation seeking. *Journal of Consulting and Clinical Psychology*, 1971, *36*, 45–52.

V

Specialization and the Varieties of Environmental Experience:

Empirical Studies within the Personality Paradigm

BRIAN R. LITTLE

Abstract: The integrative and reflexive capabilities of the personality research paradigm are here reviewed in the context of applying specialization theory to issues in man–environment research. A primary specialist typology is described along with the notion of specialization loops. Assessment techniques for measuring the cognitive, affective, and behavioral components of specialization loops are outlined and a developmental model of environmental construing proposed. The specialization model in its expanded form, which includes expressive and environmental barriers to the completion of loops, is shown to apply to students, scientists, and schizophrenics. A plea is made for an environmental psychology that is empirically reflexive. Hopefully, it will soon be difficult to find an environmental psychologist who has not been put soundly in his place—at least in his own theorizing.

While Kenneth Craik's paper has, to use his words, conveyed "the general spirit and scientific intention of the (personality) paradigm" in environmental psychology, the present contribution will take this spirit and distill it into some primary ingredients. It will then show that the paradigm's scientific intentions are honorable by presenting a set of empirical studies carried out within the personological tradition.

BRIAN R. LITTLE • Department of Psychology, University of British Columbia, Vancouver 8, British Columbia.

ESSENCE OF PERSONOLOGY: INTEGRATION AND REFLEXIVITY

We will be concerned with two essential ingredients of the personality paradigm: the field's integrative orientation and its reflexive capability. The first of these has a long history and is generally well known as a theme in personology, while the latter, despite its theoretical articulation two decades ago (Kelly, 1955), has only recently made its appearance in empirical personality research (Little, 1972b).

The Integrative Orientation of Personology

As Craik reminds us, personality theory has long traded on the notion that the various functions of man studied by psychologists need to be pieced together in a more cohesive and integral fashion, thereby providing a common source and terminus for the disparate thoughts, feelings, and behaviors that appear on the data sheets of psychology's specialists. Notwithstanding its historical and symbolic significance in personology, the integrative function has been less a concrete accomplishment than a continuing aspiration of the field. In recent years, even the aspiration to integrate has fallen from favor, and some reviewers (e.g., Adelson, 1969; Carlson, 1971) have decried the field's lapse into peripheralism.[1]

A developing perspective called specialization theory (e.g., Little, 1972b) is based on a set of assumptions that take the integrative function of personality theory seriously, particularly where it bears upon the field of environmental psychology. Without going into details of its conceptual basis, we can briefly note that specialization theory attempts to integrate a set of bipolar dimensions that have divided contemporary personality psychology into two antagonistic camps, radical personalists and radical physicalists. Table 1 indicates how these extreme groups of personologists differ in their approach to several important issues in psychological theory, research, and practice. It also indicates where specialization theory attempts to bridge the polarities and invigorate the integrative passions of personologists.

Of particular concern here is an attempt to integrate information on cognitive, affective, and behavioral responses to the environment by focusing upon a typological analysis of different "specialists" at both the lay and professional levels. Integration is also sought by developing the concept of the specialization loop, which predicts relationships between the three components of human action. Each of these approaches will be elaborated on in subsequent sections.

---

[1] Indeed, the retreat away from the study of persons toward the study of processes prompted Carlson to entitle her review of the field "Where Is the Person in Personality Research?"

Table 1. Criteria Differentiating Radical Personalism, Radical Physicalism, and Specialization Theory

Selected issues in personality theory, assessment and research	Alternative perspectives		Specialization theory
	Radical physicalism	Radical personalism	
Philosophical assumptions:			
Active vs. passive model of man	Passive model; drive reductionistic	Active model with emphasis on free–will	Developmental model: the transition from passivity to activity enacted through specialization loops.
Reflexivity	No reflexivity	Mandatory reflexivity	Optional reflexivity
Approach to assessment			
Methods used	Mechanistic, physicalistic	Intuitive and anti-measurement	Multi-method convergence of subjective and objective measures by focusing on projects
Level of analysis	Nomothetic: the establishment of general laws	Idiographic: the examination of the single case	Three interrelated levels: nomothetic–general laws of specialization; comparative and idiographic
Specificity vs. globality			
Intrinsic vs. extrinsic locus of control	Extrinsic locus of control	Intrinsic locus of control	Interaction between specialization of individual and environmental press
Person vs. situational variance	Emphasis on situational determinism		
Mode of relating to subjects, clients, etc.	I–It relationship Superior status to experimenter	I–Thou relationship Superior status to subject	You–Me relationship Equal but differently focused specialists
Focus of convenience of the theory	Behavioral systems	Persons	Personal systems: interaction of cognitive, affective, and behavioral systems
Treatment of environment	Empty person Full and physical environment	Empty environment	Primary objects serve as basis for functional man–environment theory

The Reflexive Capability in Personology

Reflexivity is that characteristic of a theory that enables it to simultaneously account for the behavior of the theorist as well as the behavior of the object being theorized about. A reflexive theory, in other words, is self-referential.[2] Within the field of personality, Kelly's (1955) personal construct theory is explicitly reflexive, being based on a model of Everyman as scientist. Kelly argues persuasively that psychology should be the prototypically reflexive discipline, and suggests that if a theory of personality cannot explain adequately the behavior of constructing a theory of personality, it has little claim as a useful theory of anything. For the Kellians, clarity begins at home.

In the environmental psychology field, Craik (1970a) endorsed a reflexive orientation in suggesting that, in developing research on the behavior of people in flood plains and other hazardous environments, we construe them as latent resource managers. We would more usefully view them as creators of theories about man–environment relations than as the victims of hopelessly irrational motives.[3]

Reflexivity is regarded by most Kellians (e.g., Bannister and Mair, 1968) as a conceptual necessity. We will regard it as a highly desirable, though not mandatory, element of a model for personality research. Furthermore, unlike most personal construct theory research, ours will take reflexivity as an empirical problem, not merely a polemical one. Thus, in specialization theory a prime goal is the systematic, empirical examination of ourselves, as well as our more conventional subjects.

PERSONS, THINGS, AND SELF: THE PRIMARY OBJECTS OF ENVIRONMENTAL SPECIALIZATION

One of the difficulties in applying the personological paradigm to the field of environmental psychology has been the lack of what might be called link concepts, processes which are directly expressive of the transactional nature of person–environment encounters, but which are also pitched at a sufficiently molar level that they will sustain the integrative needs of the personologist. The process of specialization, the selective channeling of dispositions and abilities,

---

[2] While we would not expect our geological colleagues to describe the behavior of glacial fields in the same terms as they would the development of their own geological theory and research (despite its likely utility as a metaphorical insult), the situation is rather different in psychology. A detailed treatment of the issue of reflexivity and a discussion of various routes that might be taken to offset the philosophical paradoxes that result from a disjunction between Us (as psychologists) and Them (as our subjects) appears in Little (1972b, pp.95–99).

[3] During the mid-nineteen-sixties a comprehensive movement toward interpreting lay behavior via the same constructs used to explain professional roles took place. This obliteration of the Us–Them dichotomy cropped up in many different fields of study, and it has been suggested that this "academicomimetic revolution" constituted a major shift in orientation in the behavioral sciences (Little, 1972b).

can serve the linking function adequately, involving as it does the joint consideration of a specialist and his speciality, the organism in its environment—creatures in context. Brief consideration of the traditional conception of environment in personality psychology will highlight some possible advantages of using the alternative perspective.

Conceptions of the Environment in Personological Inquiry

Wohlwill (1970) has commented on the inadequate conceptualization of the environment given in mainstream psychology, stressing that it is seen most often as being either an almost exclusively social phenomenon or as a rather nebulous generality. Similarly, in the field of personality psychology the environment is a comparatively underdeveloped resource. In a not totally whimsical mood it has been recently suggested:

> Were an alien being to attempt to draw a picture of man's environment from the information contained in personality journals it would appear as a set of disembodied significant others floating in a sea of abstractions. (Little, 1972b, p. 113)

One of the chief strategies of personality assessment has been the construction of psychological typologies out of contrasting orientations toward the environment conceived as a large, undifferentiated mass. For example, the concepts of introversion–extroversion, internal versus external locus of control, and field dependence–independence make no distinctions about the kinds of objects extroverts extrovert themselves toward; make no distinction about what types of events internals feel control over; and do not commit themselves to specifying in what kinds of fields the field-dependent person becomes embedded. It is assumed correctly or incorrectly that it makes psychological sense to distinguish between self and environment, both "writ large" and loose. What we seem to have here is a kind of psychometric brutalism, in which people are ordered on a dimension that pits a monolithic environment against an equally undifferentiated person.

At the other extreme, environmental psychologists are now developing more specific and finely honed measures both of environments (Craik, 1971; Mehrabian and Russell, 1974; Moos, 1973), and environmental dispositions (Craik, 1972; McKechnie, 1974a, 1974b, 1975), that enable the quality of environmental experience to be more precisely assessed. Because this level of analysis can assess the nuances of human response to diverse environments, with a focus upon the multiple varieties of environmental experience, we might regard this as a kind of psychometric romanticism.[4] Using the same architectural metaphor, it might be argued that specialization theory takes the approach of a psychmetric

---

[4] I hasten to add immediately that it is the conceptual rather than the mensurational characteristics of these authors' work that is romantic. In terms of methodological rigor and sophistication, they are of course certifiably classical.

functionalism. It takes a middle course between brutalistic homogeneity and romantic diversification of environmental assessment. It seeks to analyze the environment into a smaller set of objects—objects that are sufficiently basic and ubiquitous to satisfy the kind of integration and generality demanded by the personological tradition, but that, unlike a capital "E" environment, can function at the human scale—are used and loved, lifted up on one's knee, and sent to Uncle Harry for Christmas. We are concerned, in other words, with the primary objects of environmental encounters.

Primary Objects and Specialization

What, then, are the primary objects of environments to which individuals orient themselves and upon which we might begin to build a systematic bridge between environmental and personality psychology? In an earlier paper it was suggested that persons and things constitute the primary objects:

> The concept of specialization . . . stimulates consideration of those objects that are selectively attended to by psychological man. What kind of environmental objects might serve as specialities? Given the potentially limitless kinds of objects that might serve this role, can we partition the environment in some basic, primary way, so as to study systematically the largest and most substantive divisions first? We have made the provisional assumption that persons and things comprise the primary objects in our environments. While we had originally intended to partition the environment in a psychologically useful way only, it soon became apparent that this cleavage was possibly fundamental in other respects. (Little, 1972*b*, p. 113)

These "other respects" include the detailed philosophical investigation by Strawson (1959) in which he proposed that physical objects and persons were "ontologically primitive"—the "primary particulars." With respect to the separate inclusion of persons as primitive, underived particulars, Strawson suggested:

> The admission of this category as primitive and underived appeared as a necessary condition of our membership in a non-solipsistic world. Given, then, that our scheme of things includes the scheme of a common spatio-temporal world of particulars, it appears that a central place among particulars must be accorded to material bodies and to persons. These must be the primary particulars. (1959, p. 246)

If persons and things are ontologically basic they would seem to be psychologically basic as well. This is an assumption of the specialization perspective, however, the adequacy of which will be tested by the value of the facts such an assumption unfolds in the course of empirical inquiry.

THE CHARACTERISTICS OF PRIMARY SPECIALISTS

As suggested in an earlier section, an attempt has been made to integrate information on cognitive, affective, and behavioral responses to the environment

	Primary specialization	
Sample size and nature	Person-orientation	Thing-orientation
37 British University undergraduates	.76	.84
43 British occupational therapists	.82	.81
40 Canadian 12th-grade high-school students	.73	.84

Figure 1. Corrected Kuder-Richardson split-half reliabilities of items on person-orientation and thing-orientation scales (from Little, 1972a, p. 14).

by constructing a dimensional typology of primary specialists. This section will explore some of the empirical findings that have emerged in studies of the different specialist groups.

Person–Thing Orientation: Generality, Bipolarity, or Independence?

A short scale for the assessment of differential orientation toward persons and things has been developed. Starting with a large pool of potential items, the T-P scale in its present form consists of 12 items involving activities with persons, and 12 involving activities with physical objects.[5] Full psychometric analysis and evidence relating to validity is available (Little, 1972a, 1974).

Development of the T-P scale enabled the undertaking of a test of the extent to which people orient themselves toward each of the primary objects discussed above. While it may be philosophically meaningful and theoretically legitimate to distinguish between persons and things as primary objects, the empirical question has been surprisingly ignored. The question can be put quite simply: When individuals are asked to report on activities that deal with primarily social objects or primarily nonsocial objects, do they (1) show a consistent preference for encounters *within* a domain, and (2) show a consistent preference for encounters *across* the two primary domains?

The first question can be answered by looking at the internal consistency of responses to items on the T-P scale. As shown in Figure 1, there is fairly strong evidence for generality both within the person–domain and within the thing–domain. At least as assessed by the T-P scale, then, it is defensible to talk

[5] The items on the T-P scale are diversified and were chosen so as to tap a wide spectrum of environmental objects. The types of object on the person-orientation scale include children, new neighbors, old people, interviewees, and total strangers, while amongst the thing-items are stereo sets, broken watches, photographic equipment, street machinery, and a comet!

Sample size and nature	Pearson r's between		
	P-scores and T-scores	P_1 and P_2	T_1 and T_2
37 British University undergraduates	−.10		
43 British occupational therapists	.11		
40 Canadian 12th-grade high-school students	.04		
244 Females (norm group)	.07		
284 Males (norm group)	.02		
40 American University students (two-month test–retest)		.85	.89
20 British undergraduate students (two-week test–retest)		.88	.99

Figure 2. Correlations between person- and thing-orientation scores and test–retest reliability of T-P scale score (adapted from Little, 1972a, p. 15).

about a generalized disposition to be oriented toward persons and a generalized disposition to be oriented toward things.[6] With respect to the question of whether environmental orientation generalizes *across* the primary domains, three possibilities exist, each of which has received at least some theoretical endorsement. As discussed above, personologists who study broad dispositions contrasting inner with outer orientation tacitly support a generality hypothesis, and would expect that those who seek stimulation in one domain will also seek it in another, perhaps because of some common neurophysiological mechanism such as cortical inhibition that would treat stimuli as interchangeable. Under this hypothesis the correlation between person-orientation and thing-orientation scores should be positive. A second alternative, and one very widely held in the field of vocational guidance, as well as in stereotypes about professions, is that person-orientation and thing-orientation are opposing poles on a single dimension. It is assumed here that some general fund of energy is available for investment in environmental encounters, so that orientation toward one set of primary objects will draw energy away from investment in the other. This hypothesis predicts a negative correlation between scores on person-orientation and thing-orientation. A third hypothesis is that person-orientation and thing-orientation are orthogonal: that some people will focus on one primary object domain to the exclusion of the other; that some will, relative to others manifest interest in both domains; and that still others will express comparatively little interest in either persons or things. Figure 2 summarizes a set of studies look-

[6] It should be noted that several independent measures of thing–person orientation have been used in our work and there is fairly consistent evidence of convergent validity with measures such as single direct-magnitude estimates of T-P orientation, peer-ratings, and behavioral timetables relating to activities involving persons and things (Little, 1972a, 1974). See also Table 4.

ing at the correlations between person-orientation scores (P) and thing-orientation scores (T) from the T-P scale carried out on several different subject samples. There is consistent evidence that person- and thing-orientation are orthogonal. Figure 2 also shows that the test–retest correlations for both person and thing orientation are sufficiently high that the orthogonality cannot be attributed to unreliability.

The independence of person and thing orientation is further attested to in other studies. For example, King (1956) challenged what classical theories of schizophrenia had assumed to be a unitary dimension of "environmental withdrawal." King distinguished on *a priori* grounds between "interpersonal withdrawal" and "thing withdrawal" and developed two measures of each, including ward ratings of activity in the social and nonsocial domains and a measure of operant conditioning rate. King's results showed that the two thing-withdrawal measures intercorrelated significantly, as did the two person-withdrawal measures. There were no significant correlations *between* the two domains, however. He concluded that "withdrawal behavior in schizophrenia would appear to be specific to the classification of environmental referents, whether persons or things." (p. 374)

The orthogonality of thing and person orientation scores enables us to construct a fourfold table of specialists: person-specialists (high P, low T), thing-specialists (high T, low P), nonspecialists (low P, low T), and generalists (high P, high T). The four groups are graphically portrayed in Figure 3. Thumbnail sketches of the modal characteristics of people in each group appear in Table 2. Further details of the empirical work underlying these descriptions appear below.

Primary Specialists and Modes of Construing the Environment

A number of studies have been carried out to explore ways in which differential orientation, as assessed by measures of affective interest in persons and things, relate to different ways of perceiving or construing the environment.

One study (Little, 1968) examined the ways in which the different groups of primary specialists experienced three shopping areas in Berkeley, California.[7] It used an adaptation of repertory grid technique (Kelly, 1955), and subjects were asked to compare and contrast the three areas by writing down a way in which any two were alike and different from the third. After completing one such triad, subjects went on to generate as many bipolar

[7] For the afficionados of the East Bay the areas were Shattuck Avenue, Euclid, and Telegraph Avenue. The data collection was carried out by the author in 1965 as part of Kenneth Craik's graduate seminar in environmental psychology. At that time Shattuck Avenue was perceived as a fairly orthodox lower- to middle-class shopping area, Telegraph Avenue was peaking as the behavior setting *ne plus ultra* for the hippie movement, while Euclid provided a blend of each, with a preponderance of rather more middle-of-the-road, hippoid students.

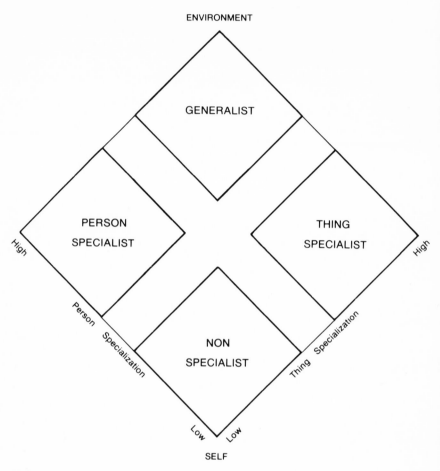

Figure 3. Schematic representation of the four primary specialist groups—nonspecialists, person-specialists, thing-specialists, and generalists.

constructs as they could in a five-minute time period. The constructs were then analyzed in terms of number generated and were content-analyzed into several categories. Results showed that the generalists used the largest number of constructs, with the nonspecialists using the least number. With respect to the content of the constructs elicited, person-specialists, as predicted, tended to construe the settings in terms of the attributes of people on the street, the personalities of some of the proprietors, and the various types of social interaction likely to take place in the setting. Thing-specialists focused significantly more

Table 2. Summary of Characteristics of Person-Specialists, Thing-Specialists, Nonspecialists, and Generalists

NONSPECIALIST

By definition, expresses comparatively little interest in either the world of things or people. Appears negativistic, rather unexpressive, and with a high general-activity threshold. Lacking specialized interest in either primary domain, tends to construe in a stimulus-inappropriate manner, seeing things personalistically, and persons physicalistically. Empirical studies confirm the hypothesis that nonspecialists tend to use a large number of self-constructs when comparing and contrasting objects in their environment. They tend to overestimate distances, and seem to avoid situations calling for either initiative or succorance. Tend to score higher than the other groups on measures of anxiety. The studies suggest that nonspecialists may be too concerned with predicting their *own* behavior to be able to attend to the world of environmental objects. They are perhaps better regarded as self-specialists.

PERSON-SPECIALIST

Expresses marked interest in a variety of encounters with people and little interest in the world of physical objects. Low threshold for activities involving affiliative, empathic, and nurturant tendencies. Has a highly developed person-construct system, thus tending to construe both persons and things in a personalistic way. Tends to focus upon emotional aspects of other people and often go too far beyond the information given during person-perception tasks. In nonverbal communication makes great use of what Mehrabian calls "immediacy cues"—standing closer during social interaction, smiling more, using first names more frequently, and being less likely to send form letters at Christmas time! Characterized by high scores on psychological femininity, their academic pursuits are most often in literary and social-service fields where they place a high value on the relevance of studies to humankind.

THING-SPECIALIST

Expresses interest in a wide range of encounters with physical objects, machines, artifacts, things. Low threshold for activities involving mechanical, manipulative, and analytic tendencies. Has a highly developed thing–construct system, thus tending to construe both persons and things in a physicalistic manner. Has strong preference for order, clarity, and pride in his practicality. In impression–formation tasks tends to "stick to the data," thus engaging in little inferential activity. Scores high on measures of psychological masculinity and tends to pursue fields such as the physical sciences or practical fields, where a stress is placed upon rigor.

GENERALIST

Expresses marked interest in a variety of encounters with both people and things. Has low general-activity threshold, with subsequent tendency to information overload. Being specialized in both domains, can construe in a stimulus-appropriate manner in both person and thing contexts. Can utilize both personalistic and physicalistic modes of experiencing the environment when the situation calls for it, and is thus the most versatile of the primary specialist types. While able to make inferential leaps in person–perception study, is able to check inferences against more solid data. Characterized by openness to both masculine and feminine aspects of self and found relatively frequently in synoptic disciplines such as town-planning or anthropology. Places a high value on achieving a balance between rigor and relevance.

upon characteristics of the physical setting; i.e., they generated a larger number of constructs relating to the nature of the spatial layout, the presence of road construction, and similar physicalistic considerations. While this difference between personalistic and physicalistic constructs had been predicted for the two extreme specialist groups, more detailed analysis showed that generalists were significantly more likely to use constructs that dealt with emergent features of the settings such as the overall ambience, the peculiar atmosphere of each shopping area. The use of these global-aesthetic constructs appeared also in the grids of nonspecialists, though not as frequently. The most significant finding vis-à-vis the nonspecialist group was, however, a proportionately high use of constructs that might be called egocentric. They made more use of constructs referring to their own personal needs and how they were satisfied in each setting, and in particular constructs that dealt with the distance, convenience, and accessibility of centers to the subject's place of residence. The great variability in the use of the latter category of constructs was noteworthy in that the subjects were all residents in the same cooperative living unit at the time of testing. The evidence on egocentric construct usage, together with other indications based on different kinds of data,[8] has led us to suggest that nonspecialists might be better labeled "self-specialists."

Table 3 lists some of the construct categories we have developed in studying a diversity of environmental elements with grid techniques.

A number of studies have been carried out using the dimensional typology of specialists presented above (Little, 1972a, 1974). The most consistent finding to emerge has been the person-specialists as assessed by the T-P scale predictably experience their environment personalistically, while thing-specialists experience it via a more physicalistic mode. For example, in an unpublished study carried out with John Saward, undergraduate male students were given the T-P scale and then asked to compare and contrast triads of short poems (ranging from highland dirges to crisp haiku). Whereas thing-specialists made more frequent use of constructs involving technical, physicalistic criteria such as differences in meter and rhyme, person-specialists evoked criteria relat-

---

[8] A study currently being carried out by Kazu Murata for an M.Arch. thesis at the University of British Columbia lends indirect support to the hypothesis that nonspecialists perceive the environment more in terms of energy expenditure and effort than other specialist groups. He was interested in examining the factors that lead to correct estimates of distance in urban settings, in particular the nature of the path between the observer and the terminal object. In analyzing his data it became clear that the environmental effects were swamped by individual differences. He had administered the T-P scale to a selection of people in downtown Vancouver, and when they were broken into the primary specialist groups, he found that they differed considerably in their estimate of distances. While there was an overall tendency for all groups to *overestimate* distances (in each case the distance they had to estimate was four miles), the greatest distortion was found for nonspecialists, who overestimated the distance to downtown locations by 45%. The most accurate assessment was achieved by generalists who overestimated by 8%, with person specialists and thing specialists occupying intermediate points (33% and 15% respectively).

Table 3. Categories for the Analysis of Personal Constructs Elicited from Subjects on Environmental Repertory Grids[a]

Personalistic	Focusing upon the inhabitants, customers, residents, etc., of places, including their personal characteristics, traits, dispositions, training, desires, relationships, etc.; e.g., nice people go there—rough people only; typical academic setting—more business-oriented
Physicalistic	Focusing upon the physical characteristics, qualities, and limitations of places, including chemical, biological, architectural (structural, not aesthetic), and mathematical-geometrical aspects; e.g., made of reinforced concrete—made of wood; crooked roofs—straight and true
Global–aesthetic	Attentive to higher-order qualitative difference between places such as general "atmosphere" or mood, qualitative differences in style that involve both personal and physical aspects; e.g., buoyant—depressed; a June-morning kind of town—middle of Novemberish
Functionalistic	Describes the use or function of places and/or relates the physical aspects of environment to behaviors of people in the setting; e.g., for studying in—designed for love; easy to navigate—impossible to find one's way in
Egocentric	Concerned with the effects of the place on oneself or with the role one has had in a location, or with any aspect of place *vis-à-vis* self; e.g., we met there—we didn't meet there; too far away—next door to me

[a] Adapted from Little (1971) and Sewell and Little (1973).

ing more to the poet's state of mind, or the feelings underlying the poem. This was seen as being consistent with the expectation that assessment of an individual's primary orientation would enable us to predict aspects of their secondary encounters with the environment—those events that involve mixes or blends of primary objects.

While typological analysis is part of mainstream personological research, it will be useful to focus upon an alternative way of approaching specialization for the remaining sections of the paper.

SPECIALIZATION LOOPS: AFFECTIVE, COGNITIVE, AND BEHAVIORAL COMPONENTS OF ENVIRONMENTAL EXPERIENCE

The dimensional typological approach to primary specialization offers one way of conceiving of man–environment relations. The notion of specialization loops supplements the typological analysis and raises some new possibilities for empirical investigation.

The Nature of Specialization Loops

In its simplest form, a specialization loop is a set of links between affective, cognitive, and behavioral components of an individual's environmental actions. Out of an almost infinitely varied set of potential foci, an individual, in the course of ontogenesis, begins the selective channelization of interest and ability that constitutes specialization. Behaviorally, specialization involves greater frequency and/or intensity of encounters with the speciality; cognitively, it involves the development of highly interrelated constructs subsuming the domain; affectively, specialization is characterized by interest in and pleasure with the specialized domain. The three components of specialization are reciprocally reinforcing as diagramed in Figure 4. An increase in any component, we hypothesize, will increase the probability of adjacent components taking on higher values. We assume that specialization loops are bidirectional. Thus, an increase in the affective components of a domain will likely increase the frequency of behavioral encounters within that domain (clockwise looping), as well as increase the level of cognitive functioning in the domain (counter-clockwise looping).

One of the main virtues of the concept of specialization is that it enables us to conceive of a family of research models operating at the idiographic, comparative, and nomothetic levels (Little, 1972b). Specialization loops, for example, would be applicable to a single individual's specialized orientation to sports cars or National Hockey League referees.[9] In the present paper, however, we wish to deal primarily at the level of the comparative analysis of primary specialization in persons and things.

The Assessment of Primary Specialization Loops

In Figures 5 and 6, two *primary* specialization loops are presented, together with greater elaboration of the nature of the three components. Also, in keeping with the methodological focus of the conference, Table 4 gives details of the assessment procedures we have been using to date in studies of specialization.

Taking as an example the primary specialization loop for people shown in Figure 5, it is predicted that with the experience of increased positive affect

[9] On the basis of the loop presented in Figure 4, then, we would predict that the greater amount an individual engaged in behavioral encounters with, say, sports cars, the greater would be her affective response to them, and the more content appropriate and structurally interrelated would be the constructs through which she anticipated and acted upon sports cars. We assume that an individual's personality can be usefully construed as a series of projects initiated and sustained on the basis of such bidirectional specialization loops. We shall not go into this level of the theory in the present paper, however.

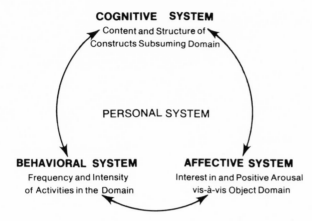

Figure 4. The basic components of a specialization loop.

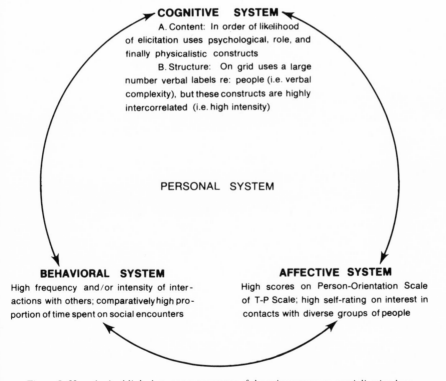

Figure 5. Hypothesized links between components of the primary person-specialization loop.

toward persons, there will be a rise in the frequency of behavioral encounters with others, an increase in the number of psychological criteria used in evaluating people, and a more intense, highly interrelated construct system used through which to anticipate and act upon the behavior of others.

Similarly, it is predicted that with increased behavioral interaction with others, the intensity of personal construct systems will increase, affect will be more positive, and so on. It is also assumed, of course, that other variables will intervene as barriers to the completion of the loop, and an example of one important variable of this sort will be given below. The critical empirical job at present is, however, the examination of evidence relating to the hypothesized relationships between the primary components of a specialization loop. Several such studies have now been completed, three of which can be briefly summarized.[10]

One study explored the relationship between the affective and cognitive components by administering the T-P scale, together with a standard repertory grid containing personally known people (e.g. your mother, your boss) as the elements to be compared and contrasted. Eighty-seven Oxford undergraduates studying in a diversity of fields served as paid volunteer subjects. A significant correlation was found between the P score on the T-P scale and the number of psychological constructs used on the grid. People who expressed positive interest toward other people, in other words, construed their acquaintances in terms of human needs, motives, and desires. Individuals expressing low interest in persons focused more upon role and physicalistic criteria. One particularly interesting aspect of this study was obtained by breaking down the results by sex. Although the correlation for the 46 male subjects between person-orientation and psychological construct usage was significant ($r = .27, p < .05$), it was low in magnitude. For the 39 female subjects, however, the correlation was very substantial ($r = .72, p < .001$). One interpretation of these results will be more credible when we consider the results of another study carried out with Canadian student subjects.

In this second study, 75 subjects were administered a grid containing places as the elements to be compared and contrasted (e.g., a place you feel comfortable in, a place you went to frequently as a child, etc.). The subjects were asked to nominate specific exemplars of each kind of place (e.g., Martha's bedroom, Mendon's corner store), and then to compare and contrast by the triadic method described above. Of particular concern here is the correlation between thing-orientation as assessed by the T-P scale and the number of physicalistic constructs used in the grid. There was a significant correlation ($r = .41, p < .01$) between these two measures when males and females were analyzed together. Broken down by sex, however, females had a marginally

[10] Unless specifically cited, the studies presented in this paper have not been previously reported.

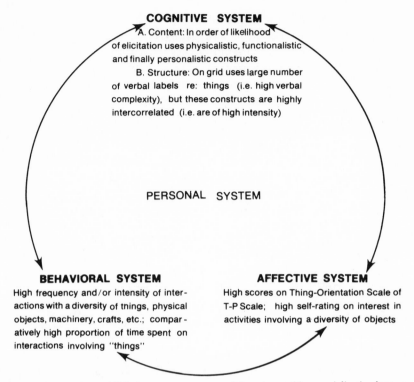

COGNITIVE SYSTEM
A. Content: In order of likelihood
of elicitation uses physicalistic, functionalistic
and finally personalistic constructs
B. Structure: On grid uses large number
of verbal labels re: things (i.e. high verbal
complexity), but these constructs are highly
intercorrelated (i.e. are of high intensity)

PERSONAL SYSTEM

BEHAVIORAL SYSTEM
High frequency and/or intensity of interactions with a diversity of things, physical
objects, machinery, crafts, etc.; comparatively high proportion of time spent on
interactions involving "things"

AFFECTIVE SYSTEM
High scores on Thing-Orientation Scale of
T-P Scale; high self-rating on interest in
activities involving a diversity of objects

Figure 6. Hypothesized links between components of the primary thing-specialization loop.

significant correlation of .30 ($N = 40$, $p = .05$), while males had a highly significant correlation of .68 ($N = 35$, $p < .001$).

Taken together, these two studies raise the possibility that sex roles may act as moderators of the relationships between components of specialization loops. It can be hypothesized that concordance among the three components of specialization will be increased to the extent that the domain in question is sex role appropriate and that the links will be weakened if the domain runs against sex-role norms. There is ample evidence that person-specialization is valued as a female sex-role activity, while thing-specialization is seen as primarily male sex-typed (Little, 1972a).[11] In terms of Figures 5 and 6, it is likely that these sex-role barriers to looping are imposed between the affective and behavioral components of the loop. Thus, while a female with interests in physical objects, mechanics, and crafts may wish (via the natural completion of a specialization loop) to enter behavior settings in which primary encounters with such objects

[11] Even though half the person and half the thing items on the T-P scale were chosen so as to be female-role-appropriate, there are still consistent sex differences favoring males on thing-orientation and females on person-orientation.

may be enjoyed, she may be precluded from so doing. There are still comparatively few girls hanging out at the local garage on Saturday morning, and the
evening classes at the local college in physics, electricity, or home repairs are
still heavily overrepresented with males. For a male with the same interests,
however, quite a different process takes place. Because there is no barrier
placed between the affective and behavioral components of his loop, a male is
able to feel the full bidirectional influence of a primary specialization loop. Not
only is the counter-clockwise bond between affective orientation and cognitive
systems felt, but the clockwise loop through the behavioral domain is un-
impeded. This dual influence on the links between components thus raises the
correlation between any two components for a speciality that is sex-role
appropriate. The same general logic can be applied to the field of person-specialization in which males, relative to females, are more likely to find barriers
preventing access to behavior settings involving intimate contact with others.

Persons as Things and Things as Persons: Developmental Progressions in Environmental Construing

In Figures 5 and 6, note was made of a developmental ordering of the
constructs used in understanding persons and things, so that as behavioral encounters and/or positive affect increase, the more "advanced" construct category is used. Figure 7 schematizes this hypothesized progression in the content
of constructs in more detail. In the person domain it is seen that physicalistic
criteria, role criteria, and finally psychological criteria are used as the bases for
differentiating people, while in the thing–domain personalistic, functionalistic,
and finally physicalistic constructs become dominant. This progression is seen
as being developmental in the same sense as organismic theory treats development (e.g., Werner, 1948; Wapner, 1969); i.e., it is felt to apply not only to
ontogenesis but to the development of systems of knowledge in general. As one
example of a nonontogenetic domain that seems to follow the progression
hypothesized for the person– domain we can cite the work of Steven Duck
(1973; Duck and Spencer, 1972), who has found that this progression of
constructs hold in the process of friendship formation. In the early stages of
friendship, similarity between students' physicalistic constructs is critical, in
middle stages role constructs become significant, while in later stages similarity
on psychological constructs is the best predictor.

As Figure 7 makes clear, we hypothesize that in the early stages of
experiencing the environment, persons are construed as things and things as
people. This ontological transposition will appear whenever there has been insufficient behavioral interaction with a primary domain and/or insufficient affective involvement in it. Thus we expect stimulus-inappropriate construing to

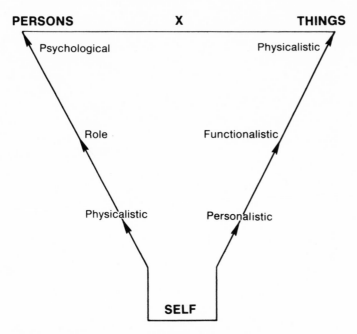

Figure 7. Hypothesized developmental progression of constructs in the person- and thing-domains. It is assumed that for adaptive purposes at least some movement toward perceiving persons psychologically and things physicalistically is necessary. "X" represents transitional objects such as abstract objects, animals, and collections of physical and social stimuli. Details of the relationship between primary construing and the interpretation of nonprimary objects will appear in later publications.

be manifested in children who have not had sufficient behavioral experience in a domain, in people who, relative to others, have not invested themselves behaviorally or affectively in a domain, and in professional scientists who, for whatever reason, may not have developed an affective bond with the object of their studies. We shall revisit this last example when we discuss how specialization theory attempts to take reflexivity into the empirical arena.

In Figures 8 and 9, some results from an early study of the ontogenesis of constructs in the person and thing domain are presented (Little, 1967). The prediction that with increased age, greater use of physicalistic constructs in the thing-domain and psychological constructs in the person-domain is confirmed (for person-domain the age main effect is significant at $p < .01$ level with neither sex nor interaction effect significant; for thing-domain the age main effect is significant at $p < .001$ with, again, neither sex nor interaction effects of significance). When older subjects are used, the trend toward sex differences be-

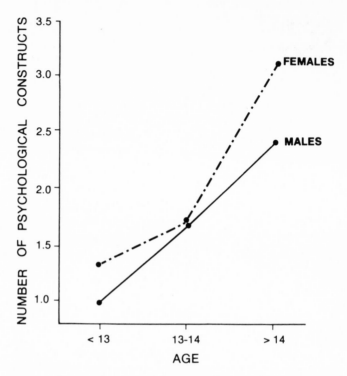

Figure 8. Number of psychological constructs used by three age groups of children when comparing and contrasting personally known individuals on a repertory grid.

comes more clear-cut, with males being more physicalistic in the thing-domain and females more psychological in the person-domain.

EXPANDING THE LOOP: SPECIALIZATION IN STUDENTS, SCHIZOPHRENICS, AND SCIENTISTS

In an important statement of the logic of test development in personology, Gough (1965) distinguished between primary, secondary, and tertiary levels of validation of concepts assessed by psychological tests. The primary level assesses whether a test is adequately measuring what it set out to measure, while the secondary level involves the explication of the psychological mechanisms underlying scores. Tertiary level analysis is concerned with unexpected relationships that the new scale unveils in the course of empirical research. We turn now to a similar tertiary analysis of the primary specialization model to discuss some studies that expand upon the loop and raise some new questions. By expanding the loop we mean two things: The loop will be generalized beyond the usual population of college students, and also, new components and/or barriers within the loop will be proposed and examined.

Expressiveness and Primary Specialization in Normals and Schizophrenics

In a study carried out with Eleanor Stephens (Little and Stephens, 1972), subjects were given a standard repertory grid and a specially constructed auditory grid. The latter involved triads of statements read by a group of actors. The triads were systematically varied so that for any triad two of the auditory statements were alike in that they were approximately equal in affective tone

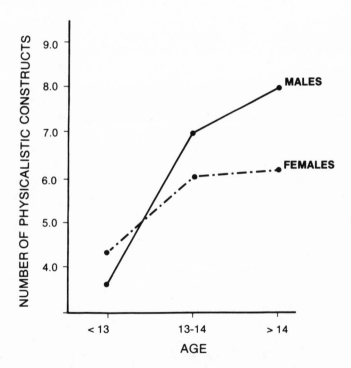

Figure 9. Number of physicalistic constructs used by three age groups of children when comparing and contrasting everyday physical objects on a repertory grid.

(e.g., both statements were said angrily, or both were said in a hesitant manner), while two of the statements were approximately equal in the "pure" content of what was communicated. Subjects were then asked to listen to a set of such triads and to write down for each the way in which any two of the three were alike and different from the third. It was thus possible to score each subject on whether they gave greater weight to expressive–affective features of auditory messages or to the content of the messages. A significant correlation was found between the tendency to use psychological constructs on the standard repertory grid, and the tendency to focus upon expressive aspects of auditory communications. It is not unlikely that in order to develop reliable psychological constructs for understanding others, it would be necessary to focus, at least in part, on the affective signals being communicated by them. For those who are more tuned to the physical and role features of individuals, it is not necessary to decode affective signals.

The confirmation of a possible link between affective decoding and one component of the primary specialization loop raised the question of whether person-specialization may also involve a disposition to *encode* affective cues more readily. Do person-specialists engage in a greater amount of expressive behavior when interacting with others than do those scoring low in this domain? In a preliminary pilot study designed to explore this question, a group of subjects who had been administered the T-P scale were asked to participate in a series of "behavioral vignettes" where they were asked to act out such things as protesting about an overly large car repair and thanking a student group for a charity donation.[12] Performances were videotaped and analyzed by a set of judges on criteria such as expressiveness, role skill, warmth, and nervousness. Two clusters emerged from the judges' ratings, one concerned with expressiveness and the other with role skill. Person-orientation scores on the T-P scale correlated significantly with the subjects' scores on expressiveness, while T + P scores (an index of generality of interest) correlated significantly with role-skill. The expressiveness finding raises the possibility that person-orientation and psychological construct usage are linked to an expressiveness factor involving both the encoding and decoding of affect.

This hypothesized link between person-orientation and encoding of affect was further confirmed in a study of individual differences in facial appearance and person-orientation. While the exploratory study looked at expressiveness as an ability manifested in a series of role performances, the second study was more concerned with the relatively enduring aspects of facial features. A facial appearance Q-deck (FAQ) was developed consisting of 150 items descriptive of human faces (e.g., bushy eyebrows, crooked teeth, etc.). Subjects were asked to complete the Q-deck as it applied to them. Subjects were also independently rated on the FAQ items by two judges who administered other scales. A

[12] I would like to thank Gordon Hobson and Margaret McCallin, who collaborated in this preliminary study.

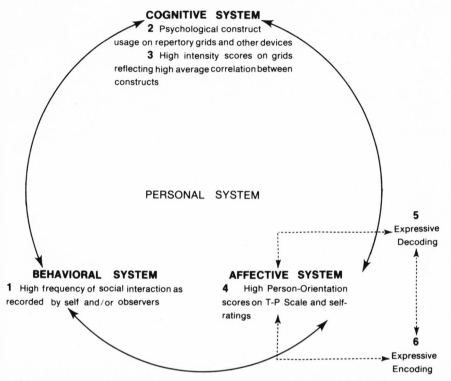

Figure 10. Hypothesized relationships within the expanded primary specialization loop.

measure of expressiveness taken from FAQ items (e.g., has mobile, expressive face; eyebrows move frequently) correlated significantly with person-orientation as assessed by the T-P scale. There was a significant positive correlation between judges' ratings and self ratings on expressiveness and both correlated with P-score. The hypothesized relationship between expressiveness and components of the primary specialization loop is graphed in Figure 10. In terms of the numbering of components in Figure 10, the previous studies summarized have empirically confirmed links between components 4 and 2, components 5 and 2, and components 6 and 4. Additional links involving the cognitive structure components that will not be discussed in this paper have been examined elsewhere (Little, 1969).

While all the subjects in studies reviewed thus far have been students, there is growing evidence that the expanded primary specialization loop of Figure 10 applies to the behavior of schizophrenics as well.[13] Dixon (1968),

[13] I am not, of course, implying that students and schizophrenics are nonoverlapping sets. The point to be made is that specialization theory attempts to develop empirical findings that generalize to highly diversified segments of the population.

demonstrated a relationship between clinical ratings of affective flattening (component 6 in Figure 10) and the use of few psychological constructs on a repertory grid (component 2). McPherson and his colleagues (McPherson *et al.*, 1970) confirmed this finding, showing that affect-flattened[14] schizophrenics used psychological construct less often and nonhuman "background" criteria more often when sorting pictures of individuals on a modified repertory grid. Williams and Quirke (1972) showed marked relationships between schizophrenic withdrawal from social interaction (component 1), the use of psychological constructs on a grid (component 2), and rated flattening of affect (component 6). Finally, there is evidence (McPherson, Buckley, and Draffan, 1971) showing correlations between psychological construct usage and the intensity of construct structure (components 2 and 3), the latter measure in use as an index of schizophrenic thought disorder.

Empirical Reflexivity: Specialization Loops in Presidents of the American Psychological Association

Specialization theory has been explicitly designed as a reflexive theory and our own professional behavior should be subsumable by our theoretical constructs. We have explored one link in the specialization loop using data supplied by other investigators on famous twentieth-century psychologists, a subset of whom became presidents of the American Psychological Association. The link explored was that between the use of personalistic constructs in one's formal psychological theory and an index of one's affective orientation toward people and things. The dimension of personalistic versus physicalistic construct usage appeared originally in Table 1, though we are now concerned with these characteristics as data about a theorist rather than a theory. In particular, we wish to explore a hypothesis nicely phrased by Abraham Kaplan in Chapter 7 of his *The Conduct of Inquiry* (1964): "It is not merely cynicism, I trust, to observe that many students of man and his ways seem to have little interest in—people!" (p. 290). It is clear from his earlier chapters, and from conventional debate about the motivational styles of different kinds of psychologists, that it is the radical physicalists who are expected to be low on interest in people. It was this contention, based more on rhetoric than research, that we subjected to empirical test by using the specialization loop as a model of professional conduct.[15] Data presented by Coan (1968) and by Campbell (1965) enabled us to test the

---

[14] Flattened affect refers primarily to a lack of expressiveness and the inability or unwillingness to exhibit nonverbal cues normally brought into play when interacting with other people.

[15] Some rather difficult, yet intriguing, issues arise when we begin to question whether the primary specialization loop serves as a theory or a model of professional behavior. While this point will not be taken up here, some preliminary considerations on the differences and similarities between theories and models can be found in Mehrabian (1968) and Little (1972*b*).

Table 4. Components of Specialization Loops and Methods for Assessment[a]

Components of loop	Tests and measures used	
	Person-domain	Thing-domain
Affective	P-orientation scale of the T-P scale (Little, 1972a, 1974); direct magnitude estimates of interest in people; peer nominations of orientation toward P-domain	T-orientation scale of the T-P scale; direct magnitude estimate of interest in thing domain; peer ratings of orientation toward variety of things
Cognitive	Repertory grid with people used as elements in matrix	Repertory grid with things, places, etc., used as elements in matrix
	A. Content: three basic categories used—psychological (e.g., outgoing-shy); role (e.g., Catholic-not Catholic); physicalistic (e.g., short-tall)	A. Content: three basic categories used—physicalistic (e.g., concrete-steel); functionalistic (e.g., for shopping in—not so); personalistic (e.g., wild factor analysts lurk there—only Freudians)
	B. Structure: number of different verbal labels elicited on list form of grid; explanation power of first factor extracted when individual grids are factored. High explanation power = high intensity	B. Structure: same techniques as used for analysis of person–domain
Behavioral	Observation of frequency of interaction with others; peer ratings of frequency and intensity of interactions; behavioral timetables showing time spent/week on social encounters	Observation of frequency of interaction with objects; peer ratings of extent of encounters involving things and nonhuman objects; behavioral timetables

[a] These are the measures that we have used most regularly in research on specialization. Other techniques such as sorting photographs taken by subjects into proportion person-oriented, recall of a set of pictures of social and physical objects, and using indices such as monthly telephone bill have also been tried, as has the observation of people's looking behavior in rooms where there are other people and physical objects to attend to. There is as yet, however, insufficient evidence on validity and reliability to warrant confidence in their use.

hypothesis that high psychological construct usage in a theorist's work (i.e., high personalism) was related to the theorist's affective orientation toward persons. Coan's data involved ratings by historians of psychology of 54 of the most influential psychologists of the twentieth century on 34 separate dimensions of theory, including methodological preferences, level of analysis, and substantive orientation. Coan factor-analyzed the test matrix and extracted six factors, which are listed in Table 5. Because there were significant correlations between factors, it was possible to reanalyze Coan's data and score each theorist on a higher order factor corresponding to the dimension of personalism–physicalism summarized in Table 1. The higher the factor score on this dimension, the more the theorist endorsed a subjective, holistic, personal,

Table 5. Basic Dimensions of Psychological Theory[a]

Highest loadings + and factor scores	Highest loadings − and factor scores
Factor 1 **Subjective–Objective**	
Conscious processes	Stress on observable behavior
Introspective reports	Determinism
McDougall, Jung	Watson, Estes
Factor 2 **Holistic–Elementaristic**	
Stress on total organization	Elementarism
Holism	Influence of past experience
Goldstein, Kohler	Titchener, Spence
Factor 3 **Transpersonal–Personal**	
Nomothetic	Persisting traits
Physical analogies	Uniqueness of individual
Koffka, Kohler	Binet, Rorschach
Factor 4 **Quantitative–Qualitative**	
Statistical analysis	Stress upon emotion
Quantitative description	Unconscious processes
Estes, Thurstone	Janet, Freud
Factor 5 **Dynamic–Static**	
Motivation	Sensation and perception
Influence of past experience	Introspective reports
McDougall, Jung	Wundt, Titchener
Factor 6 **Endogenist–Exogenist**	
Biological determinants	Social determinants
Heredity	Learning
Galton, Freud	Titchener, Skinner

[a] Adapted from Coan, 1968, pp. 717–719.

qualitative, dynamic, and endogenist position. Low scorers, conversely, stressed an objective, elementaristic, transpersonal, quantitative, and static orientation in their academic work.

Is this professional orientation at all related to the theorists' interest in primary objects? Campbell's (1965) study reported the Strong Vocational Interest Blank (SVIB) scores for 50 presidents of the APA. As we had developed person-orientation and thing-orientation scales for the SVIB that correlated substantially with T-P scale scores, we could reanalyze Campbell's data in order to assign primary orientation scores to each subject. Fourteen of Coan's subjects also appeared in Campbell's study, enabling us to run correlations between the equivalents of components 2 and 4 of the specialization loop. A significant correlation ($r = .57, p < .05$) was found between person-orientation and the tendency to endorse personalistic constructs in formal theorizing. While the individual scores are intriguing and theoretically relevant (see Little (1972a) for some further details on this study), the main point to be made here is procedural, rather than substantive: As psychologists we should not be exempt from the pressures toward convergence in the components of specialization. The loop is not just for laymen.

Environmental Dispositions and Primary Specialization

We alluded earlier to the fact that specialization theory attempts to steer somewhat of a middle road between perspectives positing massive self-environment dichotomies and those seeking more precise delineation of environmental dispositions. As much of the work exploring the more differentiated environmental dispositions was fostered by the same paradigm as was specialization theory (Craik, 1966, 1970b), it is of more than usual interest to examine the interrelationships between the specialization measures and two of the major assessment devices to come out of the personological tradition, McKechnie's Environmental Response Inventory (ERI), and Marshall's Privacy Preference Scale. McKechnie's scale (McKechnie, 1974, 1975) is meant to offer a fairly comprehensive picture of environmental dispositions where environment is seen primarily, though not exclusively, as nonhuman. It is to be expected that thing-orientation as assessed by the T-P scale should relate to a number of the scales developed by McKechnie, in particular mechanical orientation. In discussing the "personal stance" implied by each of his scales, McKechnie suggests that the high mechanical orientation scorer is one whose environmental experience leads him to see things in the following way:

> I like to know how things work, and I like things that work well. It satisfies me to be able to make and repair things. That way I don't have to become involved with or dependent upon people. If you treat a machine or a tool right, it will do what it should do, which is more than can be said for most people. (1974b, p. 28)

While McKechnie's work has been concerned with the full spectrum of responses to the environment, Marshall (1972) focuses attention upon various types of preference for privacy. As privacy can be seen as involving the spatial allocation of social encounters, it is not unlikely that scores on the various components of privacy assessed by Marshall's scales will correlate more with the person-orientation scale of the T-P scale than with the thing-orientation scale.

Figure 11 summarizes the results of two studies designed to explore the relationship between primary orientation and environmental dispositions. The first study was carried out in a small rural community in the interior of British Columbia and involved the administration of the T-P scale, the Environmental Response Inventory (McKechnie, 1974), and a detailed analysis of the town's behavior settings. Results of the correlational analysis between the ERI and T-P scale scores appear in the top section of Figure 11. As predicted, thing-orientation correlated significantly with several ERI scales, most notably with mechanical orientation and sensation seeking. The significant correlation of thing-orientation with pastoralism and environmental trust is likely due to the

Measures of environmental dispositions	Person-orientation	Thing-orientation
McKechnie's Environmental-Response Inventory		
Pastoralism	.17	.34**
Urbanism	.19	.03
Environmental adaptation	−.07	.23
Stimulus seeking	.18	.43***
Environmental trust	−.18	.28
Antiquarianism	.13	−.23
Need privacy	−.18	.17
Mechanical orientation	−.25	.45***
Communality	.01	.01
Marshall's Privacy Preference Scale		
Intimacy	.45**	.04
Not neighboring	−.01	−.11
Seclusion	.05	.19
Solitude	.01	−.16
Anonymity	−.14	−.03
Reserve	.17	.19
Total privacy preference	.22	.07

* $p < .05$, ** $p < .01$, *** $p < .001$.

Figure 11. Person- and thing-orientation correlates with environmental-response inventory and privacy–preference scale scores. The results with the privacy data were originally reported in Little and Kane (1974).

fact that several items of the T-P scale relate to adventure activities (e.g., explore the ocean bottom in a one-man submarine).

The second study, which has appeared elsewhere (Little and Kane, 1974), was carried out with university students in a large urban setting and results of the correlation between the specialization variables and the various components of privacy isolated by Marshall appear in the bottom section of Figure 11. Thing-orientation is shown to be unrelated to privacy preference, while person-orientation is strongly related to only one form of privacy—intimacy. Intimacy as assessed by Marshall's scale reflects a desire to maintain privacy while interacting closely with small groups of friends or family. Privacy for the person-specialist likely involves an approach-avoidance conflict. On the avoidance side, privacy entails diminished social stimulation, a state inconsistent with the person specialist's hunger for social interaction. On the other hand, a condition we can call overspecialization frequently occurs and in this condition privacy takes on some decidedly attractive features. Just as person-specialists seek out high rates of information about others [to use Mehrabian and Russell's (1974) terms], they are also likely to *attract* high information rates by virtue of their cues of expressiveness and warmth.[16] In terms of Figure 10, then, a loop can become so overspecialized that its rate becomes excessive; the frequency of behavioral encounters, the encoding and decoding of affect, and the appropriate use of psychological constructs are too frenetically paced to be manageable. A kind of centrifugal collapse occurs, the center cannot hold, the personal system breaks down. Under these kinds of conditions, privacy comes as a blessing. It serves as one of several barriers or filters that can be interposed between specialization components in order to slow down the pace of looping in primary specialization. The lack of a significant relationship between the overall measure of privacy and person-orientation in the Little and Kane (1974) study can be seen as being due to the canceling out of these two conflicting components of privacy for the person-specialist. Intimacy, on the other hand, would seem to be the one type of privacy that optimizes both goals of a person-specialist, the desire to attend to what matters to another individual and the need to control the pacing and spatial management of encounters. This dual utility of intimacy is reflected in the strong positive correlation reported in Figure 11 with person-orientation.

It will be noticed that McKechnie's inventory also contains a need-for-privacy scale that bears closest resemblance to the total-privacy scale of Marshall's. But whereas the correlation between McKechnie's privacy scale and person-orientation is positive, that between Marshall's scale and person-orientation is negative. While neither correlation reaches conventional levels of

---

[16] It is assumed, that is, that the affective encoding strategies of person-specialists serve as green lights to those in need of nurturance.

significance, the difference between the two correlations is significant. We might interpret this result as reflecting the different environments in which the two samples lived. In small towns a person-specialist's level of stimulation is not so high that they need to impose a general barrier to interactions with others, while in a large urban center such as Vancouver, the pacing of social encounters becomes a more difficult strategic task.[17] Further exploration of the links between different indices of privacy, the disposition to attend to single others versus groups of other people, and the quality of interaction in small towns and cities would seem to be a rewarding area for further research. Several suggestions for further empirical studies in this area are contained in the Little and Kane (1974) report.

A final issue to be discussed regarding the relationship between specialization variables and environmental dispositions concerns the joint effects of person- and thing-orientation upon selected dependent variables. When discussing the typological approach to specialization assessment, we noted that in order to assign an individual to one of the four primary quadrants it was necessary to assess *both* thing- and person-orientation. In analyzing specialization loops, however, we have focused upon one primary domain at a time. Though there is not sufficient space here to give a detailed treatment of the interaction between the two primary loops, we can cite some evidence suggesting that thing-orientation serves as a moderator variable influencing the relationship between person-orientation and other behaviors. This effect is roughly equivalent to an interaction effect when person- and thing-orientation scores are treated as fixed effects in an analysis of variance design. In Figure 12, results are presented of correlations between person-orientation scores and two measures relevant to current analyses of the quality of urban living (e.g., Alexander, 1967; Milgram, 1970)—empathy and altruism.

Hogan's empathy scale (Hogan, 1967) and Burley's (1972) behaviorally validated altruism scale have been administered to subjects together with the T-P scale. As shown in Figure 12, when subjects are dichotomized into high versus low scorers on thing-orientation, the correlations between person-orientation and both altruism and empathy are substantially changed. Person-orientation correlates with altruism and empathy only for those subjects who score above the median on thing-orientation. One possible interpretation of these results is that actions involving the direct intervention into the affairs of others require not only an affective orientation of nurturance and support, but the capacity to implement such feelings into direct action. In other words, there may be a minimal degree of task-orientation necessary before an individual can translate humanistic impulses into pragmatic helping behavior. Many a

[17] This would be particularly so for recent immigrants to Vancouver from small towns throughout the province who would have adapted to a slower loop [see Wohlwill and Kohn (1973)].

Relationships between person-orientation and tests assessing pro-social dispositions		Thing-orientation scores	
		Above median	Below median
Person-orientation and	Males	.42	−.09
Hogan's empathy scale	Females	.42	−.11
Person-orientation and	Males	.45	.00
Burley's altruism scale	Females	.31	−.05

Figure 12. Thing-orientation as a moderator of the relationship between person-orientation and test measures of pro-social behavior.

person-specialist has looked on in horror at the varieties of human degradation that pass for urban living today. It may well take a generalist to get on with the job of tackling them.

It is likely that person-orientation will serve to moderate the relationship between thing-orientation and relevant environmental behaviors. The disposition to engage in ecological activities, for example, (Sewell and Little, 1973) seems to be a conjoint function of person orientation and thing-orientation. The examination of person- and thing-orientation as mutual moderator variables is very much in its infancy but seems to hold some promise as a research strategy in the personological tradition.

Primary Specialization in Man–Environment Research: Toward an Empirical Investigation of Ourselves

As was illustrated in the section on APA presidents, a primary aim of specialization theory is the empirical examination of professionals as well as laymen. Craik (1970b) delivered a plea for the study of professional decision-makers in the environmental area and reviewed some of the preliminary studies that had been carried out to that point. Sewell and Little (1973) carried out a similar analysis of the factors influencing the behavior of professionals drawing up environmental impact statements.

It would be of considerable interest to develop a set of criteria similar to those developed by Coan for studying psychologists by which we could chart the basic dimensions of man–environment relations. The synoptic nature of the field makes it likely that the primary specialization model would account for more variation in the theoretical orientation of researchers in this area than in the field of psychology.

Consider first some of the dimensions of difference that characterize the major participants at this conference. One way of doing this would be to construct a repertory grid with the eight major theoretical proponents as elements, and through triadic sorting, elicit a set of differentiating constructs. I must confess that I began this task. After spending over an hour comparing and contrasting the following triadic sorts (Ittelson, Wicker, and Wapner; Craik, Mehrabian, and Wohlwill; Kates, Lowenthal, and Wohlwill again), I decided to pack it in. While the dimensions were interesting, and the issues they raised worth pursuing, in order to have done justice to the technique (to say nothing of the theorists), it would have taken several days of vitamin-enriched construing to have completed the full grid. The Ghost of Deadlines Past was peering too ominously over my shoulder to allow me to complete the task. I do hope it will be done someday, however, and preferably by an interdisciplinary group of judges.

We can note, however, some alternative ways of beginning a study of ourselves. The first is to simply start the listing of major issues that seem to differentiate workers in our field. As a result of the interaction provided at this conference, for example, it would be possible to construct a set of perhaps 10 major headings such as "mode of assessing environment"; "mode of assessing human behavior"; "scale used in research"; "general philosophical assumptions about man–environment interaction"; and so on. Under each major heading it would be possible to compile perhaps 20 specific dimensions. For example, under "modes of assessing environment" we might list "physical measurement of environmental features"; "consensus of expert judges; personal constructs of 'Everyman'"; "multi-method convergence"; and similar approaches to assessment. Each major theorist could then be scored on each criterion and, as in the study cited above, factor scores on the major dimensions of man–environment relations could be derived for each theorist. We might then wish to predict the different theorists' factor scores on the basis of their scores on measures of person-orientation and thing-orientation. To take just one of the quadrants, we would expect that those researchers in the person-oriented quadrant would stress a more cognitive, qualitative, experiential, and literary-historical approach to their work. We should also expect them to manifest some of the other characteristics detailed in the expanded specialization loop of Figure 10. What if a highly attentive individual with expressive eyebrows and a high need for intimacy introduces himself at the Warren Center on January 7? If he ends up being a mathematical psychophysicist, I hope he forgives me for being a little disheartened.

While the above serves to suggest what a reflexive personality theory would attempt to accomplish empirically, it is possible to take the whole process one step further and talk about *a reflexive environmental–personality psychology*. Here we would wish to include as basic data the environmental and situational features that, in interaction with personal characteristics, give rise to a theory of man–environment relations. What, then, are the environmental backgrounds of our conference colleagues? To what extent have the surrounds of our youth, the stimulational complexity of our neighborhoods, or the overmanning of our graduate programs contributed to our theoretical development? There is very little empirical data on this topic, but what does exist is intriguing. Craik (see MacKinnon, 1962) discovered that highly creative architects were more likely than their less creative peers to come from backgrounds that had involved a great deal of moving during their early childhood. Carpenter (1954) studied the birthplaces of psychologists who, in the Directory of the American Psychological Association in 1951, showed membership in the Division of Experimental Psychology and the Division of Clinical Psychology. He found that those in the more physicalistic sector of psychology were more often from the Midwest and medium and small towns, while those in the more personalistic sector were more likely to come from large cities and foreign countries. In a remarkable analysis of the environmental influences on the growth of Watsonian behaviorism in America, David Bakan (1966) develops the thesis that behaviorism was significantly influenced by the transition from rural living to urbanization during the late nineteenth and early twentieth centuries. Bakan suggests that Watson experienced great difficulties in moving from rural South Carolina to Chicago:

> The adjustment to city life was not an easy one for the young behaviorist-to-be. The rural man in America had come to terms with industrial equipment as exemplified in farm machinery. His belief in self-reliance stood him in good stead as he learned how to adjust, maintain and repair farm equipment. The movement towards a kind of scientism, essentially a belief in the ideology and success of 19th century mechanics, was natural and proper. The difficulty, however, for the young person coming into the city, the major locus of heavy industrial equipment, was that the problems which confronted him were more the peculiarities and the strangeness of the *people* whom he confronted, rather than the characteristics of machines. The power of the machine was patent, but it was under the control of people. In order to have power over the new world of the city, one had to learn how to command the actions of people. (1966, p. 10)

These few illustrations of a potential reflexive environmental psychology carried out within the personality research paradigm will hopefully, in the near future, stimulate research that is both more systematic and extensively empirical.

The personological tradition in environmental psychology, in large part initiated by the early work of Craik (1966), now constitutes one of the more lively yet well-established paradigms for research in the field of man–environment relations. It was the declared intent of this paper to extract a few essential ingredients of the personality research paradigm and to review empirical research that derived from it. By presenting some of the concepts and empirical research of specialization theory, we hope to have achieved both of those goals.

Specialization theory, it should be noted, accentuates certain aspects of the personological tradition such as its integrative and reflexive aims, but pays relatively less attention to other aspects such as the living-in assessment technique and multiple-scale inventory construction exemplified in the research of McKechnie (1974*a*, 1974*b*). It can be suggested, however, that one criterion of the fertility of a research paradigm is the diversity of specific theories that evolve from it yet that still retain the family connection.[18] By that criterion, the personological paradigm would appear to be in excellent spirits and, despite its age, ripe for affairs with strange new creatures that wear loops and go about construing themselves.

REFERENCES

Adelson, J. Personality. In P. H. Mussen and M. R. Rosenzweig (Eds.), *Annual Review of Psychology*. Palo Alto, California: Annual Reviews, 1969.

Alexander, C. The city as a mechanism for sustaining human contact. In W. Ewald (Ed.), *Environment for man*. Bloomington, Indiana: Indiana University Press, 1967.

Bakan, D. Behaviorism and American urbanization. *Journal of the History of the Behavioral Sciences,* 1966, *2*, 5–28.

Bannister, D. and Mair, J. M. M. *The evaluation of personal constructs*. London: Academic Press, 1968.

Burley, P. Unpublished masters thesis, University of New South Wales, Australia, 1972.

Campbell, D. P. The vocational interests of American Psychological Association presidents. *American Psychologist,* 1965, *20,* 636–644.

Carlson, R. Where is the person in personality research? *Psychological Bulletin,* 1971, *75,* 203–219.

Carpenter, B. Birthplaces and schools of experimental and clinical psychologists. *American Psychologist,* 1954, *9,* 637–639.

Coan, R. W. Dimensions of psychological theory. *American Psychologist,* 1968, *23,* 715–722.

Craik, K. H. The prospects for an environmental psychology. *IPAR Research Bulletin*. Berkeley, California: University of California, 1966.

Craik, K. H. Environmental psychology. In K. H. Craik, *et al., New directions in psychology 4*. New York: Holt, Rinehart and Winston, 1970. (a)

Craik, K. H. Environmental dispositions of environmental decision-makers. *Annals of the American Academy of Political and Social Science,* 1970, *389,* 87–94. (b)

Craik, K. H. The assessment of places. In P. McReynolds (Ed.), *Advances in psychological assessment* (Vol. 2). Palo Alto, California: Science and Behavior Books, 1971.

Craik, K. H. The individual and the physical environment: Assessment strategies in environmental psychology. In W. M. Smith (Ed.), *Behavior, design and policy: Aspects of human habitats*. Green Bay, Wisconsin: University of Wisconsin, 1972.

Craik, K. H. Environmental psychology. In P. H. Mussen and M. R. Rosenzweig (Eds.), *Annual Review of Psychology*. Palo Alto, California: Annual Reviews, 1973.

Dixon, P. M. *Reduced emotional responsiveness in schizophrenia*. Unpublished Ph.D dissertation, University of London, 1968.

---

[18] Wiggins (1974) makes this point in another way in his vigorous defense of trait concepts in personality. Wiggins argues that weaknesses in specific theories within the field of personality should not be mistaken for flaws in the paradigmatic foundation.

Duck, S. W. *Personal relationships and personal constructs: A study of friendship formation.* London: Wiley, 1973.

Duck, S. W. and Spencer, C. P. Personal constructs and friendship formation. *Journal of Personality and Social Psychology,* 1972, *23,* 40–45.

Gough, H. G. Conceptual analysis of psychological test scores and other diagnostic variables. *Journal of Abnormal Psychology,* 1965, *70,* 294–302.

Hogan, R. T. *Moral development: An assessment approach.* Unpublished Ph.D dissertation, University of California, Berkeley, 1967.

Kaplan, A. The conduct of inquiry. San Francisco: Chandler, 1964.

Kelly, G. A. *The psychology of personal constructs.* New York: Norton, 1955.

King, G. F. Withdrawal as a dimensions of schizophrenia: An exploratory study. *Journal of Clinical Psychology,* 1956, *12,* 373–375.

Little, B. R. Factors affecting the use of psychological vs. nonpsychological constructs on the Rep. test. Paper presented at the London Conference of the British Psychological Society, December, 1967.

Little, B. R. Psychospecialization: Functions of differential interest in persons and things. *Bulletin of the British Psychological Society,* 1968, *21,* 113.

Little, B. R. Sex differences and comparability of three measures of cognitive complexity. *Psychological Reports,* 1969, *24,* 607–609.

Little, B. R. Some methods for the assessment of environmental construing and orientation. Report for Environment Canada, Ottawa, Canada, 1971.

Little, B. R. *Person-thing orientation: A provisional manual for the T-P scale.* Department of Experimental Psychology, Oxford University, 1972. (a)

Little, B. R. Psychological man as scientist, humanist and specialist. *Journal of Experimental Research in Personality,* 1972, *6,* 95–118. (b)

Little, B. R. *Person-thing orientation: Manual for the T-P scale* (2nd ed.). Department of Psychology, University of British Columbia, 1974.

Little, B. R., and Kane, M. Person-thing orientation and privacy. *Man-Environment Systems.* 1974, *4,* 361–364.

Little, B. R., and Stephens, E. Psychological construing and selective attention to content versus expressive aspects of speech. Unpublished paper, Department of Experimental Psychology, Oxford University, 1972.

McKechnie, G. E. *Manual for the Environmental Response Inventory.* Palo Alto, California: Consulting Psychologists Press, 1974. (a)

McKechnie, G. E. Explorations in environmental dispositions: Notes for extending a paradigm (unpublished manuscript), University of California, Berkeley, 1974. (b)

MacKinnon, D. W. The nature and nurture of creative talent. *American Psychologist,* 1962, *17,* 484–495.

McPherson, F. M., Barden, V., Hay, A. J., Johnstone, D. W., and Kushner, A. W. Flattening of affect and personal constructs. *British Journal of Psychiatry,* 1970, *116,* 39–43.

McPherson, F. M., Buckley, F., and Draffan, J. "Psychological" constructs, thought process disorder and flattening of affect. *British Journal of Social and Clinical Psychology,* 1971, *10,* 267–270.

Marshall, N. Privacy and environment. *Human Ecology,* 1972, *1,* 93–110.

Mehrabian, A. *An analysis of personality theories.* Englewood Cliffs, New Jersey: Prentice-Hall, 1968.

Mehrabian, A., and Russell, J. A. *An approach to environmental psychology.* Cambridge, Massachusetts: MIT Press, 1974.

Milgram, S. The experience of living in cities. *Science,* 1970, *167,* 1461–1468.

Moos, R. H. Conceptualizations of human environments. *American Psychologist,* 1973, *28,* 652–665.

Sewell, W. R. D., and Little, B. R. Specialists, laymen and the process of environmental appraisal. *Regional Studies,* 1973, *7,* 161–171:

Strawson, P. F. *Individuals: An essay in descriptive metaphysics.* London: Methuen, 1959.

Wapner, S. Organismic-developmental theory: some applications to cognition. In P. Mussen, J. Langer, and M. Covington, (Eds.), *Trends and issues in developmental psychology.* New York: Holt, Rinehart & Winston, 1969.

Werner, H. *Comparative psychology of mental development.* Chicago, Illinois: Follet, 1948.

Wiggins, J. S. In defense of traits. Invited address to the Ninth Annual Symposium on Recent Developments in the use of the MMPI; Los Angeles, February 28, 1974.

Williams, E., and Quirke, C. Psychological construing in schizophrenics. *British Journal of Medical Psychology,* 1972, *45,* 79–84.

Wohlwill, J. F. The emerging discipline of environmental psychology. *American Psychologist,* 1970, *25,* 303–312.

Wohlwill, J. F., and Kohn, I. The environment as experienced by the migrant: An adaptation-level view. *Representative Research in Social Psychology,* 1973, *4,* 135–164.

VI

Transcendental Experience

DAVID LOWENTHAL and HUGH C. PRINCE

Abstract: To understand environmental experience it is not enough to use scientific methods. Feelings and insights that transcend those of everyday life constantly infuse and enrich our awareness of the world around us. The roles of passion and mood are perhaps best explored through imaginative literature and the arts, which enlarge experience and epitomize styles of environmental organization, preference, and symbolism. This approach is also essential in delineating national environmental attitudes and behavior. Illustrative examples suggest that relations between and beliefs about man and nature can be most cogently synthesized in categories that are unique to each country or culture.

PURPOSE

Geographers generally aim to reveal facts and relationships about how we utilize the earth's resources to make a living, to move about and communicate, and to organize political and social groups. But there is also value in research about environmental pleasure—its nature, its sources, its locales. Felicity is the leitmotiv of this approach to the study of environmental experience, an approach that focuses on what we live for, as distinct from what we live by.

"Things are interesting because we care about them, and important because we need them," as Santayana put it. "Had our perceptions no connexion with our pleasures, we should soon close our eyes on this world. . . . It is from our feelings that the great world of perception derives all its values if not also its existence" (Santayana, 1896, p. 3).

In a world so beset by calamity it may seem frivolous to shift attention from the mechanisms of living to its purposes. The poor and the hungry, it may be argued, have neither the energy nor the spirit to contemplate scenery and ar-

DAVID LOWENTHAL and HUGH C. PRINCE • University College London, United Kingdom.

chitecture, let alone landscape painting and literature. Spokesmen for America's underprivileged during the nineteen-sixties derided campaigns to clean up highways, plant trees, and remove billboards as superficial, mere beautification, a cosmetic approach meant to conceal, not cure, the country's festering social sores.

Opposition to environmental aesthetics may be absolute, as in the case of the nineteenth-century Shakers at New Lebanon, who deliberately rejected embellishment. Depressed by the homely Shaker buildings, Charles Nordhoff asked Elder Frederick Evans whether they could not devote some of their prosperity to decor. "No," Evans replied. "The beautiful . . . is absurd and abnormal. It has no business with us. The divine has no right to waste money upon what you would call beauty, in his house or his daily life" (Kouwenhoven, 1948, p. 93).

Others do not renounce environmental amenity but postpone it until economic and social inequities are resolved. Their morality is based on the premise that it is wrong for some to enjoy life while others are deprived. So the egalitarian bias of nineteenth-century Americans led them to reject the attractions of English stately homes. Similarly, their commitment to equality and social justice compels compassionate scholars today to focus on the institutional faults that cripple the disadvantaged and threaten mankind in general.

Yet such socially laudable sentiments are apt to mistake environmental enjoyment for selfish hedonism. Affective response to landscape and place is not simply a decorative façade to life, but forms its core. Attachment to locality, as Robert Coles shows for the mountain folk of Appalachia, can be a source of satisfaction that not only mitigates material poverty but enhances personal identity, family pride, and community strength (Coles, 1972).

Even those unaware of sensory stimulus are continually restored and refreshed by ordinary landscapes and townscapes. Sensory deprivation, as shown by studies in submarines and psychological laboratories and as applied in prisons and torture cells, deranges the personality and corrodes both body and mind. Our dependence on a rich sensate environment transcends our needs for food, shelter, and clothing.

The active search for environmental satisfactions, not simply their unconscious fulfillment, calls for scrutiny. We need a psychology of environment to supplement our psychology of man, a history of environmental delight to supplement our history of art, and insights into connections that make art and nature mutual metaphors. What enables us to see a collection of features as a total milieu? Why do we prefer some landscapes and townscapes to others? What leads us to embellish old and make new environments? How does imagination transform aesthetically fulfilling locales? What consequences ensue from environmental contemplation and creation? How do environmental qualities and activities enhance existence? How do mood, ambience, and circumstance affect our apprehension of environment? How do transcendental values alter everyday uses of place and space?

Such inquiries risk being subverted by utilitarian goals and econometric techniques. The economic impact of tourism and of other demands for environmental amenities has made recreation studies respectable. But social scientists focus so narrowly on the spatial and economic aspects of recreation and travel that we know next to nothing about why people prefer certain types of environments, and even less about how they envisage or experience landscapes. Whereas spatial and economic problems fit the statistical tools and questionnaire procedures behavioral scientists find congenial, questions of value and purpose require less familiar and more holistic modes of analysis. Thus, participants in a recent conference on wilderness values devoted much time and energy to refining techniques for maximizing the aggregate experience of perceived "solitude" in wilderness areas, without ever asking how visitors defined solitude or why it attracted them (Krutilla, 1972).

The farmer in his field, the weaver at his loom, the sailor on the sea—such scenes do not constitute the whole of life, not even for their principal participants. Thoreau's poet enjoys "the most valuable part of a farm, while the crusty farmer supposed that he had got a few wild apples only" (Thoreau, 1854, p. 74). All of us find some arenas and occasions—the walk to school or to the station, the sight of a new city or country, some dramatic shift in the weather or the season—that give life a special flavor, intimating that we are truly alive. Let us attend to such experiences and to the environmental things, beyond bread, that make life worthwhile.

METHOD

All insight into the relations between man and environment is grounded in experience. The paradigm for scientific observation is the ordinary behavior of normal people in their everyday surroundings. This is what social scientists generally purport to study, either in the actual world or in surrogate situations that simulate reality. In this everyday milieu, individuals communicate their experiences to one another, accept or reject consensus on the basis of comparative judgments, and act more or less in accord in a common environment.

This experience of the world seems to us so natural that only a specific shock will cause us to abandon it—"the shock of falling asleep as the leap into the world of dreams; the inner transformation we endure if the curtain in the theatre rises as the transition into the world of the stageplay; . . . Kierkegaard's experience of the 'instant' as the leap into the religious sphere" (Schutz, 1945). These other modes of experience are sources of profound satisfaction and essential to the maintenance of purpose in life. Each such province of meaning has a particular cognitive style. These alternative forms of experience shift and blur the divisions between self (or group) and environment and alter our anticipations of each. In dreams, for example, individuals may take on multiple forms and identities, and time and space often assume configurations inconceivable in everyday life. In states of trance or frenzy, the distinction between individual and universe may vanish altogether. In viewing paintings, we accept the spatial boundary set by the picture frame and adopt a different relationship to the virtual space inside it than to what lies outside. As Susanne Langer writes:

> The harmoniously organized space in a picture is not experiential space, known by sight and touch, by free motion and restraint, far and near sounds, voices lost or re-echoed. It is an entirely visual affair; for touch and hearing and muscular action it does not exist . . . This purely visual space is an illusion, for our sensory experiences do not agree on it in their report. . . . Being only visual, this space has no continuity with the space in which we live; it is limited by the frame, or by surrounding blanks, or incongruous other things that cut it off. . . . Between the picture space and any other space there is no connection. The created virtual space is entirely self-contained and independent. (Langer, 1953, p. 72)

Reading fiction—and some nonfiction—we enter into an author's created world and endow it with our own hopes, fears, and surmises. As with dreams, the chains of everyday time, space, and causality no longer bind us; we travel imaginatively to the most remote and arcane realms. The Massachusetts landscapes that Thoreau experienced, for example, were magnified by metaphorical association with the works of travel and ethnography that he constantly read and annotated (Christie, 1965). Utopian literature invites us to identify with perfected, hence impossible, circumstances.

These transcendent provinces of meaning, by contrast with the everyday world of work, are in varying degrees incommensurable, inconsistent, and unrepeatable. They have therefore habitually been dismissed or ignored by social science. Yet one must come to terms with these nebulous realms, for they are not rigidly segregated from ordinary existence, but infuse it continuously. All of us can specify times when we transcend commonplace consciousness—when we read a book, see a play, hear music, feel ill, get high, make love, dream or daydream, or are possessed by demons. The usual brevity of these intervals leads us to classify such times as unusual, the remainder of life as normal experience. The characterization is not universal; states of trance and possession are normative in many cultures, as they are in our own for those we judge aberrant or mentally ill.

The most vivid and persuasive description of these states of consciousness, and of how they relate to everyday experience, is to be found in Aldous Huxley's extended geographical metaphor:

> Like the earth of a hundred years ago, our mind still has its darkest Africas, its unmapped Borneos and Amazonian basins. In relation to the fauna of these regions we are not yet zoologists, . . . we are mere naturalists and collectors of specimens. . . .

> A man consists of . . . an Old World of personal consciousness and, beyond a dividing sea, a series of New Worlds—the not too distant Virginias and Carolinas of the personal subconscious and the vegetative soul; the Far West of the collective unconscious, with its flora of symbols, its tribes of aboriginal archetypes; and, across another, vaster ocean, at the antipodes of everyday consciousness, the world of Visionary Experience. If you go to New South Wales, you will see marsupials hopping about the countryside, and if you go to the Antipodes of the self-conscious mind, you will encounter all sorts of creatures at least as odd as kangaroos. You do not invent these creatures any more than you invent marsupials. They live their own lives in complete independence. A man cannot control them. All he can do is go to the mental equivalent of Australia and look around him. Some people never consciously discover their antipodes. Others make an occasional landing. Yet others . . . find it easy to come and go as they please.(Huxley, 1959, pp. 71–72)

Even a commonsense calculus permits us to see how insights from these transcendent realms penetrate the everyday world. The very capacity to generalize, classify, and symbolize goes beyond everyday reality to essentially mythic milieus. Response to habitual experience distills flavor from states of being that are less utilitarian, less accessible to reason.

Most of the time we find it hard to recognize these impulses, let alone to fathom their sources and linkages. In everyday environmental encounters we guard against loss of control by fencing off the transcendent into well-protected preserves, to be sampled only in specified times and places. To gain insight into these forces we might seek deliberately to confront ourselves with the strange and the unexpected—experiences that may seem outré or grotesque, precious or scandalous, obsolete or visionary. The range of responses to such encounters may lend powerful insight to everyday experience, and help us to understand why we seek here to conserve, there to alter, the world around us.

CHANGING OUR VIEWPOINTS: CHANGING OUR MINDS

Without entering into the crucial debate on whose attitudes to environment are being consulted, we may recognize that everyone has a different view from everyone else—men, women, children; residents, workers, visitors; planners, artists, landowners, developers, conservationists, foreigners—all have different views. What is more important for our immediate purpose, these views are not fixed and immutable, but are temporary and unstable. You do not have to study the behavior of a five-year-old child playing in the garden to realize how quickly a small plot of land is transformed from his nature-study laboratory into his imaginary battlefield for toy soldiers, into a picnic site, into a football ground, and back into a laboratory for observing the habits of earthworms, sparrows, and grasshoppers. The magic works for all of us. A commuter strides briskly home from the local railway station. He changes his clothes and, in an instant, becomes an amateur gardener, a local politician, a member of a sports club, or a father of his family. In each of these roles he expresses different opinions about his surroundings—rain stops a cricket match, but it waters the lawn; precious open space is to have a new school built on it, but that school will save children from the dangers of crossing a main road. In addition, his attitudes may be changed by getting drunk, by catching cold, by being bitten by insects, by treading on dog droppings, by hearing a songbird, or by sniffing the fragrance of newly mown hay. He may respond to the actions or pleas of his neighbors, he may heed the warnings of a television program, or he may feel lonely, bored, or threatened. Quite suddenly, the nature and meaning of the world are altered for him. He goes to bed at night in one world, and wakes up in another. So, when we talk about likes and dislikes, these are not responses to objects. The same objects may elicit different responses. Each new experience is unlike any previous experience, and we react to it as a new event.

LIVING DANGEROUSLY AND LOOKING FOR TROUBLE

Ignoring for the present the effects of sudden changes of mood on the responses of subjects to their surroundings, and making all allowances for the expression of a wide range of personality differences among observers, we cannot but fail to remark upon the large numbers of normal people who from time to time exhibit very curious attitudes toward their environments. In many of our preferences we may detect a taste for danger. Against the clearest dictates of reason and contrary to our will to survive, we persistently enjoy and contrive situations where life and limb are at risk. Let us illustrate by asking you to imagine you have been commissioned to prepare a newspaper advertisement for a small house located next door to the Leaning Tower of Pisa. The one idea that you must, at all costs, keep in mind is the possibility that the house may be crushed by the fall of the tower. That is the most important element in the appeal of the building. It has no special merit as an architectural monument; it does not figure in architectural histories, but tens of thousands of visitors each year pause in front of it and gasp in astonishment to find it still standing so precariously. And our admiration for the erectors of tall towers, skyscrapers, the Eiffel Tower, structures whose tops sway menacingly in the wind, is tinged by the awesome thought that one day they *must* collapse. Moreover, we secretly believe that in order to add an extra few feet to the height of a nave or a spire, most builders would not hestitate to take some risk, and that many would tax their ingenuity to the utmost to accomplish such a task. The list of medieval cathedrals whose spires toppled in the course of construction confirms our expectation that vaulting ambition must at times over-reach itself, and we are glad to be reminded of the result. The downfall of Beckford's truly Gothic horror at Fonthill in 1817 and the suspense built up in William Golding's *The*

Spire play upon this widespread fascination. To take a great risk and to triumph lends a touch of genius to a building. To crown a splinter of rock in the bay of St. Michel with such an extraordinary pile as the abbey is a breathtaking achievement. We are similarly exhilarated by the first glimpse of a Scottish baronial castle perched audaciously on a cliff-top site, or by a view of the Acropolis still proudly rising above the city after two thousand years.

Following this train of thought, we are made aware of many other examples of designers' virtuosity in defying gravity or overcoming terrifying obstacles, spanning deep gorges with bridges, cutting narrow ledges and hairpin bends on steep mountainsides, throwing lengths of roadway across quagmires. They may fall, and we, also, may fall. High bridges and tall structures without guard rails or parapets grip our nerves with numbing intensity. And this sensation is heightened and projected—out over the ocean depths—through the fiendish contrivance of a nineteenth-century pier. It is difficult to imagine the collective insanity that must have seized a worshipful mayor and his worthy corporation when they approved the first plan to construct a walkway high up on iron stilts above the sea. They may have persuaded the public that they were commissioning a cheap and efficient landing stage for steamships, a triumph of engineering skill. No amount of wedding-cake decoration, no reassuring twinkle of Chinese lanterns, no pious screen of cast-iron Gothic tracery could disguise the appalling risks that were being taken, and that visitors would be invited to accept—to walk along a flimsy plank, as from a pirate ship, over the depths of the sea. But the trick succeeded, and others wanted to repeat it, until, by the end of the Edwardian era, no seaside resort could consider itself properly equipped unless it possessed at least one of these contraptions. The pier was a novelty, but the idea of building on water had a long history reaching back to the lake dwellings of neolithic times. It finds later expression in the ramshackle burden of buildings that was laid upon the medieval London Bridge. The sixteenth-century château at Chenonceaux gains an extra dimension in charm and poise from having its long gallery suspended delicately above the waters of the Cher, and the arcades of Venetian palaces, reflected in the canals, float as if by enchantment in a Mediterranean lagoon. Anxiously, we wait for signs that the whole raft of masonry is about to sink beneath the waves.

The spice of danger is irresistible. The spectacle of a volcanic eruption, an earthquake disaster, a great conflagration, studiously mimicked for entertainment in firework displays and domestic fires, never fail to draw crowds of onlookers. Fires are not the only spectacles to bring out the crowds. Scenes of conflict from neighborhood brawls to public demonstrations, riots, and organized contests—for example, football matches, boxing matches, and motor races—may turn any of us from innocent bystanders into active supporters. And places are set aside for engaging in combat. Battlegrounds are prepared and constructed with elaborate care so that conflict may be confined as far as possible by fortresses, by walls, by barbed-wire entanglements, by sentry posts, by ditches, by gun emplacements. Periodic contests are staged and contained within the perimeter fence and behind gates of arenas and stadiums. Inevitably, the participants break out of their confinement and rampage through the streets. The path of destruction that leads from a Saturday afternoon football match is a familiar sight. Motor racing is watched not only on the tarmac ramps of Brand's Hatch, but in the dead of night along country lanes through which rallies are routed, and also from the bridges overlooking motorways, where on weekends and holidays, spectators gather to watch the thrills and spills of amateur drivers. Some anticipation of a crash is not entirely lacking among aircraft spotters who congregate on the roofs of the terminal buildings at Heathrow, and the popular pastime of gazing at work on building sites or peering at holes in the road is in no way discouraged by red-letter warnings to Beware of Danger, Men at Work.

We should, perhaps, be reluctant to admit that we cherish danger spots. But at least we should not hesitate to declare our abhorrence of violence, vice, crime, and squalor. We should not oppose the closure of brothels, the expulsion of criminals from their lairs, or the pulling-down of the haunts of alcoholics and addicts. In general terms, these measures would win approval as conducive to the maintenance of public health and safety. But, in practice, we should not welcome the clearance of Soho, or Montmartre, or the Vieux Port in Marseilles. We are not always looking for trouble, nor, on the other hand, should we wish too sedulously to avoid it. There is a place in the environment for the waterfront bar, for the football terraces, for the Leaning Tower, and for the adventure playground where life can be dangerous.

ART AND ENVIRONMENTAL EXPERIENCE

Art and imaginative literature provide invaluable routes into realms of environmental meaning. Painters and writers often epitomize styles of organization, preference, and symbolism. Works of art offer artifactual evidence of interactions between man and milieu and of the trials and tensions, promises and fruitions, inherent in environmental relations. These meanings cannot be derived simply from content analysis, from counting up features or references, or from popularity as shown by sales and prizes, prints and reprints. The purpose of aesthetic expression and the constraints of the medium must also be considered.

Artistic creations may yield more subtle insights about attitudes and behavior than inquiries into the lives of actual people. In the everyday world, people are mainly encountered conventionally; we seldom pierce their façades to discern the mainsprings of action. But we may feel intimate with literary characters almost from the start, and we do not tolerate fictional figures as flat or opaque as those we ordinarily see in real life. "When I talk to others I seldom encounter anything like a self-image," Yi-Fu Tuan has written to one of us. "Before real human beings one learns only abstractions; before fictional characters one encounters three-dimensional people." So too with environmental awareness. We have only the sketchiest notion of feelings and preoccupations about landscape and milieu, even for those whom we know best. Largely inarticulate about such matters, most people express reactions only in unusual circumstances. But painting and literature overtly disclose a wealth of response; apprehensions of environment, tacit and acknowledged, suffuse the canvas and the page. The environments of art are not only more vivid and memorable than most of those elicited by observation or questionnaires, they are also more meaningful.

This is so because books and paintings bring together their creators' own environmental experience, lend everyday vision a heightened luster, shed new light on familiar scenes. The place or milieu we perceive in a fine painting or a great novel is a metaphorical enlargement, reshaping time, space, and experience to suit transcendental realities. Monet makes us aware that trees are not always green, and that shapes change with the intensity of light and the mood of the hour. A Wilson Harris jungle is not simply a rain forest but a universe where elements and ensembles of terrain and vegetation take on mythic dimensions. Proust's Combray and Joyce's Dublin are stages for words and deeds more intense and variegated than any we ourselves are apt to fabricate. The artist's strength of feeling enriches our excursions through places and past things with tension and passion.

That the artist's viewpoint often becomes our own is the clearest link between art and life. We can scarcely visualize Provence except as a creation of Cézanne, the American desert other than through Hollywood and TV Westerns, or Dorset save as a scene in a novel by Thomas Hardy. What we see is filtered through an artist's stylistic and social sensibilities. Works of art alert us to such influences and connect our views with those of epochs past.

Art also magnifies environment by distilling memories. We appreciate scenes only when they arouse recollections of previous scenes that were strikingly similar or different. Works of art enable us to compare our own experiences and responses with those of past observers. Just as landscapes accrete meaning over time, so do paintings, poems, and novels possess diachronic qualities; the portrayal freights present impressions with past associations. Thus works of art are more lifelike reflections of our environmental relationships than are the raw data of social science. They embody the social constructs, the subconscious drives, and the temporal condensation inherent in our environmental responses, but seldom articulated in everyday discourse, much less in the language of behavioral science. As Robert Coles says:

> We hunger after certainty. We want "orientations" and "conceptual frameworks" and carefully spelled out "methodological approaches." We want things "clarified"; we want a "theoretical structure," so that life's inconsistencies and paradoxes will somehow yield to man's need for a scrupulous kind of "order." . . . Lives, as opposed to problems, may puzzle the fixed notations of theorists, while at the same time adding confirmation to what has been revealed by such keenly sensitive (if "methodologically untrained") observers as Dostoevski or Zola, Orwell or Agee, who have managed, regardless of time or place, to set down something both comprehensible and enduring about human beings the rest of us have merely pigeonholed (Coles, 1972, pp. 25–26).

Works of art are in fact doubly historical. Those that antedate the present distill a past generation's experience in a recognizably antiquated style. They encapsulate in the present moment a whole lifetime (and more, because our experience subsumes all we have learned about times past before we were on the scene).

Yet works of art are not wholly congruent with everyday experience, as the words distill and encapsulate imply. Selecting and crystallizing, highlighting some features and shadowing others, they resemble landscapes of memory more than those of actuality. This is a function not only of the art work itself, but also of our involvement with it. When we look at a picture or read a poem or a novel, we suspend our normal sense of time and place to enter imaginatively into another realm, just as we do when we consciously recall our own past; and we attend to this other mode of being for its own sake rather than for some practical purpose. This is not to say that we never read a book or look at a picture for mundane and instrumental motives, to identify a fact, say, or to pass an examination, just as we may cudgel our memory to recall some point essential to livelihood. But artistic enjoyment, like memory, characteristically transcends such needs.

That works of art enrich rather than simply reflect life can be seen by comparing a landscape painting with a photograph; the photo simply records what already exists, the painting creates a new reality. Landscape photographs are typically left unframed because, unlike paintings, they have no virtual space of their own. Similarly, the slice-of-life novels of Robbe-Grillet and Sarraute simulate reality by recording events and perceptions in the most minute detail. Like an Andy Warhol movie, art fails when it only imitates life. Aesthetic representations sift out and dispose of empty spaces and trivial events, heightening the meaningful clusters of experience.

NATIONAL AND CULTURAL STYLES

With individual responses to milieu so complex, ambiguous, and mutable, how can one hope to ascertain the environmental attitudes and behavior of communities and states? Just as personal style is embedded in one's life history, so are cultural and national configurations part of an ongoing historical flux; any description of attitudes necessarily conflates what is already passé and what is just becoming recognizable with what is in full bloom. Moreover, national, like individual attitudes toward environment, are really segments of more comprehensive value sets, in which social views play a crucial role.

Faced with conditions so multiform, the student of group attitudes may choose one of two general approaches. He may restrict his enquiry to some more or less measurable kind of evidence, such as the consumer-marketing surveys used by D. Elliston Allen (1968) in *British Tastes* (in fact an essay in regional differentiation rather than on national characteristics), or to questionnaire responses such as H. E. Bracey (1964) used in *Neighbours* to distinguish British and American housing preferences. Alternatively, he may try to embrace the whole of national experience, in the hope that intuition and familiarity will disclose an appropriate analytic framework, some principle of selection and classification that will provide a convincing holistic portrait. Such a method will forgo statistical demonstration for interpretive synthesis, hard proof for empathy and analogy, and will seek to stimulate and entertain while suggesting fruitful ways of ordering ideas. To cite Coles again, "It is enough of a challenge to spend some years . . . and come out of it all with some observations and considerations that keep coming up, over and over again—until, I swear, they seem to have the ring of truth to them, . . . distinct and unforgettable" (Coles, 1972, p. 42).

Our attempts to categorize landscape attitudes in England and in the United States illustrate these methods and underscore their difficulties. For England, it was not hard to identify preferences that are mirrored in pervasive and distinctive visual qualities. A diversified, small-scale terrain, a hierarchical social order based more on the countryside than the city, and a long history of relatively peaceful occupance have engendered fondness for the old, the rustic, the picturesque, and the tidy. These preferences, which diffuse from elite to working class with little resistance, find tangible expression in landscape and townscape. Although much of the country now looks quite different, the essential England beloved of most inhabitants is a land whose urban and rural façades reflect the comfortable commingling of man and milieu and the pleasure of dressing structures and localities in appropriate costumes (Lowenthal and Prince, 1964, 1965).

For the United States, no comparable consensus was discernible. By contrast with England, the United States comprises regions widely dissimilar in climate and terrain, with inhabitants of many unlike backgrounds who lack a common recognition of fused social experience. Moreover, elite tastes in America gain no such ready popular approval as in England; on the contrary, Americans incline to disregard the preferences, as they do the very existence, of the ruling class. As a consequence, the elite tend to lack confidence in their own style, and to mute its material evocations on the ground. Thus America has its great houses, though not nearly so many as England, but they are usually concealed from public view to avert invidious comparisons between rich and poor. Few Americans have any idea what the Rockefeller brothers' compound in Pocantico Hills looks like. Hearst's San Simeon is invisible from the California coastal highway; one would hardly guess that anything of consequence is up there among the mesquite and sage, let alone a multimillion-dollar mansion crammed with the treasures of Europe. The happy rural seats of the English gentry were not initially all that easy of access either, to be sure, but their owners felt confident enough of public approbation to make their landscaped parks, if not their houses, realms of conspicuous display.

In all events, it was difficult to find American features that evinced common environmental attitudes, beyond a professed lack of interest in the everyday landscape. The uniformities that do emerge seem to stem less from explicit preferences than from the economic and social pragmatism that are responsible for the grid pattern in town and countryside, the massive highway net and roadscape, the featurist domestic structures, and the absence of any framework to cluster, consolidate, or delimit aggregations in the landscape. Landscape attitudes are seldom expressed in visual terms and appear to have little impact on the fabric and texture of the environment as a whole.

American environmental attitudes and embellishments seem, instead, to fit a different rubric of analysis, one that emphasizes gulfs and conflicts between ideals and realities. Hence the tendency to move whatever is thought desirable—wilderness areas, historical preserves, pedestrian malls—out of the everyday landscape into remote or special locations, protected against the incursion of the commonplace. Once anything is seen to be worthy of attention, it becomes a precious commodity that must be taken out of general circulation. Early Americans were conscious that their landscape was devoid of human history and therefore lacked features of interest. This view hardened into an assumption that anything noteworthy was *ipso facto* exotic. Meanwhile countryside and cityscape at large, beyond the bounds of special concern, remained untended and suffered the consequence of social and visual neglect (Lowenthal, 1968). Thus, Anthony Sampson finds that American cities "each look alike, with their desert in the middle, the same crumbling office blocks . . . surrounded by desolate car parks, as if King Kong had been through them all." But he fails to realize that this landscape is partly a consequence of another fact he notes, that "most Americans . . . simply don't seem to notice and care about cities as much as Europeans do" (Sampson, 1974, p. 11). Other attitudinal polarities—private versus public, freedom versus control—have parallel environmental consequences.

These methods of categorizing attitudes are not inherently English and American; they stem from our own particular minds. The two national styles could certainly be interpreted in other ways. But however idiosyncratic our modes of interpretation may be, they do reflect apparently incommensurable differences between English and American realms. Still other frameworks are likely to be needed to express the landscape tastes and imagery of other nations. Indeed, interactions between physical environment and social history might well produce as many unique configurations, both of values and of ways of categorizing them, as there are separate cultural realms.

Australian attitudes, for example, might be seen as a reflection of British settlers' utter unfamiliarity with the antipodean environment and their continuing preference for European features. Australia is now a nation of suburbanites who habitually polarize urban and rural, the sprawling cities little distinguishable from urban milieus elsewhere, the rural areas despised and neglected. Only in recent years has a felt need for Australian identity induced a nostalgia not only for outback and desert but for all the features of the countryside formerly thought weird or disagreeable, from gum tree to billycan to blowfly. Still lacking a unified environmental perspective, Australians nonetheless believe that they have domesticated their diversity (Boyd, 1972; Lowenthal, 1975).

In the West Indies, landscapes that have pleased European and American senses for centuries have quite another significance for residents' of predominantly African and Asian ancestry. Historical degradation as slaves and indentured servants, together with continued control of resources by outsiders, has meant that the land and its fruits were not their own. Environmental appreciation beyond sheer livelihood is consequently seen as a mockery of urgent social and economic needs. Local rejection of local landscapes also reinforces the imperial view, internalized by the colonists, that Europe and North America are better places: The temperate metropolis, not the tropical backwater, is how things *ought* to look. The pattern of rejection, however, is not the same as in Australia. The West Indians concentrate on the small private realms they actually possess—the house, the yard, the plot of land. Attitudes toward milieu are differentiated by scale: The island or state receives perfunctory homage; the immediate personal domain gets devoted care and attention. Only in the smallest and least hierarchical islands does the sense of stewardship extend beyond one's own acres to the entire realm (Lowenthal, 1961, 1973).

Attempts to classify any group's environmental attitudes and behavior come up against grave difficulties. Can one know enough about value systems in several cultures to make valid comparisons of them? If not, how can any study be properly assessed, and how can people in the country concerned validate one's interpretations? For what is delineated must stem in part from traits the inhabitants are unaware they hold and may indignantly repudiate.

Environmental attitudes, like other aspects of world views, include public statements affirming or rejecting certain positions, together with reflections of unconsciously held views revealed by close scrutiny of behavior, artifacts, and expressive style. "Covert culture" is significant for environmental (as for other) values partly because it is unconscious. In public statements expressing mid-nineteenth-century American pleasure in industrial advance and faith in its beneficent effects, imagery and metaphors nonetheless reveal a sense of dread and danger, and a revulsion against the inhuman, even demonic monsters spawned by technology. American environmental practice and attitudes reflect the unacknowledged conflict between public enthusiasm for technology and the largely unconscious rejection of it (Bowron, Marx, and Rose, 1957).

It may be less difficult, however, to limn attitudes and behavior than to describe what a country is actually like. Uniqueness and idiosyncrasy characterize actual conditions more than they do beliefs and behavior patterns (though admittedly the latter are a feature of the former). Geographical expressions of national quality—significantly labeled "personality" in studies of Britain, France, and Mexico—are profoundly idiographic. Cultural views are more ordered and less heterogeneous than cultural milieus because social groups require a comprehensible cosmos. We adopt consensual taxonomies to satisfy our need for system. We accept such categories even when we know that our information is incomplete or partly erroneous, because we would rather endure contradiction than forgo order altogether. The environmental attitudes that emerge may reflect how far a people have achieved a consensus and how much that consensus conflicts with other widely held values or departs from environmental behavior.

CONCLUSION

These comments are intended to illustrate our own perspectives, predilections, and preferred methods of analysis. Our subject matter as well as our approach depart radically from that of the other papers in this book. We have focused on aspects of environmental experience whose measurement or experimental manipulation would be difficult, if not profitless; and we have conjured with stylistic configurations that may be too complex to characterize at all, let alone to set in a precise comparative framework. But this is, after all, what life is mostly like—not so much a system or a structure as an ongoing flux, in which patterns are only fleetingly discerned and partially understood. Environmental experience is most fully apprehended, we suggest, when the otherwise banal or amorphous circumstances of everyday existence are enlarged and transformed through the medium of mystery and art.

REFERENCES

Allen, D. E. *British tastes: An enquiry into the likes and dislikes of the regional consumer.* London: Hutchinson, 1968.

Bowron, B., Marx, L., and Rose, C. Literature and covert culture. *American Quarterly,* 1957, *9,* 377–386.

Boyd, R. *The great great Australian dream.* Australia: Pergamon Press, 1972.

Bracey, H. E. *Neighbours: On new estates and subdivisions in England and the U.S.A.* London: Routledge & Kegan Paul, 1964.

Christie, J. A. *Thoreau as world traveler.* New York: Columbia University Press, 1965.

Coles, R. *Children of crisis, II: Migrants, sharecroppers, mountaineers.* Boston, Massachusetts: Atlantic–Little, Brown, 1972.

Huxley, A. *The doors of perception* and *Heaven and hell.* Harmondsworth, England: Penguin Books, 1959.

Kouwenhoven, J. A. *The arts in modern American civilization.* New York: W. W. Norton, 1948.

Krutilla, J. V. (Ed.). *Natural environments: Studies in theoretical and applied analysis.* Baltimore, Maryland: Johns Hopkins University Press, 1972.

Langer, S. K. *Feeling and form.* London: Routledge & Kegan Paul, 1953.

Lowenthal, D. Caribbean views of Caribbean lands. *Canadian Geographer,* 1961, *5*(2), 1–9.

Lowenthal, D. The American scene. *Geographical Review,* 1968, *58,* 61–88.

Lowenthal, D. The Caribbean region. In Marvin W. Mikesell (Ed.), *Geographers abroad.* Chicago: University of Chicago, Department of Geography Research Paper No. 152, 1973, pp. 47–69.

Lowenthal, D. Perceiving the Australian environment: A summary and commentary. In George Seddon (Ed.), *Man and landscape in Australia,* 1975. In press.

Lowenthal, D., and Prince, H. C. The English landscape. *Geographical Review,* 1964, *54,* 309–346.

Lowenthal, D., and Prince, H. C. English landscape tastes. *Geographical Review,* 1965, *55,* 186–222.

Sampson, A. The great American morality play. *Observer (London),* Sept. 15, 1974, p. 11.

Santayana, G. *The sense of beauty.* New York: Charles Scribner, 1896.

Schutz, A. *The problem of social reality* (1945). Reprinted in Mary Douglas (Ed.), *Rules and meanings.* Harmondsworth, England: Penguin Books, 1973.

Thoreau, H. D. *Walden* (1854) *and other writings.* New York: Modern Library, 1937.

VII

Experiencing the Environment as Hazard

ROBERT W. KATES

Abstract: The environment as hazard has been under intensive study for some 20 years, and has mostly focused on natural hazards. Industrialized countries exhibit a pattern of declining death rates and increasing damage, despite substantial investment in technical means for coping. In developing countries, both damage and deaths are high. A conceptual model in which hazard events and consequences arise from the interaction of environment and society and are mediated by coping actions helps to explain these divergences. The observed and perceived experience are described for each of the model elements.

The paper concludes with an observation that for most people everywhere, on balance, the everyday is more secure, the exceptional may be less so; and with a deep concern that the central role of experience as social learning in coping with the hazards of the natural environment is a missing ingredient in coping with the newly created or recognized hazards of technology.

Environment is that which surrounds us, the ambience of individuals, of social groups, of our species. So all-pervasive is environment that in its totality it escapes our comprehension, at least in this mode of consciousness. Inevitably we fraction it and destroy it, to reconstruct it in more narrow comprehensible slices. How we choose to emphasize the environment—as nurture, haven, or home; as deprivation or stimulation to the senses; as myth or symbol; or as threat and hazard—is partly the essence of the conference. Our topic, the emphasis of the environment as threat or hazard, is no more or less pure than other emphases. Indeed, it is inevitable that each environmental plane we slice intersects with others. Thus, the environment as hazard is integral to the environment as nurture or resource; men encounter hazard in the search for the

ROBERT W. KATES • Clark University, Worcester, Massachusetts.

useful. The environment as hazard serves as a source of stimulation, and is rich in the mythical and the symbolic.

This choice of emphasis arises not out of some conceptual insight, but out of the accident of research thrust and the concern with applied human and social problems of man-environment interaction. Nevertheless, the study of *homo in extremis* is a useful focus for insights beyond the problems at hand. Reasoning from the extremes, be they of environmental stress or any other set of data, is an ancient and honorable practice of scientific and philosophical inquiry. In this paper, we consider each of the five major conference approaches to experiencing the environment, emphasizing what we know of each from our studies of the environment as hazard. We begin by describing these studies and our current concept of their underlying structure.

STUDIES OF THE ENVIRONMENT AS HAZARD

The environment as hazard has been under intensive study for some 20 years. Most attention has been given to the study of hazards of the natural environment, more recently to that of the made environment and little to that of the social environment. Participants in these studies have expanded from a small group of teachers and students at a single university (Chicago, 1955–61) to groups at several universities (Chicago, Toronto, Clark, and Colorado, 1962–68), to collaboration through the interested organizations of a single discipline (International Geographical Union, 1969–72), to international collaboration through many disciplines (Scientific Committee on Problems of the Environment, 1973–). While geographers have been prominent in the leadership of these studies, economists, engineers, psychologists, and sociologists have been active as well.

In specific terms, much of the early effort concentrated on flood studies in the United States, and as recently as six years ago, we had available substantial studies of other hazards only for North America and Britain. In these studies, we had followed a simple research paradigm which sought to: (1) assess the extent of human occupance in hazard zones; (2) identify the full range of possible human adjustment to the hazard; (3) study how men perceive and estimate the occurrence of the hazard; (4) describe the process of adoption of damage-reducing adjustments in their social context; and (5) estimate the optimal set of adjustments in terms of anticipated social consequences.

In general, these studies provided evidence for a pattern of declining death rates and increasing damage, despite substantial investment in technical means for coping with hazard. In so doing, they raised serious questions as to the efficacy of the prevailing approach to natural hazard loss reduction. But six years ago we knew little as to the prevalence of this pattern in the nonindustrialized world and were at a loss for ways of systematically comparing hazards of varied origins and impact. Thus, we sought to organize, with the collaboration of many colleagues, a series of field studies, which when concluded told us in some detail about the ways in which people adjust to different hazards. They raised more questions than they answered, but they did outline some of the patterns of hazards and adjustments in roughly comparable form.

Specifically, we compared findings from local studies of: tropical cyclones in Bangladesh, the United States, Puerto Rico, and the Virgin Islands; droughts in Australia, Brazil, Kenya, Mexico, Nigeria, and Tanzania; floods in India, Malawi, Sri Lanka, the United Kingdom, and the United States; volcanoes in Costa Rica and the United States; and coastal erosion, frost, urban snow, volcanoes, and high winds in the United States. These studies, which comprised 28 studies at 73 sites and interviews with approximately 4,800 households, revealed the diversity of adjustments for coping with natural hazard.

Although five of the studies involved habitats where the vulnerability to extreme events is uniform, the others embraced a wide range of risk. The frequency of damaging events was high in some places and rare in others: In contrast to San Francisco and its decades without serious earthquakes, residents of Boulder reported high winds on an average of three times per year, and farmers in the Ganga flood plain noted floods once in five years on the average.

By design, the people interviewed were mostly men who were heads of their households, between the ages of thirty-seven and fifty-four with families. They varied in education from almost wholly illiterate pastoralists in northern Nigeria to sites in the United States where almost all those interviewed were at least high school graduates; in income from Shrewsbury, England, with perhaps $2,000 per capita yearly, and from Sri Lanka where the annual income is less than $200; in occupation the studies included sedentary farmers, shifting cultivators, fishermen, city laborers, artisans, small businessmen, manufacturers, teachers, and government workers.

In no sense, however, was the set of study areas representative of the world's population at risk; nor was it intended to be a statistically valid sample. Rather, it was a selection from different cultures and hazard situations, drawn partly by intent and partly by the fortuitous cooperation of investigators. The results permitted initial probing of the immense variety of the earth's patterns of hazard in the environment.

Seven sets of these studies were of sufficient breadth as to constitute studies of the national experience for a single hazard where the research paradigm was applied in a reasonably consistent and comprehensive manner. The comparative research design called for at least one comprehensive study in both a developing and industrial nation for each of several natural hazards, and for at least one hazard of substantial human origin. To complete the set of studies, we had to draw upon United States experience in two cases, floods and hurricanes. We were not able to develop a comprehensive study of air pollution (the hazard of substantial human origin) in a developing country. Instead we drew upon some limited findings and reports from Mexico to provide some measure of comparative experience. The seven studies that emerged from the collaborative effort were studies of drought in Australia and Tanzania, floods in Sri Lanka and the United States, hurricanes in Bangladesh and the United States, and air pollution in the United Kingdom with supplementary data from Mexico. Detailed analysis for 21 sites has been published (White, 1974), and an overall synthesis will be published this year (Burton, Kates, and White, in preparation).

In addition to the studies of air pollution, which were consciously chosen to bridge hazards arising from the natural and made environment, a growing body of data dealing with the made environment or interaction between the natural and made environment has been collected in roughly the same tradition. These include studies of water quality (Baumann, 1969; White, Bradley, and White, 1972), water quality technology (Baumann and Kasperson, 1974), weather modification (Sewell, 1966, 1968), and work currently underway into the hazards of nuclear power production. Formal study of the hazards of the social environment has been limited to a few comparisons (Golant and Burton, 1969, 1970), reading the work of others, and some preliminary collection of statistics of hazard risk and occurrence. All of the foregoing can be integrated into a simple conception of the environment as hazard emphasizing the approaches of our conference.

THE ENVIRONMENT AS HAZARD: A CONCEPTUAL MODEL

In the terminology of this conference, the environment becomes hazard in the course of being acted upon by society, such interaction leads to the generation of hazard events, and consequences of those events, which in turn are reacted upon by individuals and societies seeking to cope with the threatening consequences. This process is shown schematically in Figure 1 and is elaborated on by drawing primarily from the natural hazard findings supported by insights from studies of the hazards of technology and the made environment.

In describing the environment as hazard in these categories, caution should be exercised in interpreting these. Acting upon, experiencing, reacting to—these are categories of convenience; they try to relate to the approaches of the conference organizers, and serve to order the presentation of finding

ACTING UPON   EXPERIENCING   REACTING TO

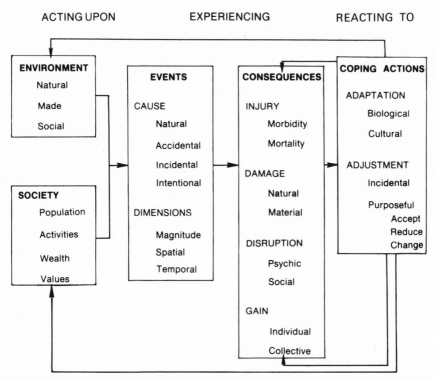

Figure 1. The environment as hazard.

and insight. But they are not a sequence of human behavior, neither in the world of life, or of hazard; the schema of such behavior escapes the dimensionality of graphics or words and at our best we only approximate it, in inner understanding.

Acting upon Environment: An Interactive View of Hazard

The earth suddenly shakes, houses collapse, people are buried in the ruins, fires start, disease spreads, the rescue teams move in. The world knows that an earthquake has occurred. The rains do not come, the crops (planted in expectation of rain) wither and die, the water holes dry up and the cattle fall ill, there is less food, the people perish. The world knows there is a drought. In the conventional wisdom, these events are ascribed to nature, to the environment, or to God.

Much of the content of natural hazard research, the way it is structured and written and the information incorporated in it, arises from a set of ideas and definitions about the nature of natural hazard. The first idea views nature as neutral; catastrophic events are seen as human events, a product of man. If man is absent from an area in which an extreme natural event occurs, then he is not usually affected by it. Insofar as man is present, the density and distribution of population, the style and level of economy, the shape and size and character of his buildings, patterns of production, consumption, and leisure all affect in significant and powerful ways the consequences of the event. The most important idea, therefore, is that natural events are indeed natural and that hazards—the threat potential for man and his works—are by definition human phenomena. If we extend Bishop Berkeley's dictum, it can be said that not only is there no sound when the tree falls unwitnessed in the forest, but there is also no danger from falling trees.

A second fundamental idea is that interaction between man and nature involves many transactions, some of which are beneficial to man, others harmful. It is the harmful that we can hazards. Many elements in nature cannot be easily allocated to either beneficial or harmful categories. They may be both simultaneously. But it is the human search for the beneficial that often results in the harmful. Invariably, the events that cause harm can only be quantitatively, not qualitatively, distinguished from the normal circumstances of nature—the flood from the rains that water the plants, the storm from the winds that bring the moisture.

The idea that the search for utilization of natural resources creates hazard can be extended to both the made environment and the social environment that surrounds us. In making and using things, we create threat as well; buildings can burn, cars can hit, and drugs can poison. Similarly, in joining with others in complex social relationships, we become vulnerable to violence from war and crime, to illness from propinquity and social mixing, or to deprivation from unemployment and inflation.

Experiencing the Environment as Hazard: Events

The environments—natural, made, and social—are the sources of events that only necessarily become hazardous as they intersect human populations carrying on activities, possessing material wealth, and having values. Using the national studies of natural hazards, estimates of the population at risk from some of the major hazards considered are between 5% to 15% of the national population with two exceptions: drought in the peasant society of Tanzania (90%) and air pollution in the urbanized society of the United Kingdom (50%). These exceptions can be generalized: Hazard events of natural origin affect the greatest number in rural societies; hazard events of the made and social environments affect the greatest number in urbanized societies.

The distinctions between events originating in natural, made, or social environments are constructs of the author; how is the cause or source actually experienced? Embedded in our language and our law is the distinction between the Act of God (or Nature?) and the Act of Man. The Acts of Man, in turn, can be seen as either intentional acts (with good or bad intentions) or accidents (with or without imputed negligence). We can also try to distinguish the accidental—a chance failure or unintended happening, from the incidental—what we might do without failure or intention in the course of the pursuit of other ends.

Historically, yesterday's Act of God frequently becomes today's Act of Man as more and more control and responsibility for environment is achieved or assumed. For many, the Act of God is not accidental, more intentional than Acts of Man. Thus, while the distinction may hold meaning in any given society, universal meaning for these categories appears unlikely.

Events not only have causes, they have generalized dimensions independent of their interaction with society. These dimensions describe the size and the spatial and temporal distributions of events with hazard potential. In turn, these dimensions seem to collapse into a continuum between the pervasive or chronic and the intensive or acute. *Intensive* hazard events are characteristically small in areal extent, intense in impact, of brief duration, sudden onset, and poor predictability. *Pervasive* hazards are widespread in extent, have a diffuse impact, a long duration, gradual onset, and can be predicted more accurately.

The sets of natural hazard events that fall most easily into the intensive class are earthquakes, tornadoes, landslides, hail, volcanoes, and avalanches; and those that fall into the pervasive class are drought, fog, heat waves, excessive moisture, air pollution, and snow. Other hazards are less susceptible to grouping, and examples can be found at both ends of the spectrum as in the case of floods, for example. These might be described as *compound* hazards, displaying mixed characteristics. Some flash floods are close to intensive events, while others—the great riverine and deltaic floods—are very close to pervasive events. Other events such as tropical cyclones, while less variable as between upstream and downstream flooding, have some characteristics of both and are intermediary between the polar events. We would further include among compound hazards extreme winds, blizzards, tsunamis, and sand and dust storms. The pervasive-intensive continuum provides a way in which we can make comparisons between hazards and seems to influence the resulting pattern of adjustment and choice.

A typology of the events of the made and social environments is yet to be developed, but it seems possible that similar characteristics will be found. The distinction between acute and chronic disease in medicine, between rapid onset, short duration and slow onset, long duration (Wingate, 1972) suggests such similarity.

Experiencing the Environment as Hazard: Consequences

The consequences of events involve threats to person: morbidity and mortality, damage to activities and wealth both natural and man-made, disruption to psychic and social activities and well-being, and although often forgotten, the antithesis of the foregoing instances of individual and collective gain.

The ultimate experience with consequences of hazard is death, but fortunately, such experience is limited. In developed countries, the natural environment contributes little to what is primarily the burden of age and disease. Out of slightly less than two million Americans who died in each of recent years, perhaps 500 died as a consequence of natural hazard, 50,000 from the violence of others (war and crime) and of self (suicide), 100,000 in accidents with the made, built, and machine environments. More difficult to give quantitative expression to is the effect of environmental events on disease rates: natural and man-made radiation on birth abnormalities and malignancies; the pollutants of the made environment on respiratory diseases and cancer; the hazards of poverty and poor housing on childhood mortality; or the pace of society on cardio-vascular disease. In developing countries, these proportions may be reversed; as many have died from natural hazard in Bangladesh as from heart trouble in the United States. A graph of global disaster (Figure 2) suggests that disaster of the made environment is more frequent and less costly than natural disaster.

The monetary value of damage is considerable as well. Damage and preventive measures for natural hazard cost an estimated $10 billion per year in the United States; air and water pollution, $30 billion; accident, wage, and health, $25 billion; and fire losses, $2.5 billion.

Psychic and social disruption are poorly documented, although in an out-of-court settlement the Pittston Coal Company paid the survivors of the Buffalo Creek disaster $6 million over and above direct losses for community disruption, the first case so recorded. Individual and collective gains range from the grocer who temporarily profits from his competitor's flood or fire, to the sense of well-being and solidarity some communities and nations evidence when performing well in the face of a disaster.

To experience events does not imply experiencing consequences, although in common language, the events and consequences of many hazards are confused. Floods can mean high water flowing over the bank of a stream or

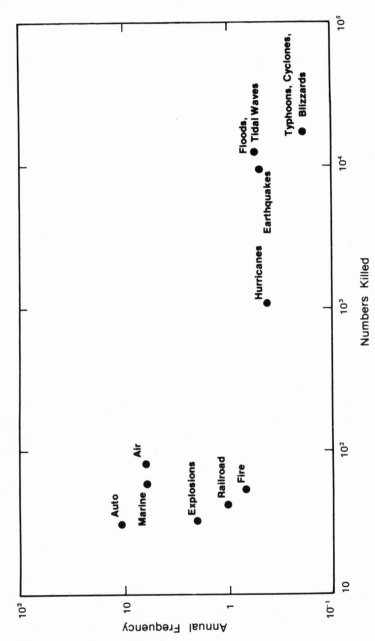

Figure 2. Comparison of risk from various types of disaster (world). (Based on Sinclair *et al.*, 1972.)

high water that drowns people, destroys buildings, washes away soil. All of us employ the familiar phrase, "It was only an accident, no harm done."

But, in many ways, it is important in understanding hazard experience to separate events from their consequences. For example, a puzzling problem of early hazard research was why experience of a recurring hazard event was not more strongly linked to the future expectation of such an event. The lack of such expectations seemed to become more rational on further analysis. It was discovered that, while there are many who felt that hazard events may recur, they also felt that they may not experience them, and even if experienced, they may not personally suffer the potential consequences (Kates, 1962). Similarly, a point of contention among highly skilled analysts of nuclear power hazard is whether the probability of accidental event sequences is independent of consequences and therefore multiplicative, or whether there are chains of closely linked events (common made failure) and consequences.

Reacting to the Environment as Hazard: Coping

People survive and indeed prosper in the face of environmental hazard because they cope with the hazard by adaptations and adjustments. Adaptations are long-run responses that are deeply ingrained as part of human biology or culture. Adjustments are short-run responses purposefully or incidentally adopted. Together they work to reduce the hazard consequences to some level of general tolerability.

Starr suggests that for developed countries there are two general levels of tolerance. One is related to voluntary exposure to death hazards at risks of 10^{-3} to 10^{-6} fatalities per hour of exposure and a thousandfold more stringent standard for involuntary exposure (Starr, 1972). Both levels of risk are related to the curve of potential benefits (Figure 3).

An example he cites is aviation safety. In the 1920s, risk from commercial aviation was about the same as general (private, pleasure) aviation today. But over that period, adjustments were developed to reduce such risk to the present level, which while maintained in the face of new aircraft, routes, etc., will probably not be diminished. Commercial aviation in its infancy, he implies, was a voluntary risk, as is general aviation today. Over time it becomes a necessity with stringent control until a balance is reached of societal risk and effort. Similarly, the low death rates from natural hazards in the United States may be close to the reasonably preventable annual minimum, and the focus is on reducing property damage losses and preventing catastrophic deaths, rather than further prevention of isolated deaths.

Adjustments take three major forms: measures to accept losses by bearing, sharing, or distributing losses; measures to modify events or reduce the vul-

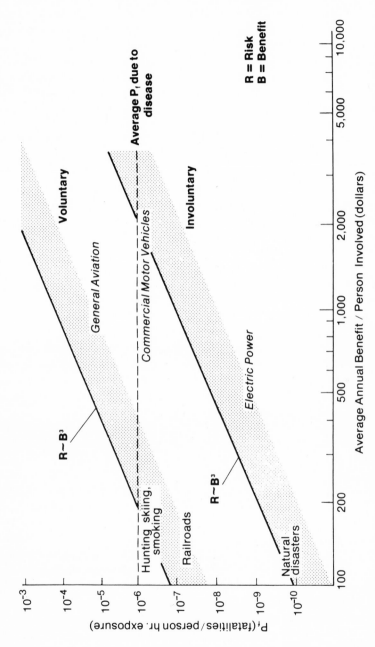

Figure 3. Risk versus benefit. Voluntary and involuntary exposure. (After Ch. Starr, benefit-cost studies in socio-technical systems, April, 1971.)

nerability of society to loss; and on rare occasions, changes in basic location or livelihood systems. These purposeful adjustments vary tremendously by hazard and society, but nevertheless are universally found. Almost all individuals and societies have more than one such adjustment at hand, though seldom is any individual or collective group aware of the entire range of adjustments. In the comparative study of natural hazards, separate adjustments enumerated range from a low of seven for drought in Yucatán to 263 for floods in Sri Lanka.

Over most of the globe, and for most of mankind throughout human history, there has been little or no external assistance. If drought or flood threatened, those directly affected were left to cope as best they could; the national government, if it existed at all, had at its command neither the resources nor the technical capacity to respond. Under such circumstances, individual and community adjustments flourish. Studies of folk or pre-industrial societies reveal the enormous ingenuity that is employed to develop and adapt adjustments to natural hazards.

On the Ganges delta lands in Bangladesh, farmers have developed many ways of protecting themselves against the hazard of cyclonic storms and the accompanying tidal floods (Islam, 1971, 1974). Small protective levies or bunds are constructed to keep out the sea water. Tanks are excavated for water supply, and the material removed is used to construct elevated platforms of refuge where people and livestock may find safety above the level of the surrounding flood waters. Shelter belts of trees are planted. Houses built of dried mud, wood, and grass are designed to withstand strong winds and some flooding. Special anchoring devices and supports are constructed. These adjustments are effective in saving property and preventing loss of life in the smaller cyclonic storms. When disaster strikes in the form of an extreme magnitude event, however, these adjustments are of no avail, and high loss of life results. Damage to property and livelihood may also be total, although the actual value of the losses in cash terms may be small as measured by international standards. Similar patterns, with less tragic consequences, are seen in the studies from Tanzania and Sri Lanka.

The pattern of folk or pre-industrial response to natural hazards may be characterized in general terms. The number of adjustments is large, and often a high rate of adoptions is found among individuals and communities. They often involve modifications of behavior or of agricultural practices more in harmony with nature than in attempts to control or manipulate environment. The adjustments are low cost and may often be added to in small increments. To this extent, they are flexible, easily increased, or reduced in scale. While in use, they may be closely related to social customs and supported by norms of behavior and community sanctions. Technological and capital requirements are commonly low. The adjustment pattern may require cooperative action by community or local groups, but not depend at all on outside assistance either in the form of technical knowledge, financial assistance, or legal approval. The pattern of adjustments adopted is in this sense flexible and may vary quite drastically over short distances, according to local variations in hazard severity or cultural practice.

Although effective in preventing property losses and loss of life from low-magnitude hazard events, the folk or pre-industrial pattern is ineffective in the prevention of major disasters. When such events occur, a high level of government or social organization may be needed to intervene. At such time, national governments in pre-industrial societies commonly respond by offering relief, emergency food supplies, and assistance. The scale of this help may very well be small in relation to the losses suffered. It may be sufficient, however, to permit a population to recover slowly and become reestablished in the same hazard area. Theoretically, the available adjustments at individual and community levels continue to include any folk or pre-industrial choices, even in highly complex industrial societies. Commonly, however, these choices have ceased to be adopted and have been replaced by adjustments at the community and national levels.

In the modern industrial state, a different pattern has emerged as technological capacity to manipulate and manage the environment has grown and theoretical alternatives have developed at the national level. Governments have been drawn steadily into activities designed to protect citizens from natural hazards. The expanded role for national governments in modern states arises largely from the opportunities provided by new technology. The construction of dams, major irrigation projects, sea walls, the design of monitoring forecasting and warning systems with complex equipment, is clearly beyond the scope of individual action. The large indivisible capital requirements also place many such adjustments beyond the reach of community or regional resources.

What emerges, therefore, is a picture of great complexity in the many ways individuals and societies can react to hazard, but the range of purposeful adjustments does not account for the entire set of mechanisms that enable human beings to survive and even prosper in the face of extreme environmental variation. These include: (1) adjustments, the choice for which is never made because they are part and parcel of the habitual activity of daily and seasonal life and work; (2) activities whose purposes are varied and remote from hazard adjustment, but whose net functional effect is to diminish the burden of hazard; and (3) unconscious shifts in individual cognition and affect in the direction of reducing the perceived or felt sense of threat and loss. These habitual, incidental, and unconscious adjustments may rival and even prove more significant than the outcomes of more conscious choice.

PERCEIVING AND COGNIZING THE ENVIRONMENT AS HAZARD

Events, consequences, adaptations, and adjustments—these are the categories of a set of scientific observers. How are these perceived and cognized by those who live and work in areas of recurrent hazard? Again, we draw heavily on comparative studies of natural hazard, touching lightly on hazards of the made environment, even more lightly, on the social environment.

In a rough and ready way, the interaction we hypothesize between the environment and society is widely recognized. Most people can list clear advantages related to life, livelihood, and location for their site. Some, not all, will list the hazard as the principal disadvantage, and these are mainly in rural areas and areas of high vulnerability. Most also recognize that others in similar settings have similar problems with hazards, and some, mostly at rural sites, believe that there are sites somewhat less exposed than theirs, where they might earn as good a living.

It is uncommon to find people who are totally unaware or ignorant of risk from the natural hazards prevalent in their location. At the same time, the knowledge of events is often less than the best scientific record. Events more recent are better known than those farther removed in time. Events more frequent are better appraised than those that are not. Events with greater impact on everyday life and livelihood are more accurately assessed than those with trivial outcomes. All of this, up to a point—most people cannot extend their imagination beyond the commonly experienced; many see order in random events; some are blissfully ignorant.

Yet, in contrasts between the best scientific estimates of the magnitude and probability of events, there is less of a gap between trained observers and residents of hazardous areas than most surmise, and greater limitations on both the formally and informally trained than most realize. For example, we held an early hypothesis that one significant distinction between scientific and lay perceptions was the concept of probability and randomness (Burton and Kates, 1964). Our recent work, however, shows that, worldwide, 74% of our respondents choose the random explanation in a story format for the recurrence of events—hazards can occur at any time. Slovick, Tversky, and Kahneman (Slovick, Kunreuther, and White, 1964; Tversky and Kahneman, 1974), in their studies of cognitive bias, show subtle and significant biases in the appraisal of probability even by skilled and experienced scientists. Overall, in the hazard literature, the distinction between trained and untrained assessors has given way to varying, sometimes contradictory, interpretation—some choosing to focus on the relatively widespread knowledge and partial accuracy of folk appraisal, others on the divergence of such appraisal from the best scientific knowledge.

The most careful comparison comes from the London, Ontario, study (Hewitt and Burton, 1971; Moon, 1971):

> In the study of the hazardousness of London, Ontario, an effort was made to compare for the first time in a systematic way "lay" appraisals with more "objective" assessments across a range of hazards. Expectations of frequency of hazard events were investigated by asking respondents how often a given event could be expected to occur in the next 50 years. Responses are plotted in Figure 4 together with the objective estimates.
>
> Events were described as more likely to occur 5, 10, 15, or 20 times in 50 years rather than the odd values of 4, 7, 9, or 11, 14, or 16 and so on. A preference for round numbers is to be expected. The distributions of responses for tornadoes, hurricanes, and floods, all show a pattern highly sheered to the left. This coincides well with observed frequencies. While all three hazards are thought of as rare events, tornadoes appear to pose the greatest threat in the minds of London residents. This may be because of the dramatic effects of tornadoes that are frequently reported in the Midwest of the United States including areas in southern Michigan contiguous to southern Ontario. That 140 people consider that no floods will occur in the next 50 years is very likely due to the high degree of confidence placed in the Fanshawe Dam, which does reduce flood peaks. Most significant about tornadoes, hurricanes, and floods, however, is the fact that the subjective estimates of frequency coincide so closely with objective assessments.
>
> The expectations of frequency of ice storms and blizzards are quite clearly in a different category. Both have a bi-modal distribution with marked peaks toward each extreme. Ice storms are expected to occur between 1 and 5 times in 50 years by 86 people and between 46 and 50 times by 62 people. Similarly blizzards are expected to occur 5 times or less in 50 years by 148 people while 59 others expect blizzards to occur 46 times or more in 50 years. This suggests a major discrepancy in definition of ice storms and blizzards. Most dramatically in the case of blizzards, people tend to see them as common events occurring almost every year or as rare events occurring only a few times in 50 years. In neither case do the peaks of subjective frequency coincide with objective estimates based on the observed record. In fact the reverse is true, and the objective frequency tends to fall in an area of very low subjective expectation (Moon, 1971). The significance of these observations is that they strongly shape the propensity of individuals or households to adopt adjustments to specific hazards where the perceived frequency is low. Differing concepts of what a hazard signifies may also affect the receptivity of populations to warnings or other advise about adjustments. (Burton, Kates, and White, in preparation.)

Despite the large number of available actions for coping, many, but not most, know of one or more actions that can be taken to reduce damage from the hazard. Many take some positive action to reduce losses, but few take preventive action much in advance of the hazard event, and few choose a large number of adjustments. In general, more people bear losses than share losses, more accept losses than reduce damages. Of those that reduce damages, more seem to try to modify events than to prevent effects, and many more seek to reduce damages than change their livelihood or land use. Fewer still move their residence even when the hazard is severe, and those that do move are likely to be low-income farmers fleeing drought, dwellers in the path of lava flows, or residents of eroding coastlines. Our overall impression of human effort expended in coping is shown in Figure 5.

Consequences, like the events, are widely recognized. Some people, espe-

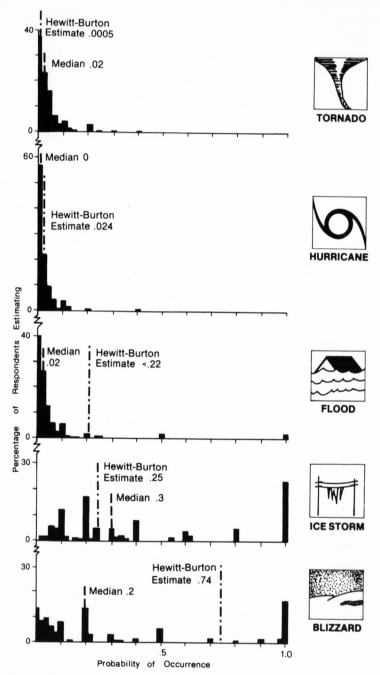

Figure 4. Experts and lay people: an appraisal of the hazardousness of London, Ontario.

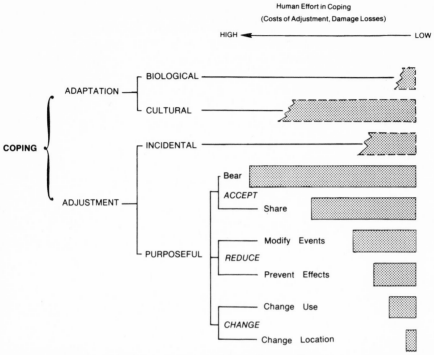

Figure 5. Coping actions and human effort.

cially at rural sites or places of high vulnerability, regard resultant damages as substantial. But everywhere, as with events, consequences are not easily seen to exceed experience, and collective experience does not necessarily portend individual fate. As with events, the gap between perceived consequences, between scientist and lay person, may be less than assumed. A list of 126 diseases has been scaled by both patients and doctors as to the seriousness of the disease with a rank correlation of .95 between both groups (Wyler, Masuda, and Holmes, 1968, 1970). Yet, if compared with the actual risk of death, the perceived seriousness of both patients and doctors is poor. Leukemia, cancer, multiple sclerosis, etc., are all perceived as more serious than the more frequent strokes and heart attacks.

These same researchers have tried to measure the seriousness of social readjustments, all of which may have some stress, but not all of which might be called hazards. While values may have changed somewhat in the seven years since the study was done, it is still sobering that divorce is viewed as more stressful than a term in jail, which in turn is viewed as more serious than a death in the family (Holmes and Rahe, 1967).

We know little of how the events and consequences from each domain of nature, *urb,* and society are comparatively appraised. Golant and Burton found that 58 Torontonians using semantic differential ratings discriminated between natural hazards, man-made hazards, and quasi-natural hazards of air and water pollution along factorial clusters of concepts related to disruptiveness, cause or source, and magnitude (Figure 6).

In a related study, they analyzed the risk avoidance of 206 respondents of 12 hazards classified as natural, physical (direct injury to person), and social (psychic-social distress). Hazard experience is compared with perceived serious-

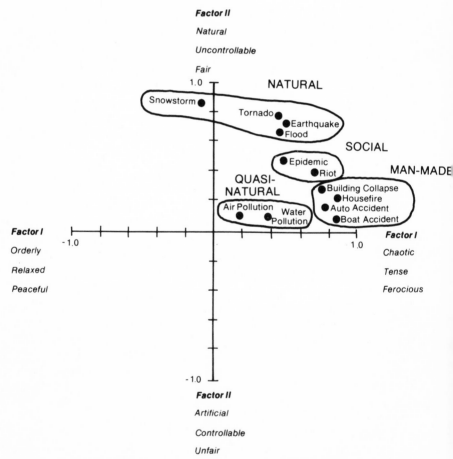

Figure 6. Some evidence for the causal distinction between natural, made, and social environmental hazard events is found in the groupings of the factor analysis of semantic scales of concepts and hazards. (Adapted from Golant and Burton.)

Table 1. Ranking of Hazards Based on Respondents (Total Sample) Greatest Avoidance Measures and Experience

Avoidance rank	Hazard	Avoidance No.	%	Experience No.	%	Experience rank
1	Auto accident	160	77.7	127	61.7	4
2	Attacked and robbed	127	61.6	11	5.3	12
3	Tornado	110	53.4	19	9.2	11
4	Forest fire	107	51.9	29	14.8	8
5	Earthquake	106	51.5	27	13.1	9
6	Failing in school or job	105	50.9	68	33.0	7
7	Illness	95	46.1	166	80.6	1
8	Loneliness	79	38.4	152	73.8	2
9	Flood	74	35.9	27	13.1	10
10	Public embarrassment	73	35.4	108	52.4	5
11	Being disliked by someone you admire	72	35.0	90	43.7	6
12	Thirst	55	26.7	128	62.1	3

ness (preferred risk avoidance) in Table 1. With the exception of auto accidents, the least experienced are the most feared. A similar study is now being done in Austria.

The environment as hazard is perceived, cognized, acted upon and reacted to in varied ways. But, on a global level, there is some limited order and structure. The varied environments of hazard provide significantly different sets of events characterized as pervasive/chronic or intensive/acute. The perceived events reflect this intrinsic difference. Coping actions and resultant consequences vary with the flexibility of livelihood systems, and the available resources, knowledge, and efficacy of adjustments. These are structured by the nature of societal development.

Contained within the structure of environment and society is the "prison of experience" accounting for much of the variation in human behavior. In 1962 I described the prison of experience in relation to flood hazard:

> A major limitation to human ability to use improved flood hazard information is the basic reliance on experience. Men on flood plains appear to be very much prisoners of their experience, and the effect of such experience is not consistently in the direction of taking individual action to reduce flood damage.

> Improved flood hazard information would include data on floods greater than those flood plain managers have experienced. The observations in LaFollette and elsewhere suggest that managers have a great deal of difficulty conceptualizing and acting upon this information.

> Floods need to be experienced, not only in magnitude, but in frequency as well. Without repeated experiences, the process whereby managers evolve emergency measures of coping with floods does not take place. Without frequent experience, learned adjustments wither and atrophy with time.

Conversely, limited experience encourages some managers to feel that floods are not so bad after all, and they lose their motivation to seek further for alternatives. With limited experience, other managers appear to decide that they have received the flood that Nature has had in store for them and that they will not have another flood for some time.

Recently experienced floods appear to set an upper bound to the size of loss with which managers believe they ought to be concerned. Since much flood damage is caused by floods greater than have recently been experienced, this experience serves to negate the effect of improved information that seeks to expand the expectation of the flood plain manager.

Today, the prison of experience still seems central to perception and cognition but less rectangular and more trapezoidal in shape, being lesser and greater at the same time than the reality it could contain. The perceived experience of hazard is lesser than the reality—human memory being biased to the recent and impressionable; cognition, biased to the ordered and determinate. It is also greater than the reality we can share in the memory of others close to us, experience by empathy, myth, and symbol. But the distortions, whether they narrow or enlarge our perspective of experience, do not really provide in meaningful ways substitutes for experience. The bars, be they steel or rubber, contain us and in that we face some peril, for environmental hazard for which we have little or no relevant experience is increasing.

EXPERIENCING THE UNEXPERIENCED

For most people everywhere, on balance, the everyday is more secure, the exceptional may be less so. The life expectancy of people rises, rapidly in poor nations through increased survival of the young, slowly in rich nations pressing on a ceiling of medical, life, and environmental understanding. We live longer in America today than 50 years ago, die less of infectious disease, and more of stress, diet, and malignancy. Cars kill us more frequently than in the past, but other accidents less; the balance is in our favor. Least of all, we die from natural hazards. In this, we are fortunate. Deaths from nature have climbed elsewhere in the world, despite the relative constancy of 30 global disasters per year over the past 25 years (Dworkin, 1974).

In places of rapid social change, the social environment may be less secure but not necessarily less satisfying. Our own society appears somewhat more perilous in recent times. Crime rates, while dropping, are higher than we have been accustomed to; business failures and unemployment are up, while inflation is frightening. Global peace is obtained at the price of great peril, and the price of more restrained warfare continues to be high.

The hazards of the made environment seem to offer much recent concern, both to scientists and the public alike (Figure 7). Scientific reports of man-made

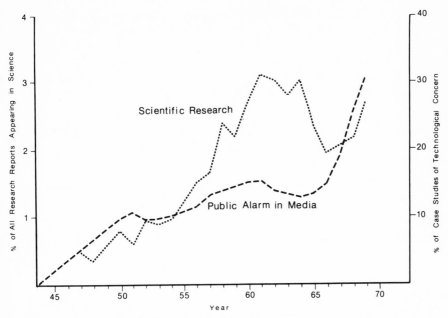

Figure 7. The graph of public alarm in the media is a 5-year running average of public alarm over technology based on 45 case studies of alarm as evidenced by major newspapers and periodicals (Lawless, in press). The graph of scientific research is based on analysis of research reports appearing in the interdisciplinary journal *Science* (Halverson and Pijawka, 1974).

environmental hazard have climbed more or less steadily until some 5% of all reports in *Science* concern them (Halverson and Pijawka, 1974). Public concern evidences similar trends: Forty percent of 45 major public alarms over technology peaked over the last four years (Lawless, in press). By and large, these newly created or recognized environmental hazards are too new to assess or measure their consequences; we have yet to experience their peril. Can we?

The central role of experience as social learning in coping with the hazards of the natural environment is a missing ingredient with newly created or recognized hazards of technology. Such risk appears removed from everyday experience; we are buffered by special assessors of hazards or guardians of the environment, both self- and societal-appointed. It is not clear from what we know that we can simply tell others about hazards, even when we are relatively sure about them. Experience with smoking and seat belts does not augur well for the prevention of less common risks through informational or educational activity. With such less common risks, the events and consequences are much more uncertain. Nor will the uncertainty be easily resolved; the hazards are too new and too many, they may affect many before we detect them, act upon us for a long time before we control them.

There are, of course, ways of substituting for experience. Science and poetry try to do so by analogue, metaphor, or simulation. We are asked to transfer experience in one realm to another. But we are indeed constrained by what we know, and there is question if we can know beyond the experiential.

We might ask how well we might fare by reflecting on how others fared in unknown lands. Martyn Bowden has reflected on this:

> Coping with risks of unknown magnitude is the challenge of the explorer (and to a lesser extent of the frontiersman). The former faces unknown regions peopled by fantasies, the latter is a heroic figure who leaves the comfortable and the known for a period of adaptation during a self-imposed disaster. The experiences of both tell us much about contemporary man's conceptions of unknown risks. Both were essentially uniformitarian through and through. The maps showed terrae incognitae in the regions traversed first by explorers; sailors crossed seas where serpents swam (on maps) to lands where dragons and gorgons dwelt; settlers of the west moved into regions labeled "desert"—the unknown lands, serpentine seas, and irreclaimable deserts were not parts of their adventurous imagery. Rather they projected into these regions what they wanted to find (usually a world familiar to them, an idealization, a simplification of the familiar world they had left). Terrae incognitae were really known by projection from the familiar, by principles of symmetry, latitudinal analog, projection, and extension of the known to the unknown. At the most, the unknown lands were simplifications, exaggerations of the known brought together, perhaps in unfamiliar combinations. (Bowden, personal communication, 1974)

More sophisticated analyses seemingly recognize the limitations of the known but cannot escape it. The Rasmussen report on reactor safety is an assessment of accident risks in U.S. commercial nuclear plants (U.S. Atomic Energy Commission, 1974). It attempts to estimate the likelihood of accidents that release large amounts of radioactivity to the environment and to assess the consequences of such releases. It deals with an event that begins with an accident the likelihood of which is estimated at 1 in 17,500 per reactor year. It draws upon the experience of perhaps 40 reactors for a total of 200 reactor years. To bridge the gap, it reconstructs all conceivable (to the assessor) sequences that could lead to the accident, working back from the unknown to the known; reducing the unknown accident rate to the known failure rates of small parts, bits of metal, pipes, and people. The logic is known as fault-tree analysis, and it cost $3 million. It is more rigorous and searching than sailors and frontiersmen; nonetheless it is still constrained by experience. To reduce the unknown into knowable parts or to extend the known into the unknown appear structurally alike.

It may be that the limits of experience are adaptive, for if we knew more of the perils, we would be less venturesome and deny ourselves the blessings of new lands or new power. But we become each day more clever at creating, recognizing, and disseminating threat; we lag in our ability to attend to and cope with threat. In the absence of experience, we may never know what happened.

ACKNOWLEDGMENTS

This paper, while written by the author, draws heavily on his shared work with Ian Burton and Gilbert F. White and their forthcoming volume entitled *The environment as hazard,* to be published by Oxford University Press; ideas and words of close colleagues Martyn Bowden and Anne Whyte; the research and fellowship of the many members of the Commission on Man and the Environment of the International Geographical Union; and the financial support of the National Science Foundation.

REFERENCES

Baumann, D. The recreational use of domestic water supply reservoirs: Perception and choice. Chicago, Illinois: University of Chicago, Department of Geography Research Paper No. 121, 1969.

Baumann, D., and Kasperson, R. Public acceptance of renovated waste water: myth and reality. *Water Resources Research,* August, 1974, *10*(4), 667–674.

Bowden, Martyn. Personal communication, 1974.

Burton, I., and Kates, R. The perception of natural hazards in resource management. *Natural Resources Journal,* January, 1964, *3*(3), 412–441.

Burton, I., Kates, R., and White, G. *The environment as hazard.* New York: Oxford University Press. In preparation.

Dworkin, J. Global trends in natural disasters, 1947–1973. Boulder, Colorado: University of Colorado, Natural Hazard Research Working Paper No. 26, 1974.

Golant, S., and Burton, I. Avoidance-response to the risk environment. Chicago, Illinois: University of Chicago, Natural Hazard Research Working Paper No. 6, 1969.

Golant, S., and Burton, I. A semantic differential experiment in the interpretation and grouping of environmental hazards. *Geographical Analysis,* April, 1970, *II*(2), 120–134.

Halverson, B., and Pijawka, D. Scientific information about man-made environmental hazards. *The Monadnock,* June, 1974, *XLVIII,* 7–20.

Hewitt, K., and Burton, I. *The hazardousness of a place: A regional ecology of damaging events.* Toronto: University of Toronto Press, 1971.

Holmes, T. H., and Rahe, R. H. The social readjustment rating scale. *Journal of Psychosomatic Research,* 1967, *11,* 213.

Islam, M. A. Human adjustment to cyclone hazards: A case study of Char Jabbar. Boulder, Colorado: University of Colorado, Natural Hazard Research Working Paper No. 18, 1971.

Islam, M. A. Tropical cyclones: Coastal Bangladesh. In Gilbert White (Ed.), *Natural hazards: Local, national, global.* New York: Oxford University Press, 1974. Pp. 19–25.

Kates, R. Hazard and choice perception in flood plain management Chicago, Illinois: University of Chicago, Department of Geography Research Paper No. 78, 1962.

Lawless, E. Technology and social shock—100 cases of public concern over technology. Washington, D.C.: National Science Foundation. In press.

Moon, K. The perception of the hazardousness of a place: A comparative study of five natural hazards in London, Ontario. Unpublished masters research paper, University of Toronto, 1971.

Reactor safety study: An assessment of accident risks in U.S. commercial nuclear power plants, 14 volumes. Washington, D.C.: U.S. Atomic Energy Commission, 1974.

Sewell, W. R. D. (Ed.). Human dimensions of weather modification. Chicago, Illinois: University of Chicago, Department of Geography Research Paper No. 105, 1966.

Sewell, W. R. D. Human dimensions of the atmosphere. Washington, D.C.: National Science Foundation, 1968.

Sinclair, C., Marstrand, P., and Newick, P. Innovation and human risk: The evaluation of human life and safety in relation to technical change. London: Centre for the Study of Industrial Innovation, 1972.

Slovick, P., Kunreuther, H., and White, G. Decision processes, rationality, and adjustment to natural hazards. In Gilbert White (Ed.), *Natural hazards: local, national, global.* New York: Oxford University Press, 1974. Pp. 187–205.

Starr, C. Benefit-cost studies in sociotechnical systems. In *Perspectives on benefit-risk decision making.* Washington, D.C.: National Academy of Engineering, 1972. Pp. 17–42.

Tversky, A., and Kahneman, D. Judgment under uncertainty: Heuristics and biases, *Science,* September 27, 1974, *185*(4157), 1124–1131.

White, G. (Ed.). *Natural hazards: Local national, global.* New York: Oxford University Press, 1974.

White, G., Bradley, D., and White, A. *Drawers of water.* Chicago, Illinois: University of Chicago Press, 1972.

Wingate, I. *Penguin Medical Dictionary.* London: Penguin Books, 1972.

Wyler, A. R., Masuda, M., and Holmes, T. H. Seriousness of illness rating scale. *Journal of Psychosomatic Research,* 1968, *11*, 363–374.

Wyler, A. R., Masuda, M., and Holmes, T. H. The seriousness of illness rating scale: reproducibility. *Journal of Psychosomatic Research,* 1970, *14*, 59–64.

VIII

From Church to Laboratory to National Park:

A Program of Research on Excess and Insufficient Populations in Behavior Settings

ALLAN W. WICKER and SANDRA KIRMEYER[1]

Abstract: We offer here a presentation of conceptual and empirical refinements of Barker's work on manning of behavior settings. The laboratory research followed an ecological, social systems approach in creating different conditions of manning and measuring their effects. Different manning levels produced differences in the subjective experiences of group members, but not in group performance or in patterns of verbal interaction. The manning levels to which they were previously exposed affected group members' judgments of personnel requirements. Subsequent conceptual work has focused on behavior settings in which staff members provide services to clients. Effects of staffing and population levels on both types of setting occupants are considered in terms of McGrath's stress model. Adaptive mechanisms designed to avoid problems of client overpopulation in service behavior settings are also discussed. Illustrations of research on these problems are provided by recent work in Yosemite National Park.

INTRODUCTION

In the national office of a liberal Protestant church, a researcher looks up and down a row of yearbooks of the 112 dioceses of the church. He selects one, looks for the listing of a particular local church, and copies down the church's average worship service attendance, average church school attendance, number of pastors, and number of church school teachers.

ALLAN W. WICKER and SANDRA KIRMEYER • Claremont Graduate School, Claremont, California.

In a social psychology laboratory on a college campus, another researcher listens to the conversation of four students as they race a slot-car around an obstacle-laden track in an attempt to improve their team's performance. She codes each statement into one of nine categories.

In a heavily visited National Park, a third researcher greets a Park Service ranger who has just finished a busy and difficult work shift. She asks the ranger to complete a questionnaire regarding his day's work.

In the same national park, a fourth researcher supervises a work crew installing a network of posts and chains for channeling people (a queuing device) at a heavily used bus stop where he and another researcher have been observing loading procedures for the previous three weeks.

Behavior Settings

We have used the above research activities to study some of the ways human behavior and experience interact with the immediate social–physical environment, or *behavior setting*. As conceived and studied by Barker and his associates (Barker, 1960, 1963, 1965, 1968; Barker and Gump, 1964; Barker and Schoggen, 1973; Barker and Wright, 1955), behavior settings are places and activities, such as banks, piano lessons, church worship services, Lions Club meetings, bus routes, and baseball games. More precisely, a behavior setting has the following characteristics:

1. One or more standing patterns of behavior; that is, regularly occurring human activities: For example, at a church worship service, these activities would include ushering, preaching, and singing.
2. Coordination between behavior patterns and the inanimate objects nearby: Behaviors at a worship service are coordinated with the location and physical characteristics of the pews, altar, hymnals, and offering plates, for example.
3. Definite time–place boundaries, such that the behaviors outside the boundaries are readily discriminable from those within: The boundaries of the worship service, say, would be between 10:00 and 11:00 A.M. on Sundays, and within the walls forming the church sanctuary.
4. Lack of dependency on specific individuals: The people inhabiting a behavior setting are largely interchangeable and replaceable. Members attending a worship service, or even the church pastor could change and the setting would function much as before.
5. A hierarchy of positions that influence the behavior setting or have responsibility for its functions: An usher at a church service has more

influence and is more essential than a single member who merely attends; the pastor has more authority and responsibility than the usher.

6. The capacity to generate "forces" necessary for its own maintenance; that is, pressures develop to assure that the program of the behavior setting is adhered to, that necessary components (people or materials) are brought into the setting, shaped, or if necessary expelled when they become disruptive: Thus, a crying child at a worship service may produce forces leading to such actions as glances from people trying to listen to the sermon, or a parent carrying the child out of the room.

(In the present paper, the terms behavior setting, setting, and environment will be used interchangeably to denote the above concept.)

Much of Barker's work has been devoted to cataloguing and extensively describing all of the public behavior settings in several small towns (cf. Barker and Schoggen, 1973). The present concern, however, is with a more dynamic aspect of settings: how they influence, and are influenced by, their inhabitants. The interdependence between people and behavior settings could be studied in an almost unlimited number of ways; indeed, much research in environmental psychology can be conceived as being addressed to this general question. Similarly, numerous theoretical approaches can also be applied to the question of how person–environment influences operate (cf. Wicker, 1972).

Manning Theory

Barker's discussion of the dynamics of behavior settings has focused on the interplay between people and their environments under different conditions of *manning*[1] (Barker, 1960, 1968). Undermanning, the condition of having insufficient or barely sufficient personnel in a setting to carry out the essential tasks or functions, represents a threat to the setting and to the satisfactions that occupants receive from it. In order to maintain the setting under these adverse conditions, the occupants both receive and produce more frequent, stronger, and more varied messages regarding the carrying-out of the setting's essential activities than would be the case if the number of persons available were at or above the optimal level.

This greater *claim* of undermanned behavior settings is said to produce the following consequences for setting occupants:

1. Greater effort to support the setting and its functions, either by "harder" work or by spending longer hours

---

[1] The choice of the term, *manning*, is perhaps unfortunate due to the sexist connotations it may have for some people. As will be seen, we have replaced it with more neutral terms in our recent conceptual work.

2. Participation in a greater diversity of tasks and roles
3. Involvement in more difficult and more important tasks
4. More responsibility in the sense that the setting and what others gain from it depend on each individual occupant
5. Viewing oneself and others in terms of task-related characteristics, rather than in terms of social–emotional characteristics
6. Greater functional importance of individuals within the setting
7. Less sensitivity to and less evaluation of differences between people
8. Setting of lower standards and fewer tests for admission into the setting
9. A lower level of maximal or best performance
10. Greater insecurity about the eventual maintenance of the setting
11. More frequent occurrences of success and failure, depending on the outcome of the setting's functions

This set of propositions has stimulated a number of investigations, most of them comparing schools and churches differing in size of membership. The research has been recently reviewed elsewhere (Wicker, 1973) and will not be summarized here. We will, rather, continue from about the point where that review ended, and present the latest three- or four-year slice of our research program, beginning with the conclusions from the archival study of churches, which led to a reformulation of the manning notions (Wicker, McGrath, and Armstrong, 1972). We will then report in some detail two laboratory studies based on the reformulation and using the slot-car task. Finally, we will discuss our latest thinking on the theory of manning, and show how it guided our recent research in Yosemite National Park.[2]

From the archival study of churches, and for reasons we will not repeat here, Wicker et al. (1972) concluded that future research on manning should be conducted at the level of specific behavior settings, rather than at the organizational level. They also suggested that the definition of manning conditions needed to be refined and made more precise in a number of ways: by introducing the concept of behavior setting capacity, by clarifying the distinction between optimal manning and overmanning, and by allowing different levels of manning to be specified for different types of occupants in the same behavior setting.

A Reformulation of the Manning Notions

In an attempt to deal with these needs, Wicker et al. (1972) proposed the following reformulation: Degree of manning should be determined separately

[2] In this set of studies we have attempted to follow a number of methodological procedures that are often recommended but infrequently followed by social scientists: within the context of a program of research, to use a variety of settings, research designs, types of subjects, and response measures. We have also become acutely aware of a less well-publicized aspect of these recommended procedures: They involve a considerable "retooling" cost.

for two kinds of setting occupants identified previously by Barker: *performers*, who have assigned responsibilities in the setting (for example, the managers, players, umpires, and concessionaires at a baseball game); and *nonperformers* (consumers, clients), who do not have such responsibilities (for example, the baseball fans in the stands). Thus, there can be differential degrees of manning of the same setting. For example, a one-man barber shop having insufficient customers would be adequately manned or overmanned at the level of performers but undermanned at the level of nonperformers; and a crowded physician's office would be undermanned at the level of performers yet overmanned at the level of nonperformers.

According to this reformulation, the following basic concepts are applied to each class of potential setting occupants (i.e., to performers and to nonperformers) to determine the degree of manning of a setting: the smallest number of persons required in order for the setting to be maintained (the *maintenance minimum*); the largest number of persons the setting can accommodate (*capacity*);[3] and the total number of persons who both seek to participate and meet the eligibility requirements (*applicants*).

The maintenance minimum of performers in a behavior setting is the smallest number of functionaries required to carry out its *program*; i.e., the time-ordered sequence of events that must occur in the setting. A baseball game requires 18 players (9 per team), for example.

In the case of nonperformers, the maintenance minimum is the smallest number of persons who must be present as consumers (audience, members, customers) in order for the setting to continue. A quorum is the maintenance minimum for a business meeting, for example.

A behavior setting's capacity for performers may be constrained both by physical and social structural factors. The backstage area of a theater may limit the number of persons who can serve on the stage crew, and the size of the choir loft in a church may effectively limit the size of the choir. The program of the setting may also limit capacity. Examples would include rules specifying the size of the roster of athletic teams, scripts specifying the number of actors in a play, by-laws of organizations, and the like.

The capacity for nonperformers in a setting is largely constrained by physical factors, such as number of seats and available floor space, but social structural factors may operate as well. For example, safety regulations may limit the number of persons who can be admitted to an auditorium to a figure below the absolute physical capacity.

The applicants for performer roles in a behavior setting are those persons who are both eligible to participate at the performer level and who wish to do

---

[3] In fact, it is probably more reasonable to think of both the maintenance minimum and the capacity of a behavior setting as ranges rather than as points. For example, a business office might be able to get along with one exceptionally fast and accurate typist, or two persons who type with average speed and accuracy; a church sanctuary might seat 350 thin people in its pews, but only 325 people of average build.

so. A person is eligible for a setting if he can attend at its specified time and place and if he meets all admission standards.

Applicants for nonperformer roles are simply those people who meet the admission requirements and who can and wish to enter.

These concepts can perhaps be more clearly understood by relating them to a particular kind of behavior setting. For example, in a high school play, the maintenance minimum for performers would include the director, members of the cast, persons to handle lighting, props, and costumes, a ticket seller, and possibly a few others. The maintenance minimum for nonperformers would be the smallest audience size that would be tolerated before the setting would be altered or eliminated. Capacity of performers would be the total number of persons who could be accommodated in all functional roles, including in addition to those listed above, ushers, a house manager, an assistant director, understudies, concessions sellers, and others. Capacity of nonperformers would be the number of persons who could be seated in the auditorium. Applicants at the performer level would be the number of people who sought to or at least were willing to serve as a functionary in the settings; i.e., to direct, act, usher, serve on the stage crew, and so on. Applicants at the nonperformer level would be the number of persons who have the admission fee and seek to enter the play performance.

According to Wicker *et al.* (1972), the condition of manning of a setting depends upon where the number of applicants falls relative to the maintenance minimum and capacity. If the number of applicants is below the maintenance minimum, the setting is *undermanned.* If the number of applicants falls between the maintenance minimum and capacity, *adequate manning*[4] exists. When there are more applicants than capacity, *overmanning* is present. More recently, two subdivisions of adequate manning were also specified: *poorly manned,* when number of applicants barely exceeds the maintenance minimum, and *richly manned,* when number of applicants approaches capacity (Wicker, 1973).[5]

Adequate manning is a quasi-stationary state and produces no strong internal pressures toward change. However, in the poorly manned and richly manned regions, the pressures described below would begin to increase as number of applicants approaches the maintenance minimum and capacity, respectively.

Both undermanning and overmanning are unstable and generate forces toward adequate manning. Undermanning, whether at the performer level or nonperformer level, results in pressures to increase the number of applicants, perhaps by recruiting from among the eligibles or by lowering eligibility standards, and/or to reduce the maintenance minimum, perhaps by reducing the

---

[4] The term, *adequate manning,* was deliberately chosen over Barker's term, *optimal manning,* to avoid the connotation of a specific, ideal level of manning in a behavior setting.

[5] The terms, *poorly manned* and *richly manned,* were suggested by a colleague, Stuart Oskamp.

scope of the setting or by reorganizing it. Overmanning at either level results in pressures to reduce the number of applicants, perhaps by reducing recruiting efforts or by raising eligibility standards, and/or to increase the setting capacity.

In the example of a high school play, overmanning at the performer level would exist if more students sought to be in the cast than there were acting parts available. In this case, the eligibility standards might be raised so that only the best actors would be selected. Or, an additional cast might be set up ("double casting") to perform on a different night so that twice as many people could serve as actors. At the nonperformer level, the capacity of the play behavior setting might be increased either by dealing with physical features of the setting (adding more chairs, allowing people to stand at the back of the theater, finding a larger theater) or by repeating the performance.

In many instances, however, adjustments to overmanning or undermanning cannot be made immediately. Thus, these conditions, although unstable, may persist over sufficient amounts of time for them to be studied.

Questions for Research

The clearer distinction between optimal or adequate manning and overmanning, which the above reformulation provides, led Wicker (1973) to propose that the ecological psychology literature be applied to the study of excess human populations. He suggested that three basic questions be examined empirically over the range of manning conditions:

1. *Are different degrees of manning sufficient causes for differential experiences and behaviors of group members?*

Previous research had shown that members of small organizations, whose voluntary activities were presumably undermanned, were more often performers, and had more experiences of feeling important, being needed, having worked hard, and so on, than members of large organizations, whose activities were presumably adequately manned or overmanned. While the findings were consistent with Barker's theory, these studies were limited in that they (a) used correlational designs, (b) compared organizations and not behavior settings known to differ in degree of manning, and (c) provided no information on differences between adequate manning and overmanning.

2. *Are there differences in group verbal interaction patterns as a function of different manning conditions?*

Barker's theory suggests that with increasing degrees of manning (i.e., from under to adequate to overmanning) there are decreases in (a) task-related comments, (b) evaluative comments about the setting and its occupants, and (c) comments that are directed toward modifying the behavior of others, as opposed to comments that seek to eliminate the others from participation. No previous studies had observed group process in settings varying in degree of manning.

> 3. *Does the degree of manning in a setting have carry-over effects on experiences and behaviors in subsequent situations?*

There were no direct data on this question. However, studies at the organizational level suggested that members' subjective experiences in organization behavior settings were related to the size of the organization with which the members had previously been affiliated.

A LABORATORY STUDY OF MANNING

Two studies dealing with the above questions have been completed. The first investigation (Hanson, 1973; Hanson and Wicker, 1973) examined (a) the differential effects of performer overmanning and adequate manning on group subjective experiences, admissions standards, and group performance, (b) possible carry-over effects on experiences due to the immediately prior manning condition, and (c) possible carry-over effects on experiences due to the manning conditions of settings in the subject's everyday environment. We had reasoned, following Helson's (1964) adaptation-level theory, that both immediately preceding manning conditions (*contextual* stimuli) and earlier manning conditions of activities in everyday environments (*residual* stimuli) might displace ratings of experiences in the current situation.

Carry-over effects of the immediately prior environment were studied by exposing subjects to two successive conditions or stages of manning, while carry-over effects of settings in the subject's everyday environment were studied by means of a questionnaire that asked about manning conditions of several different kinds of settings (work, voluntary organizations) he entered regularly. We found no evidence for carry-over effects due to the everyday environment, and only one carry-over effect due to the immediately preceding manning level. With that one exception, the experimental design and findings to be reported thus pertain only to the first of the two stages of manning to which subjects were exposed.

Groups of two or three male college students worked on a task designed for either two or three persons. There were three experimental conditions: (a) groups of size three when only two could be accommodated (three-person, overmanned groups, of which there were 24), (b) groups of size two when two were required (two-person, adequately manned groups, of which there were 12), and (c) groups of size three when three were required (three-person, adequately manned groups, of which there were 12). As can be seen, this design experimentally isolates the variables of group size and degree of manning.

The task for this study was adapted from Petty and Wicker (1974). Each group ran a miniature car, a slot-car, 55 laps around a track as quickly as possible in competition for a prize to be awarded to the fastest group in the experiment. The roles of the participants were *driver*, who controlled the speed of the car by means of a hand-trigger mechanism, and who was blindfolded, and *crew member*, who was not blindfolded, and whose job it was to lift obstacles (snap-back hinges mounted across the track) in order to allow the car to pass unhindered each time it completed a lap of the track. Crew members also replaced the car on the track when it went off, informed the blindfolded driver of the location and running speed of the car, and directed him when to change the car's speed.

The minimum number of persons required in order to complete the task was varied by having either one or two track obstacles in operation during the run. For example, in overmanned groups, there were three group members with only one obstacle operating. Thus, only two people were required: the driver, and one crew member to lift the obstacle, replace the car, and provide feedback to the driver. Prior to the 55-lap run, there was a practice session in which each group member drove the car 10 laps around the track without a blindfold, after which his running time was announced to the group. The groups then decided on role assignments for the 55 competition laps; i.e., the number of laps each member would drive and the number of laps each would be a crew member and/or (in overmanned groups) a watcher.

On the basis of Barker's theory, it was expected that members of overmanned groups, relative to members of adequately manned groups, would (a) have lesser experiences of: being needed, having an important role, being involved with the task, being concerned about the group's success, being depended upon, having contributed to the group, having worked closely with others, and having worked hard; (b) set higher standards of admission into the group; and (c) show higher levels of performance on the group task. Since it was believed that manning level, and not group size, is the primary determinant of the dependent variables studied, the two sizes of adequately manned groups were not expected to differ in experiences, admissions standards, or performance.

Group members' perceptions of personnel requirements, subjective experiences, and admissions standards were measured by a semantic differential-type questionnaire administered after the 55-lap run. There were two performance measures recorded for each stage: running time taken to complete the 55 laps, and number of penalties. Penalties were assessed each time the car went off the track, which was usually due to the car's going too fast to make a curve. For each penalty, one second was added to the running time.

For all analyses to be reported, the unit of analysis was the mean of each experimental group, rather than individual scores of group members. Three comparisons were made on variables of interest: (a) overmanned versus two-person adequately manned, (b) overmanned versus three-person adequately manned, and (c) two-person adequately manned versus three-person adequately manned.

Responses to two rated validator items (more men were needed, and an additional member would be desirable) and to an item asking subjects' judgments about the appropriate number of persons for the task revealed that the present manipulation was rather weak. There were four comparisons of the rated items on which differences were expected: for each of the two items, over versus two-person adequate and over versus three-person adequate. Although for each comparison the means were in the expected direction, only one was significant beyond the .05 level: Over versus two-person adequate on the item, more men were needed. The two adequately manned condition means did not differ on these items. As expected, adequately manned groups with three members gave a larger mean judgment of number of people appropriate for the task (3.0) than did adequately manned groups with two members (2.2, $p <$ .001) or overmanned groups (2.7, $p <$ .005). However, the average of 2.7 people considered appropriate by overmanned groups was significantly greater ($p <$ .001) than the judgment of two-member adequately manned groups (2.2), despite the fact that the task setup was identical. Apparently, the number of people present influenced subjects' judgments about personnel requirements.

There were eight subjective experience items dealing with manning theory (see above). Seven of the eight were found to intercorrelate highly; a composite index was derived by summing the standard scores for each of the seven items. The composite revealed the expected outcome: The pattern of feeling needed, involved, and so on, was less prevalent for overmanned groups than for two-person adequately manned groups ($p <$ .01) or three-person adequately manned groups ($p <$ .05). The means for the latter two conditions did not differ.

No support was obtained for the hypothesis that higher standards of admission are set by members of overmanned groups. Average ratings of minimal qualifications required of new group members (based on seven items, such as patience, quickness) did not differ for any comparison.

Adequately manned groups tended to spin the car off the track more, and therefore were assessed more penalties than overmanned groups ($p <$ .10, $<$ .05), but there were no differences among conditions on the running-time measure of performance.

Other analyses revealed that scores on the subjective experience composite tended to be higher for subjects who drove for the entire 55 laps than for those who were crew members or who merely watched for the entire period. Half of the groups in each condition chose to have one driver for all 55 laps; the remainder shared the driving responsibilities.

The carry-over effect due to prior manning conditions was found on the three validator items listed above. In a comparison of adequately manned groups, half of which had previously been overmanned and half of which had been adequately manned, it was found that the groups with a history of overmanning indicated that more people were needed ($p < .01$), that an additional member would be more desirable ($p < .001$), and they gave larger mean judgments of the number of people appropriate for the task (2.6 vs. 2.0, $p < .001$). Although the differences are not statistically significant, means for all three validator items also suggest that overmanned groups with a history of adequate manning felt that fewer people were needed than did overmanned groups with a history of overmanning. These results thus suggest that estimates of present personnel requirements in a behavior setting can be considerably influenced by the prior manning conditions occupants have experienced in the same setting.

The pattern of data for the validator items may be at least partially due to the fact that, despite our attempts to structure the task roles somewhat rigidly, some overmanned groups in effect increased the setting capacity by fractionating the crewman role. We observed in some cases that the person designated as the crewman would merely remove the obstacle and replace the car on the track, while the other person (nominally a watcher) would give feedback to the driver regarding the car's location and speed.

Even with this weakening of the manipulation, the study showed that the present manipulations for conditions of adequate manning and overmanning did produce differences in subjective experiences that cannot be attributed to group size. The study produced inconsistent evidence regarding the effects of manning on quality of group performance, and no evidence to support the assertion that admissions standards vary in groups differing in degree of manning. Carry-over effects of manning conditions were limited to perceptions of personnel requirements. We felt these results were sufficiently promising for us to conduct a second laboratory study of manning to examine several other questions of interest.

A FOLLOW-UP LABORATORY STUDY OF MANNING

In planning and developing the next investigation, we sought to follow more closely than in the previous study, an "ecological, social systems" orientation (Altman, 1973). That is, while we set up the basic experimental conditions, we also sought to avoid excessive experimental control. Groups were

allowed more flexibility in dealing with the experimental task (e.g., more opportunities to change roles, equipment), and accurate, periodic feedback on task
performance was provided. Moreover, we sought to employ measures of several
different levels of behavioral functioning that could be monitored over time, and
whose interrelationships could be determined. Some of our considerations in
setting up the study are given below.

Design, Equipment, and Procedure

The slot-car task was retained, as was the two-stage experimental
procedure exposing subjects to successive conditions of manning. An attempt
was made to strengthen the manning manipulation, and the range of manning
was extended to include undermanning. Group size was set at four members
for all experimental conditions. Degree of manning was manipulated by varying the number of necessary jobs: undermanned, six jobs; adequately manned,
four jobs; and overmanned, two jobs. In the second stage, all groups were
exposed to the overmanned condition. As before, number of jobs was varied by
changing the number of track obstacles in operation. In the undermanned condition, crew members had to run from one end of the table to another to
remove the obstacles so that the car could pass freely.

Two major equipment changes were made: The track was made longer
and more difficult by adding more curves, and table-mounted dials were installed to control the car speed, replacing the less reliable hand-held trigger
devices.

The number of laps run in each stage was reduced to 23; these were
broken down into four "segments" of 6, 6, 7, and 4 laps by "pit-stops." At the
pit-stops, group members were told their running time and penalties for the
laps run since the previous stop. Teams were then give a fixed amount of time
to discuss strategy for the next set of laps. During these pit-stops, members
could decide to reassign roles (driver, crew, watcher), change from one to the
other lane of the race track, and/or change from the slot-car they had been using to one of three others provided. Each segment thus contained two distinct
types of tasks: planning strategy for the next set of laps, and actually running
the laps. This arrangement permitted an analysis of the influence of type of
task on group interaction, in addition to manning influences.

Dependent Variables

The questionnaire measuring subjective experiences and validation of the
manipulation was revised and expanded. It included questions on the manning
experiences, and, in addition, questions about experiences that have been
reported in the literature (e.g., Steiner, 1972) to be a function of group size (e.g.,

perceptions of how well organized the group was, and how much influence the member felt he had on the group's decisions and performance). We were interested in learning if responses to these items would vary with degree of manning when group size was constant. A more explicit validator item asked subjects to consider the number of obstacles that had been operating in the experiment and then to estimate the most appropriate number of people for the setup in order to get the car around the track as fast as possible. Finally, several questions were asked about experiences suggested in the literature (e.g., Stokols, 1972) as consequences of crowding (e.g., feelings of frustration, pressure, being restless).

A second questionnaire administered to all subjects after the second stage of the experiment sought to measure individual differences in reactions to situations requiring waiting and/or inaction. It was reasoned that people with different generalized reactions to waiting might report different subjective experiences and show different behaviors in overmanned situations. The format (adapted from Wicker, 1971) was a series of described hypothetical situations to which subjects responded in terms of the likelihood they would remain in the setting to wait or would leave the setting. Some of the 18 situations described were: being told there will be a 45-minute wait at one's favorite restaurant before being seated; being the 12th man on a basketball team and thus having little opportunity to play; being repeatedly asked by a dormitory telephone operator to hold the line when trying to reach a girl to ask for a date.

The group performance measures were the same as in the previous study: running time to complete the assigned number of laps, and number of penalties assessed.

An observational measure of the distance subjects positioned themselves from the board on which the group running times and penalties were posted was employed as a possible index of members' involvement in the group and its task. An observer looking through a one-way mirror took this measure at the beginning of each pit-stop, just as the performance data were being announced by the experimenter. Bits of tape were placed on the floor of the experimental room at predetermined distances from the board to make the measurement more reliable.

Observation Scheme

In an attempt to study group interaction patterns in settings differing in degree of manning, we devised the following set of nine interaction categories,[6]

---

[6] It had been planned also to include in the coding scheme, categories corresponding to Barker's "deviation countering mechanism," i.e., comments aimed at correcting the inappropriate behavior of others, and his "vetoing mechanism," i.e., comments directed toward eliminating others from continued participation. Pilot testing revealed, however, that for the present task, there were insufficient numbers of comments in the categories to retain them.

some of which were adapted from Bales (1951) and from Carter, Haythorn, Meirowitz, and Lanzetta (1951):

1. Proposes game strategy or role for self or other
2. Shows agreement concurrence, compliance, acknowledgment
3. Shows disagreement, skepticism
4. Questions, asks for information, opinion, or evaluation
5. Gives information, opinion, evaluation, explanation
6. Gives directions
7. Satisfaction or supportive evaluation of setting
8. Dissatisfaction or negative evaluation of setting
9. Incidental comments, joking

Categories 1 through 8 were considered task-related comments, and categories 7 and 8, evaluative comments. Complete descriptions of each category, with examples, are presented in Kirmeyer (1974).

The unit of analysis of this scheme was the smallest portion of a verbal utterance that had meaning independent of the rest of the statement; it could be a complete sentence, a phrase, or a single word (cf. Bales, 1951). The verbal interaction of each group was tape-recorded for later analysis. All tapes were coded by two raters, and inter-rater agreement was periodically monitored by a third researcher. When a decline in agreement was detected part way through the experiment, the two raters worked on pilot tapes until their former high level of agreement was achieved. Mean inter-rater reliability for the entire experiment was .80 for content classification and .86 for unit classification. (Mean r's are based on z-transformations.)

Subjects

Since it was felt that there would be more group interaction if members were acquainted with one another prior to the experiment, subjects were recruited by asking volunteer male college students to bring three male college friends to the experiment. This differs from the earlier study, in which groups were composed of strangers. A total of 180 persons participated; there were 15 four-man groups in each of three manning conditions.

Results

The results to be reported are of two basic kinds: comparisons of manning conditions on the various dependent variables, and interrelationships between the dependent variables across manning conditions.

Effects of Manning Conditions

In contrast to the previous study, the validator items for Stage 1 showed highly significant differences across manning conditions ($p < .01$): Mean judged appropriate group size was 4.7 for undermanned groups, 4.0 for adequately manned groups, and 3.3 for overmanned groups. It should be noted, however, that participants in the undermanned and overmanned groups did not perceive the task as requiring the exact number of participants intended by the experimenters (six and two, respectively). As in the previous study, judgments were displaced toward the number of people present. In Stage 2, when all groups were overmanned, a residual effect of prior manning conditions on perceived personnel requirements was again noted: Mean judged appropriate group size was 2.4 for previously undermanned groups, 2.6 for previously adequately manned groups, and 3.1 for previously overmanned groups ($p < .01$).

Correlational analysis[7] revealed reasonably high intercorrelations among the eight subjective experience items derived from Barker (1968) (median $r = .52$) and among four of six items designed to measure subjective experiences presumably associated with group size (median $r = .45$). The eight Barker items were combined into a single manning experience composite by summing their standard scores, and a group size experience composite based on the four items was calculated in the same way. As expected, in Stage 1 the pattern of feeling needed, expending effort, feeling one's role was important, and so on, was most characteristic of undermanned groups ($\overline{X} = 2.68$), followed by adequately manned groups ($\overline{X} = .28$), and then by overmanned groups ($\overline{X} = -2.96$) ($p < .01$). It was also found that in Stage 1 the pattern of feeling one's group was well organized, that one has an influence on group decisions and on group performance, and that group experience is a pleasant one (i.e., the group size experience composite), was most characteristic of undermanned groups ($\overline{X} = .77$), followed by adequately manned groups ($\overline{X} = -.08$), and then overmanned groups ($\overline{X} = -.69$) ($p < .05$). Neither composite showed significant effects of manning condition history in Stage 2. No differences were found between manning conditions in the frequencies with which subjects reported feelings based on the crowding literature, with one exception: feeling crowded. Although one might expect that felt crowding would be more prevalent in overmanned groups, we found that members of undermanned groups more often indicated they felt crowded than did members of adequately manned or overmanned groups. Stokols (1974) has suggested a plausible explanation: The greater physical movement and coordination required of the three crewmen to operate five obstacles successfully in undermanned groups might have led to feelings of crowding.

[7] Matrices were calculated for individual and group data for both Stage 1 and Stage 2. Only group data for Stage 1 are summarized here, since the patterns were essentially the same across levels of analysis and across stages.

Neither measure of group performance (running time, penalties) was affected by manning condition, either in Stage 1 or in Stage 2. However, as might be expected, there was a strong ($p < .01$) practice effect in Stage 1, with both time and penalties declining with each successive segment. The Stage 2 running time data showed similar patterns, but the penalties data did not.

It was expected that when running times were posted at each pit-stop, members of undermanned groups, who presumably were more involved in the task, would position themselves closer to the board than would members of adequately manned groups, who would be closer than members of overmanned groups. The Stage 1 mean distances differed significantly ($p < .01$) across manning conditions: undermanned, 81 in.; adequately manned, 105 in.; and overmanned, 87 in. The contrast between the former two conditions is the largest and is consistent with expectations. It is also less ambiguous than other comparisons because in both undermanned and adequately manned groups, all members had a station at the table (either an obstacle or the speed control) that they had been manning. In contrast, two members of overmanned groups did not have such stations and in the small experimental room, one of the two members nearly always watched from an open area just in front of the board. Thus, his proximity to the board was generally not due to his moving forward to learn how well the group performed. This explanation, however, cannot readily account for the pattern of the distance data in Stage 2, when all groups were overmanned. Distances for the groups, by prior manning conditions, were: undermanned, 77 in.; adequately manned, 97 in.; and overmanned, 83 in. ($p < .05$). Correlational data reported below, however, lend credibility to the view that the distance measure may be an indicator of involvement.

Turning now to the group interaction data,[8] contrary to expectation, manning levels did not affect the frequencies of task-related or evaluative comments. While the group interaction profiles for the three manning conditions were not significantly different at either stage, the profiles for strategy and run sessions were markedly different, as shown in Table 1. At each stage, the strategy-run X coding category statistical interaction was highly significant ($p < .001$), and accounted for more than 50% of the variance in the frequency data. As might be expected, in strategy sessions there were more proposals of how to improve group performance and in runs there were more directions given. Perhaps less obvious are the findings that strategy sessions showed more frequent

---

[8] The present discussion of results of analyses of the group interaction data does not reflect the actual complexity of the statistical treatment of the data. For example, since the strategy sessions had the same duration (eight minutes) for each group, but the run sessions varied in length, all frequency data for the run sessions were statistically adjusted to eight minutes. A square-root transformation was then applied to the strategy frequencies and the time-adjusted run frequencies to meet the assumptions of the analyses of variance that were computed. Two five-way anovas (one for each stage) were applied to the time-adjusted, transformed data. The factors were: manning condition (three levels), coding category (nine levels), rater (two levels), strategy-run partition (two levels), and partition for before-after remedial coder training (two levels).

Table 1. Interaction Profiles for Strategy and Run Sessions
Stages 1 and 2

	Stage 1		Stage 2	
Coding category	Strategy	Run	Strategy	Run
1. Proposes strategy	30.4	3.2	16.7	2.5
2. Shows agreement	22.3	3.4	12.5	3.6
3. Shows disagreement	3.4	1.1	2.0	.9
4. Asks for information	23.7	10.4	15.2	9.4
5. Gives information	59.5	59.0	40.7	63.5
6. Gives directions	3.2	85.6	2.1	88.1
7. Expresses satisfaction	5.9	22.5	6.1	26.1
8. Expresses dissatisfaction	3.0	10.2	2.6	11.1
9. Incidental comments	22.8	5.5	27.0	7.3

Note. Mean frequencies are reported. Frequencies for run sessions were adjusted to equate observation time with strategy sessions (eight minutes). See Footnote 9.

expressions of agreement and disagreement, more requests for information, and more comments unrelated to the task, while run sessions had more expressions of satisfaction and dissatisfaction.

There was a tendency in Stage 1 for overmanned groups to share the driver role more than groups in the other conditions ($p < .10$). The numbers of groups (out of 15 in each condition) that used more than one driver for the four segments were: undermanned, 4; adequately manned, 2; and overmanned, 8. This pattern was even more pronounced in Stage 2 when all groups were shifted to overmanning: previously undermanned, 3; previously adequately manned, 0; and previously overmanned, 8 ($p < .05$). There was thus a pronounced carry-over effect of manning conditions on choice of role assignments.

Interrelationships between Dependent Variables

We will limit our discussion of correlational results to a summary of significant relationships of the manning experience composite with other variables.[9] As shown in Table 2, subjective experiences associated with undermanning (higher composite scores) were more prevalent for *persons* who: (a) stood closer to the board when running times were announced, (b) had more central

[9] At this writing we are still digesting results of other correlational analyses; e.g., relationships between group performance and types of verbal interaction.

Table 2. Correlation Coefficients Relating
Manning Experience Composite with Other
Variables

Variable	Stage 1	Stage 2
Distance from board	−.19*	−.15
Role index [a]	−.36**	−.50**
Judged appropriate	.18†	.16*
group size		
Hypothetical waiting situations:		
all conditions	.14	.18*
Hypothetical waiting situations:		
overmanned condition in Stage 1	.19	.33*

Note. n = 180, except for last row of coefficients, for which n = 60.
* p < .05.
** p < .01.
[a] An index of the subject's roles for one stage was formed by summing the nu-
merical values assigned to the roles (1 = driver, 2 = crew, 3 = watcher) each subject had during the four segments of the stage.

roles in the experimental task, (c) estimated greater personnel requirements for
the experimental task, and (d) reported that they were more inclined to wait in
the hypothetical situations described (especially subjects in the overmanned
condition). *Groups* scoring higher on the manning composite also tended to
show: in strategy sessions, more expressions of agreement and task-related
comments; in run sessions, more expressions of satisfaction, comments providing information, and task-related comments.

Conclusions from the Completed Research

Our experience in conducting the two laboratory studies of manning has
convinced us of the value of the ecological, social-systems approach with its
emphases on mutual influences of persons and environments, multiple modes of
response, and adaptive behaviors over time (Altman, 1973). There are a
number of benefits that may follow from loosening tight experimental controls
and allowing a wide latitude of response in laboratory experiments: One may
find effects that are understandable after the fact, and indeed consistent with
existing theory, but that were not anticipated at the outset of the experiment.
Examples are our findings that overmanned groups tended to fractionate the
crewman role, and to share the driver role to a greater extent than other
groups. One may also find reliable and comprehensible results that were not
anticipated. Our finding that perceived personnel requirements are a function

of the number of people present to work on a task and of the prior manning conditions in the same setting is an example. One may also be able to examine the same relationships among variables in different ways. We found, for example, that subjective experiences related to manning theory varied not only with different manning conditions, but also within manning conditions, depending upon subjects' task roles. A broad, multiple variable approach may also provide results that suggest promising strategies for future study. An example would be our finding that type of task greatly influenced group interaction profiles, but manning did not. Conceivably, manning effects might be found if the present observation scheme were applied to groups working in a setting where the nature of the jobs to be done changed with shifts in degree of manning. In any case, the relationships between manning conditions and task roles should be further explored. Finally, we would also like to note that researchers who begin to use the ecological, social systems approach in the laboratory may have to develop a greater tolerance for complexity and ambiguity, and learn to focus on patterns of results rather than rely on the significance of statistical tests on one or a few variables.

While we were concluding our analyses of the laboratory studies, we were also considering the questions of what would be the most profitable next steps in developing the theory of manning, and in what kinds of settings future research should be conducted. Consistent with the ecological orientation, we decided that we should return to real-life situations while attempting to expand the theory. Our long-range goal is to develop a more comprehensive and more "balanced" theory of excess and insufficient populations in behavior settings by focusing upon inner psychological states, such as cognitions and feelings, and related behaviors, and by elaborating upon the consequences of overmanning.

FOCUS ON SERVICE BEHAVIOR SETTINGS

In working toward the above goals, we have narrowed our conceptual focus from behavior settings in general to *service behavior settings*; i.e., those in which the performers are employees or entrepreneurs whose primary function is to provide a service to consumers, users, visitors, or other nonperformers. In the following discussion, we refer to performers in service behavior settings as "staff," and nonperformers in these settings as "clients." Examples of service behavior settings would be grocery stores, post office lobbies, attorneys' offices, privately owned campgrounds, police patrols, massage parlors, or hospital emergency rooms. While the focus on service settings eliminates from present consideration a number of other kinds of settings, such as most voluntary organization activities and work environments in which nonperformers are not present, it nevertheless clearly includes a sufficient number and diversity of settings to be of general interest.

One advantage of focusing on service behavior settings is the fact that in such settings, there is an inverse relationship between manning levels for staff and clients. Increases in number of clients result in greater job demands for staff; decreases in number of clients lessen job demands on staff.[10] In the following discussion, we use the terms, "understaffed," "adequately staffed," and "overstaffed" to refer to manning conditions among staff, and the terms, "underpopulated," "adequately populated," and "overpopulated" to refer to manning conditions among clients. Three different setting conditions are possible: (a) understaffed-overpopulated; e.g., a crowded dentist's office, (b) adequately staffed–adequately populated, and (c) overstaffed-underpopulated; e.g., a beauty shop with more operators than customers. Obviously, staffing and population conditions in service behavior settings can fluctuate widely over periods as brief as a few minutes due to changes in numbers of clients and/or staff. Variations also occur over hours, days, weeks, months, and years. While the selection of a time period for research purposes is somewhat arbitrary, such decisions should take into account the program of the setting, the range of staffing and population conditions that exist in the setting, and whether the investigator is interested in reactions of staff or clients or both.

In our thinking about service settings, we have considered two related, yet somewhat distinct problem areas: One focuses more directly on people, and examines in greater detail than has been done previously, the effects of staffing and population conditions (i.e., manning conditions) on the cognitions, feelings, experiences, and behaviors of setting occupants. The other focuses more directly on selected features of settings, and deals with the adaptive mechanisms that have been developed to avoid or reduce setting overpopulation. Our work on both problem areas is in a formative stage, as will be seen.

Effects of Staffing and Population Levels on Occupants of Service Behavior Settings

Conceptual Considerations

In an attempt to elaborate upon the cognitions and feelings of occupants of service behavior settings, we have drawn upon the psychological stress literature, particularly the concept of overload. Several writers have linked departures from adequate manning with stress (Barker, 1968; McGrath, in press;

---

[10] Barker's (1968) implicit assumption that the boundary between performer and nonperformer roles is permeable, i.e., that when more performers are needed, nonperformers present take over those duties, seems inappropriate for service behavior settings.

Weick, 1970). Barker and McGrath have proposed very similar models, which deal with the steps by which individuals deal with environmental threats. For Barker (1968), the threats are conditions or events in a behavior setting that jeopardize the functions of the setting and hence the satisfactions of setting occupants. He suggests that when such events are perceived (by a "sensory mechanism"), they are evaluated and a course of action is chosen (by an "executive mechanism"), and then enacted (by an "action mechanism").

McGrath (in press) considers sources of stress to be environmental situations that are "perceived as presenting a demand which threatens to exceed the person's capabilities and resources for meeting it. . . ." He proposes a four-stage, closed-loop cycle for stress situations that we will relate to staffing and population conditions in service behavior settings. The stages are the following:

1. The objective situation, as it might be recorded by an observer
2. The perceived situation, as it is experienced by the focal person
3. Response selection, the strategy chosen by the focal person for dealing with the threat
4. Behavior, the actual responses emitted to affect the objective situation

The objective situations of interest are two of the three conditions specified earlier, namely, service behavior settings that are either (a) understaffed and overpopulated or (b) overstaffed and underpopulated. In the first condition, task *overload* is a potential stressor for staff, who must deal with large numbers of clients over whom they may have little control. For clients in this condition, waiting with nothing to do could be a stressor, particularly if they are not aware of the procedures and policies that constrain the staff's activities (cf. Kahn and French, 1970, pp. 255–256). In the second condition, both staff and clients might also experience stress: staff, due to a task *underload* (i.e., few people to be served [cf. McGrath, 1970, p. 19]), and clients, due to an uncertainty about the quality of the service (e.g., wondering if lack of restaurant patrons means that the food is not good).

The next two stages in the stress cycle, perceived situation and response selection, occur within the focal person. McGrath (in press) and other writers have emphasized the importance of the individual's perceiving the objective situation as stressful. Thus, one aspect of the perceived situation is essentially validational. In the understaffed-overpopulated situation, the following feelings might be expected: among staff, feelings of having too much to do, being under pressure, feeling rushed, needing help; and among clients, feelings of impatience, boredom, wasting their time. In the overstaffed-underpopulated condition, we should find among the staff feelings of boredom, not having enough to do, having too many co-workers; and among clients (in some cases, at least), feelings of insecurity and uneasiness. Since previous research (cf. Glass and

Singer, 1972) has suggested that unpredictable, uncontrollable stressors may have greater effects than predictable, controllable stressors, it might further be expected that these feelings would be more prevalent for unexpected shifts in staffing and population conditions.

Another important aspect of the perceived situation is causal attribution for the stress; i.e., who or what is believed to be the source of the offending condition (cf. Heider, 1958; Weick, 1970). Attributions can be made to the self, or to persons or conditions outside the self. For staff in the situations of interest, not only the self but also persons who interact with the focal person in the job situation and who are dependent upon him, may be considered to be responsible for the stress. These would include the people being served, one's co-workers, and one's immediate supervisor. Staff could also attribute the stress and its effects to components of the broader organization, such as an employer or the physical features of the behavior setting, such as equipment, the arrangement of physical objects, or amount of available space. For example, a bank teller in an understaffed setting might consider the long queue of people at his window to be due to his own inefficiency, the unreasonableness of the customers, the inefficiency of his fellow tellers, the failure of his supervisor to assign enough people to windows, the failure of the organization to hire enough tellers, an insufficient number of windows, or the absence of a queuing device. For clients, attributions could be made to the self, the staff offering the service, others being served, the organization as an employer, or physical features of the setting. For example, a person waiting for service at the bank teller's window might consider his condition to be due to his own failure to arrive at a less busy time, the inefficiency of the teller, the unreasonableness of the other customers, the failure of the bank to employ enough tellers, or the failure of the bank to provide enough windows.

The third stage in McGrath's stress cycle is response selection, the process by which the focal person selects a strategy from among possible alternatives to deal with the perceived threat. An important factor in response selection is undoubtedly the source to which the stress is attributed: A staff member who sees his own inefficiency as being responsible for a long queue might try to work faster. The attribution–response selection linkage often may not be direct or one-to-one, however. A staff member might also attribute a long queue to his co-worker's inefficiency, yet try to relieve stress by working faster himself.

Among the response alternatives a staff member might consider in dealing with different staffing conditions are the following: spending less or more time per client served; purposefully reducing or increasing the quality of the service he renders; ignoring or attending to low priority tasks; inducing his co-workers to change their rate or quality of work; asking his supervisor for additional help or for permission to leave his post; communicating his feelings to persons higher up in the organization; activating or deactivating a queuing mechanism (e.g., a "take-a-number" device). A client's response alternatives to various setting population conditions might include the following: leaving the behavior setting; switching from one waiting line to another; complaining to the other clients or the staff in the setting; questioning other setting occupants about the reasons for the small number of people present; attempting to advance in a queue by cutting in or using other unauthorized methods to obtain service more quickly; releasing emotion, e.g., honking one's horn, stamping one's feet; making resolutions for the future, e.g., never or always to return at that hour, to make reservations or not to bother with them, to communicate his feelings to others by letter or in conversation (cf. Saaty, 1961, p. 10).

Some of the alternative responses described above were derived from Milgram's (1970) discussion of the reactions to sensory overload shown by residents of large cities and from Meier's (1962) list of responses to communications stress. Milgram also suggests two other responses that are probably gradual adaptations to overload, rather than consciously considered strategies; these would most directly apply to persons who repeatedly and/or continuously experience understaffing. They are (a) interacting with clients only in terms of job role prescriptions; i.e., only on an impersonal and relatively superficial level, and (b) lacking empathy with or sensitivity to the problems or concerns of the persons served. Another possible adaptation is the development of stereotyped perceptions of clients by the staff; i.e., classifying clients into a small number of broad and often derogatory categories.[11]

The notions derived from Milgram may seem somewhat contradictory to Barker's theory, which would predict increasing feelings of job involvement, importance, and concern as staffing levels decrease. Conceivably, this relationship may be stronger in voluntary activities (e.g., settings in schools and churches, laboratory experiments) than in work situations. Also, the temporal factor may be crucial: First experiences of understaffing may well lead to greater involvement, with later chronic understaffing producing cynicism and dissociation from the task.

The fourth stage in the stress cycle is the actual behaviors by the focal person to deal with the threat. The behaviors will presumably be a subset of the response alternatives considered in the third stage. The outcome of these behaviors in the objective situation is then perceived, considered, and further acted upon if necessary, according to the McGrath (in press) model.

---

[11] For example, Washington, D.C., supermarket checkout clerks have developed the following categories for the people they serve: "hawks," who closely watch the cash register as items are rung up; "scavengers," who attempt to get reductions on prices for dented cans, damaged produce, and the like; "aristocrats," who ask clerks for services no longer provided, such as leaving their station to collect items the shopper could not locate; and "self-servers," who shoplift in a variety of ways (McCarthy, 1973). And among National Park Service employees, "turkeys" refer to park visitors who bring large motor homes or trailers to parks. Such visitors are said to "gobble up" all of the resources.

Empirical Research

We attempted to examine some of the above notions in Yosemite National Park in the summer of 1974.[12] With the cooperation of the local park administration, we obtained questionnaire responses from National Park Service employees in several different kinds of jobs that involved extensive contact with park visitors. Our sample included some people whose work allowed them to move about, and others who had to stay in a single, rather confining location: patrolling rangers, ranger naturalists, entrance station attendants, and campground kiosk attendants. The employees answered questions about specific work days that we had judged from external criteria to be heavy, average, or light in terms of job demands. Questions dealt with such topics as the extent to which the employee felt involved in his work, the extent to which he felt under pressure, the extent to which he saw himself or others as being responsible for the pressure, the alternatives he considered for dealing with the pressure, and what he actually did. Other questions asked about general working conditions (e.g., how often the amount of work the employee had to do interfered with how well he was able to do the work, how much freedom he had in deciding the amount of time to spend with any given park visitor); and about perceived characteristics of park visitors (e.g., the percentage of visitors who understand the problems that park employees have to deal with, the percentage of visitors who try to minimize the environmental impact of their visit). Unfortunately, we were not able to obtain comparable data from park visitors due to regulations that severely restrict the administration of questionnaires and interviews to visitors on Federal recreational lands. Results of the Yosemite research are not available at this time, as we are just beginning the data analysis. Among other things, we hope to determine the effects of both level of job demands and type of job on the subjective experiences, attributions, and perceptions described above.

Adaptive Mechanisms for Avoiding or Reducing Overpopulation of Service Behavior Settings

Conceptual Considerations

We are also struggling with ways to conceptualize and study adaptive mechanisms that have developed spontaneously or that have been introduced into service settings to lessen problems of overpopulation; i.e., having more

---

[12] While there are both conceptual and methodological similarities and differences between our Yosemite research and the laboratory studies reported earlier, it should be understood that we view the Yosemite work as an examination of our most recent elaboration of the manning notions, and not simply as a field replication of the earlier laboratory investigations.

clients present than can readily be served. There appear to be at least three basic ways these mechanisms function: by regulating (a) the entrance of clients into the setting, (b) the capacity of the setting, and (c) the length of time clients spend in the setting. Each basic type of regulation may be achieved in a number of different ways, as illustrated below[13]:

A. Regulation of the entrance of clients into the setting
  1. Scheduling entrances
     Example: A dentist might require his patients to make an appointment before being allowed to see him.
  2. Varying recruiting activities
     Example: A restaurant whose business is good every night might stop advertising.
  3. Adjusting standards of admission
     Example: A National Park whose wilderness areas are heavily visited might begin to require all backpackers to demonstrate a knowledge of how to minimize the environmental impact of their visit before issuing them wilderness permits.
  4. Channeling clients into holding areas
     Example: Patrons of a busy restaurant might be directed to the cocktail lounge to wait until a table is free.
  5. Preventing unauthorized entrances
     Example: A bus driver might eject a would-be passenger who entered the bus in a discharging zone to avoid waiting in line at the loading area.
B. Regulation of the capacity of the setting
  1. Altering physical facilities and spaces
     Examples: Ushers at an Easter worship service might place folding chairs at the back of a church sanctuary to accommodate a large crowd of worshipers. On holiday weekends, additional queuing device stanchions might be placed in the waiting area for a popular amusement park attraction.
  2. Adjusting duration or occurrences of the setting
     Example: A popular tavern might extend the hours and/or the days of the week it is open.
  3. Adjusting size of staff
     Example: A bank manager might assign an additional employee to teller duty on Fridays.

[13] This list is tentative and undoubtedly incomplete. The list and examples have been drawn from our casual observation of service behavior settings, introductions to queuing theory (Cox and Smith, 1961; Goode and Machol, 1957; Panico, 1969; Saaty, 1961), the literature on sensory overload (Milgram, 1970; Meier, 1962), manning theory (Barker, 1968; Wicker, et al., 1972), and general systems theory (Miller, 1971, 1972).

    4. Varying assignments of nonservice tasks to staff
      Example: Lifeguards at a beach might be asked to suspend all
      equipment maintenance tasks during heavy visitation periods.
C. Regulation of the amount of time clients spend in the setting
    1. Varying rate of processing clients
      Example: A barber with a number of customers waiting might
      spend less time on each haircut.
    2. Varying limitations on length of stay
      Example: A public campground might allow campers to stay only
      seven days during the summer, but 21 days during the rest of the
      year.
    3. Activating a graduated fee structure based on time spent in the
      setting
      Examples: Campers in a public campground might be charged a
      higher fee each successive night they spent there.
    4. Establishing priorities among clients in the setting on such bases as
      time of arrival, waiting costs, service time required
      Example: A hospital emergency ward might have a policy of at-
      tending to the most seriously injured first. A computer consultant
      might first serve those clients having brief questions before helping
      those with more involved problems.
    5. Altering the standing patterns of behavior by means of procedures,
      rules, and/or physical facilities that affect the rate of flow of clients
      into and out of the setting
      Examples: A hamburger stand might be re-arranged so that cus-
      tomers place their orders at one counter and pick them up at
      another. A busy bus system might begin to accept only the exact
      fare. A rest room in a large sports arena might be redesigned with
      separate entrance and exit doors. A savings and loan bank might
      post signs asking customers to complete their own deposit slips
      before approaching a teller.

In addition to the above mechanisms which are aimed at physically processing clients in ways to avoid or reduce overpopulation, there are other mechanisms which seem to be oriented toward reducing clients' *perceptions* and *experiences* of overpopulation and its consequences without really affecting the objective situation. One such mechanism is a distracting or entertaining stimulus located where it can be viewed by people waiting in line. An example would be a closed-circuit television which shows ski movies placed near a queue of skiers waiting for a lift. Another such mechanism is a queuing arrangement which leads people waiting in line to believe that the number of people ahead of them is smaller than it actually is. For example, inside the building housing an amusement-park attraction, there may be a 100-foot queue that is not visible to those waiting in line outside. A somewhat related mechanism is leading clients to believe they are making progress by introducing a number of discrete steps in obtaining service. For example, a patient in a physician's office may first check in with a receptionist, then wait in a waiting room until his name is called, then be escorted to an examination room where he waits until a nurse comes to take his temperature and pulse, then be escorted into still another room where he waits until the physician arrives. Another of these mechanisms involves concealing the setting capacity from clients. A dentist may have several patients in chairs and rotate from one to another without their knowing how many others he is seeing at the same time.

Empirical Research

In Yosemite National Park, we have studied an adaptive mechanism designed to reduce problems of overmanning at a bus stop. The mechanism was a queuing device made of posts and chains arranged in such a way as to get passengers to line up in an orderly fashion in preparation for boarding. In the study, we first systematically observed and recorded a number of measures of the orderliness and rate of loading at two of the busiest bus stops on the free Yosemite Valley shuttle-bus system. During these observations, there were many instances when people were stranded at the stop because the bus filled before they were able to board. There was also much pushing and shoving. After three weeks of observations, with the help of the Park Service work crews, we installed the queuing device at one of the two stops. Over the next three weeks, we again took the same measures at both stops and also observed the frequency of violations of the queuing procedures. At the end of this period we gave questionnaires to the bus drivers to get their reactions to the device. It is our impression that the queuing device was successful, but we will be better able to make an evaluation and recommendations regarding its use after the data are analyzed.

We believe that further knowledge of the ways service settings avoid or reduce overpopulation would be valuable, both for theoretical and practical reasons. Such knowledge might come from attempts to elaborate and refine the above list of mechanisms, and/or from other intensive studies of specific mechanisms in selected settings. The potential conceptual payoffs include a greater convergence between the study of adaptive mechanisms and the study of subjective reactions to staffing and population conditions, and increased understanding of the *processes* by which these mechanisms operate (cf. Wicker, 1972) and of the ways various mechanisms are related to one another. The potential practical payoffs include detailed information on how, and how well, certain mechanisms operate, and availability of a comprehensive list of adaptive mechanisms that could be consulted by persons in charge of settings threatened with overpopulation.

POSTSCRIPT

In this paper, we have tried to *illustrate* the recent activities in our program of research, rather than to make formal or general statements about our orientation to the study of how people experience their environments. Given the nature of programmatic research, it also seems appropriate that the paper should end by alluding to data still being analyzed and by posing questions for future study.

Acknowledgment

The first author was primarily responsible for the theoretical sections of this paper; the second author had a major role in the empirical work reported. The following persons also participated in the empirical research: in the slot-car studies, Lois Hanson and Dean Alexander; in the Yosemite National Park projects, Lois Hanson, Richard LeBlanc, and Scott Buehler. We are indebted to Joseph E. McGrath for helpful comments on an earlier version of this paper. The research reported here was supported by Grant No. GS 34998 from the National Science Foundation.

REFERENCES

Altman, I. Some perspectives on the study of man-environment phenomena. *Representative Research in Social Psychology*, 1973, *4*, 109–126.

Bales, R. F. *Interaction process analysis.* Cambridge, Massachusetts: Addison-Wesley, 1951.

Barker, R. G. Ecology and motivation. *Nebraska Symposium on Motivation*, 1960, *8*, 1–50.

Barker, R. G. On the nature of the environment. *Journal of Social Issues*, 1963, *19*(4), 17–38.

Barker, R. G. Explorations in ecological psychology. *American Psychologist*, 1965, *20*, 1–14.

Barker, R. G. *Ecological psychology: Concepts and methods for studying the environment of human behavior.* Stanford, California: Stanford University Press, 1968.

Barker, R. G., and Gump, P. V. *Big school, small school: High school size and student behavior.* Stanford, California: Stanford University Press, 1964.

Barker, R. G., and Schoggen, P. *Qualities of community life.* San Francisco: Jossey-Bass, 1973.

Barker, R. G., and Wright, H. F. *Midwest and its children.* New York: Harper & Row, 1955.

Carter, L., Haythorn, W., Meirowitz, B., and Lanzetta, J. The relation of categorizations and ratings in the observation of group behavior. *Human Relations*, 1951, *4*, 239–254.

Cox, D. R., and Smith, W. L. *Queues.* New York: Wiley, 1961.

Glass, D. C., and Singer, J. E. *Urban stress: Experiments on noise and social stressors.* New York: Academic Press, 1972.

Goode, H. H., and Machol, R. E. *System engineering.* New York: McGraw-Hill, 1957.

Hanson, L. Effects of overmanning on group experience and task performance. Unpublished masters thesis, Claremont Graduate School, Claremont, California, 1973.

Hanson, L., and Wicker, A. W. Effects of overmanning on group experience and task performance. Paper presented at the meeting of the Western Psychological Association, Anaheim, California, April, 1973.

Heider, F. *The psychology of interpersonal relations.* New York: Wiley, 1958.

Helson, H. *Adaptation-level theory.* New York: Harper & Row, 1964.

Kahn, R. L., and French, J. R. P., Jr. Status and conflict: Two themes in the study of stress. In J. E. McGrath (Ed.), *Social and psychological factors in stress.* New York: Holt, Rinehart and Winston, 1970.

Kirmeyer, S. The effects of manning condition on group interaction. Unpublished masters thesis, Claremont Graduate School, Claremont, California, 1974.

McCarthy, C. Checking out the faces on the supermarket assembly line. *San Francisco Examiner and Chronicle,* December 30, 1973, Sunday Punch, p. 7.

McGrath, J. E. A conceptual formulation for research on stress. In J. E. McGrath (Ed.), *Social and psychological factors in stress.* New York: Holt, Rinehart and Winston, 1970.

McGrath, J. E. Stress and behavior in organizations. In M. D. Dunnette (Ed.), *Handbook of industrial and organizational psychology.* Chicago, Illinois: Rand-McNally, in press.

Meier, R. L. *A communications theory of urban growth.* Cambridge, Massachusetts: M. I. T. Press, 1962.

Milgram, S. The experience of living in cities. *Science,* 1970, *167,* 1461–1468.

Miller, J. G. The nature of living systems. *Behavioral Science,* 1971, *16,* 277–301.

Miller, J. G. Living systems: The organization. *Behavioral Science,* 1972, *17,* 1–182.

Panico, J. A. *Queuing theory: A study of waiting lines for business, economics, and science.* Englewood Cliffs, New Jersey: Prentice-Hall, 1969.

Petty, R. M., and Wicker, A. W. Degree of manning and degree of success of a group as determinants of members' subjective experiences and their acceptance of a new group member. *JSAS Catalog of Selected Documents in Psychology,* 1974, *4,* 43, (Ms. No. 616)

Saaty, T. L. *Elements of queueing theory.* New York: McGraw-Hill, 1961.

Steiner, I. D. *Group process and productivity.* New York: Academic Press, 1972.

Stokols, D. A social-psychological model of human crowding phenomena. *Journal of the American Institute of Planners,* 1972, *38,* 72–83.

Stokols, D. The experience of crowding in primary and secondary environments. Paper presented at the meeting of the American Psychological Association, New Orleans, August, 1974.

Weick, K. E. The "Ess" is stress: Some conceptual and methodological problems. In J. E. McGrath (Ed.), *Social and psychological factors in stress.* New York: Holt, Rinehart and Winston, 1970.

Wicker, A. W. An examination of the "other variables" explanation of attitude-behavior inconsistency. *Journal of Personality and Social Psychology,* 1971, *19,* 18–30.

Wicker, A. W. Processes which mediate behavior-environment congruence. *Behavioral Science,* 1972, *17,* 265–277.

Wicker, A. W. Undermanning theory and research: Implications for the study of psychological and behavioral effects of excess populations. *Representative Research in Social Psychology,* 1973, *4,* 185–206.

Wicker, A. W., McGrath, J. E., and Armstrong, G. E. Organization size and behavior setting capacity as determinants of member participation. *Behavioral Science,* 1972, *17,* 499–513.

IX

The Nature of Environmental Experience

WILLIAM H. ITTELSON, KAREN A. FRANCK, and TIMOTHY J. O'HANLON

Abstract: This paper discusses a series of presuppositions that have traditionally directed research in environment and experience. It describes, alternatively, a methodology based on different assumptions that will enable the researcher to avoid the biases and conclusions these presuppositions necessitate, and relates a series of studies that display the salient elements of environmental experience. The results of these studies have suggested a number of characteristics of environmental experience and specific modes of experiencing the environment. The fundamental tenet is that environmental experience is that continuing product of an active endeavor by an individual to create for himself a situation within which he can optimally function and achieve his own particular pattern of satisfaction. Finally, it is concluded that no single mode or combination of modes of environmental experience represent a "true" view of the environment, and that as scientists we should emulate the individual and develop a view of the environment that will optimally enable us to carry out our goals both as students and as concerned human beings.

I have two desks[1]; one is quite far physically and psychologically from here. As I sit at that desk, which I can visualize at this very moment, I can look out of a window directly in front of me. The window is attached to an adobe house that is a little over 8,000 feet above sea level. It is on the outskirts of the highest settlement in that part of New Mexico, although there are some cabins up another couple of thousand feet. Nine miles away to the east the highest peak in that area rises to 13,000 feet. This is not visible through my westward-look-

---

[1] Experience is personal, and we take as our starting point the first-person experience of one of the authors.

WILLIAM H. ITTELSON, KAREN A. FRANCK, and TIMOTHY J. O'HANLON • Environmental Psychology Program, The City University of New York, New York, New York.

ing window, but what I do see as I settle comfortably in my chair is a field gently sloping off for 300 to 400 yards and then dropping fairly precipitously into the Rio Grande valley. The river itself is visible 2500 feet below and about 15 miles away. Beyond that the landscape stretches westward, seemingly endlessly, rising and falling, the air so clear that one cannot identify the farthest visible landmark. The scene changes continuously as the sun and clouds cast shadows. There is an occasional rainstorm throwing a shaft of black down into the valley. If I move my chair a little, I can see the cows in the next field. There are three of them and two calves, and although I cannot see them, I can hear the mare and her colt in a nearby field.

But all this passes through my mind as I sit at my other desk. It, too, faces a window through which I can look across 43rd Street in Manhattan and into the windows in the red-brick façade of the building on the other side of the street. I can see into several offices quite clearly when the lights are on and I can observe the comings and goings of the nameless occupants with whom I feel a strange sort of kinship. Directly across from me stretches a hallway which terminates in an abrupt right turn, and like Alice, I wonder where one goes when one makes that journey. My reverie is interrupted by the harsh sounds of fire sirens as the engines leave the station house directly across from me. If I approach the window, I can look down into the street five stories below. If I do so, I become more conscious of the steady drone of noises, to which the fire siren is only a punctuation mark. The street and sidewalk, almost independent of the weather, are full of busy people and impatient automobiles and trucks. I move away from the window, retire within my four walls and contemplate the painting on the wall across from my desk.

How easy and how obvious it is to assume that I have described two environments, each of which I experience in a particular way due to the characteristics it possesses. Each environment sits out there—New Mexico and New York—each sublimely indifferent to my experience of it or indeed of my existence at all, but each tolerantly willing to let me come and experience it if I so choose. An easy assumption to make and a comfortable one, for it dictates a familiar and straightforward path of inquiry. It represents one possible mode of environmental experience. However, as investigators of the nature of environmental experience, we must steadfastly refuse to make that assumption, for in doing so we are committing the "fallacy of the forest fire."

For the elucidation of this fallacy, we are indebted to the U. S. Forest Service as reported in *The Sciences* (Libassi, 1975). The Forest Service has as one of its objectives the preservation of our national forests in their natural state. One very obvious way of preserving natural forests is to keep them from burning down. This makes such obvious sense that elaborate fire-fighting techniques such as helicopter drops and airborne sprays have been developed over the years.

However, only recently has it been realized through studies conducted by the Forest Service that presevation of the forests actually may mean allowing forest fires to occur.[2] For example, it was found that certain plants and animals depend on nutrients provided by post-fire vegetation for food. In addition, the cones of certain species of pine will not open and release their seeds without being exposed to fire. Inadvertently, then, by suppressing all forest fires in past years, the Forest Service has been changing the ecological patterns within forests. The present policy of the Forest Service is to use fires to restore and preserve the natural ecology of the forest.

Within this framework, it has become a tactical question for the Forest Service whether they should put out fires started by man or by natural events, e.g., lightning. These decisions will depend on whether a fire is necessary to restore or preserve the natural ecology of the forest. Indeed, at times it might be necessary for the Forest Service to start their own fires.

In this case the Forest Service's recognition of certain anomalies and their interest in preserving natural forests led to a redefinition of the natural forest and the actions necessary to maintain that definition. The policy of the Forest Service with regard to fires changed. The forest that is now being preserved and restored through the use of forest fires is not the same forest that was formerly harmed by forest fires. This changing definition of forest suggests that the forest ranger never functioned as an isolated and independent agent able to manipulate and preserve the forest that hypothetically existed independently of him. Rather, he is an integral part of the process through which the forest exists. Whatever he chooses to do, he cannot escape that ultimate fact.

While the new strategy of the Forest Service makes good sense, it illustrates the contradictions inherent in pretending that we are able to identify and preserve a separately existing external environment. On one level the parable of the forest fire points out how difficult it is, operationally, to distinguish between the processes of nature and man. On another level it illustrates the theoretical problems inherent in trying to identify and preserve an environment independent of human conceptions and considerations. Man's conception of the environment is related to his conception of himself and his actions, and change in the conception of one affects the conception of the other.

The "fallacy of the forest fire," then, is the conceptual separation of man and environment into two separate, independently existing entities. However, as we have suggested, this is a common mode of environmental experience and is reflected in the word itself. The environment is literally that which surrounds. In this way of thinking, the environment is something that surrounds something else. And what does it surround? It surrounds us, of course, so that

---

[2] The use of forest fires as an aid in silviculture has been an issue of great controversy within the Forest Service since the early part of this century. Scientific evidence of its value was initially suppressed or degraded by the Forest Service because it conflicted with their preconceived notions about the nature of forest fires (Schiff, 1962).

there we sit, surrounded by an environment that in principle we can know and that our knowledge does not affect in any way.

But this man–environment dichotomy is just the tip of the iceberg of con-ceptual dichotomies most of us bring to the study of man and environment. Man himself is split into man, the responder to environments on the one hand, and man, the actor on environments on the other hand, each being considered the special province of a particular set of disciplines. The environment, in turn, is split first into natural versus man-made and then each of these is further sub-divided into those aspects of the environment that evoke human response and those aspects that are the product of human action. Each element of these various dichotomies is treated separately and differently as the special territory of particular groups of professionals.

Man as responder to environmental stimuli traditionally has been considered to be the subject matter of social scientists in general and psychologists in particular. This concern has been conceptualized and investigated in many different ways, but the methodological and theoretical details need not concern us here; they have been spelled out amply elsewhere. What is important is the overall view we as psychologists tend to take of man as a responding mechanism. In this view, man creates a psychological environment by the nature of his responses to environmental stimuli. The question of environmental experience in this context is reduced to the question of identifying the particular kinds of responses made by particular individuals to identifiable elements of environmental input.

Man acting on the environment would certainly seem to be an equally valid topic for consideration in any study of environmental experience. It is, however, an interesting historical fact that the social sciences in general have been rather uninterested in the study of man as an environment maker, although it seems obvious that man not only responds to the environment, he actively creates it. Relative to other organisms, man is probably unique in the extent to which he self-consciously builds the environment in which he functions. It should not need elaboration that man, the tool maker and tool user, man, the manipulator of his environment, man, the builder of his environment, is a unique biological event. Indeed, a noted biologist has stated that "what is unique about man is his technology" (Medwar, 1973). It is almost self-evident that this aspect of man is important in determining the nature of his experience of the environment. Yet, until very recently psychologists have not been interested in the study of man as the designer and builder of environments. This line of thought has been dealt with by designers, architects, and to a somewhat lesser extent, by geographers and some anthropologists.

This division of labor, growing out of a fundamental conceptual division of man himself, has made virtually impossible any study of the interconnections between these two modes of human activity. It is our belief, which will be indicated in more detail later, that it is precisely at this junction that the important elements of environmental experience are to be found. The way man responds to his environment affects the way he acts on it; the way he acts on it affects the way he responds. Out of this continuing process emerges a picture of man as the active creator, psychologically and physically, of the environment within which he functions.

On the other side of the man–environment dichotomy the environment fares no better. The fallacy of the forest fire has already shown us the danger inherent in the common distinction between natural and man-made environments. It is dangerous first because there is no operational or theoretical way of distinguishing between the two. Operationally, man is part of nature, or perhaps more correctly, man is nature in the sense that man has become the dominant force in determining the direction of natural development on this planet. Theoretically, the distinction between man and nature represents a restatement of a particular line of thought with a long history, rather than a necessary, unique, and unavoidable conclusion. It represents one mode of environmental experience with no demonstrable superiority over others. Secondly, it is dangerous in the present context because it leads to the temptation to speak of the experience of natural environments and the experience of man-made environments as if they represented theoretically and empirically distinct and different categories.

Beyond the distinctions between natural and man-made, as we have already pointed out, the environment is dichotomized conceptually into those aspects to which man responds and those aspects that are the product of man's action. This split exactly corresponds to the division of man into responder and builder. Psychologists and other social scientists interested in man as responder see the environment as made up of elements which elicit responses, either in the form of stimuli or in the form of reinforcers. Those disciplines interested in man the builder see the environment as a product of man's technological and architectural activities.

In summary, the conventional wisdom which most of us bring to our study of environmental experience separates man from environments, divides man into responder and builder, divides environments first into natural and man-made and then each of these into environment as stimulus and environment as product. Furthermore, each of these various components is associated with a tradition of thought that is for the most part separate from that of the others. It is not our purpose here to try to demonstrate that this picture is false, but rather to assert that if one builds it into the start of one's inquiry, it will most certainly emerge at the end of the inquiry. So perhaps the principal methodological concern in our studies of environmental experience has been to become self-consciously aware of our preconceptions and of the influence that they will have on the outcome of any study. We have outlined what we consider to be a common but unfruitful set of assumptions about the nature of environmental experience. We can suggest an alternative point of view that has guided our work.

We believe as a fundamental premise that environmental experience and environmental action cannot be separated. How one experiences the environment affects both general strategies in dealing with it and specific actions in concrete situations. In this way environmental experience is a set of predictive guidelines for acting in the environment. However, environmental strategies and actions in turn affect the range of future possibilities for experiencing the environment and confirm or deny the relevance of previous experiences. In this sense environmental action is a set of predictive guidelines for future experience. Environmental actions affect environmental experience, environmental experience affects environmental actions. We believe these two aspects cannot be separated theoretically or operationally without destroying the subject which we are setting out to study.

Paradoxically, this conclusion comes not at the end point of a program of study of environmental experience but rather is preliminary to such a study. The scientist no less than the object of study is a participant in this process. The ways in which we experience the environment will influence the ways we go about studying the nature of environmental experience. Few other areas of study are so susceptible to the influence of the presuppositions of the investigator. If we uncritically assume on the basis of our personal and cultural history that we know the nature of the environment, then we will have inevitably written the answer into the way we ask the question. Since no one can be without environmental experience, no one can be without preconceptions as to the nature of the environment and how to study it. Environmental experience is a deeply important part of all of us, but those who choose to study it have an obligation to examine and make explicit our preconceptions and how they relate to our work. Our working assumption is that the individual cannot be separated from the environment. He is a part of the system he is experiencing, and the ways he experiences it become part of the environment he in turn experiences.

The direct methodological implications for us are twofold. The first is to treat every study as a simulation of the situation to which we hope to generalize and to understand the differences between the simulation and the larger context. Thus, laboratory simulation can be of primary value in providing insights and hypotheses for elaboration and study in other more naturalistic settings. The second is to use a wide variety of different procedures, recognizing that no single one is going to provide definitive answers, but that the convergence of many may approximate what we are looking for. In terms of situations we have ranged from the controlled laboratory to the fully naturalistic setting; the role of the experimenter has ranged from detached observer to full participant; the role of the subject has ranged from object for study to co-investigator; and our data collection techniques have included direct observation, cognitive maps, interviews, questionnaires, diaries, other forms of self report, and formal scaling techniques. In this paper we will briefly report three studies of environmental experience: one a laboratory experiment, the second a controlled field experiment, and the third a naturalistic field study.

THREE STUDIES OF ENVIRONMENTAL EXPERIENCES

Novel Environment Laboratory

The novel environment laboratory represents an attempt to simulate within the laboratory some of the principal features involved in the experience of a novel environmental situation. The laboratory has been described in detail elsewhere (Nahemow, 1971). At this point it is sufficient to say that it is a large room in which vibrating mirrors, various sounds, flashing lights, and changing colors all combine to create a rather unusual and previously unexperienced situation. Subjects in a series of studies were introduced singly into this room; their only instructions were that they would be asked some questions about it afterward. Their behavior in the room was observed and recorded and, following a period of five to fifteen minutes within the room, they were questioned concerning the general nature of their experience, their awareness of object properties of the room, and their awareness of the environmental contingencies. In some studies, the situation was random; in others, predictable sequences were built in but not under control of the subject. In the two studies (Ittelson and Krawetz, 1975) to be mentioned here, the sequences of light and sound were actually under the control of the subjects in the sense that predictable events followed specific actions on the part of the subject. In the earlier work it was found that subjects' descriptions of the situation could be categorized as either "experiential" or "structural." Experiential descriptions consisted of moods, feelings, impressions, and other forms of self-report, while structural descriptions contained references to the physical features of the room as though it consisted of a series of objects apart from the subjects' own experiences. In the present studies three categories (structural, experiential, and mixed) were derived from the subjects' written descriptions of the situation.

In addition, two other measures of the subjects' experiences were used: total activity and awareness of specific contingencies. The lights, sounds, and mirrors were controlled by the activity of the subject, and the more he explored the room, the more opportunities for controlling it he encountered. The number of changes the subject activated were recorded and used as a measure of his total activity. To determine whether the subject's activity was random or based on his learning the contingencies of the room, each subject was questioned as to how many of the eight possible contingencies he knew.

The results indicated that the mode of describing the situation (structural, experiential, or mixed), the amount of activity, and the learning of contingencies were all positively related. Structural descriptions were related to more activity and to greater learning of contingencies. Activity varied from a very low level to a fairly high level, ranging from zero to 151 changes in 15 minutes. Reported experience ranged from concentrating on the room exclusively as a physical place to concentrating entirely on one's own inner experiences. Reports of environmental contingencies varied from having no idea that there were such contingencies to having a fairly complete and adequate grasp of them, ranging from zero to seven out of the eight possible contingencies. Enjoyment or boredom in the room was unrelated to any of the above measures.

Controlled Field Experiment

The aim of the controlled field experiment was to analyze the nature of the problem of spatial orientation in the New York City subway system, and to evaluate the adequacy of the official New York City subway guide as an aid in this orientation (Bronzaft, Dobrow, and O'Hanlon, 1975). The essential task of the subway rider is to transform knowledge about the structure and operation of the subway system into patterns of action necessary for traveling between an origin and a destination. The usual sources of this knowledge are maps, structural design and details of the system, public announcements, graphics, past experience, and communications from other people. In the experiment 20 subjects were divided into two groups of 10. The subjects within each group were assigned the same trip with four connected segments, and they were asked to travel their routes in the shortest possible time. For the trip each subject was given a copy of the New York City subway guide and a log sheet for recording his use of trains and stations. In order to assess the value of the subway guide for those who would be dependent on it, the subjects were newcomers to New York City, and they were instructed not to ask for directions from others while on their trips. When the subjects completed their subway trips, they were interviewed and asked to complete a questionnaire on their traveling experiences. During the interview the subjects were asked to reconstruct the events of their trips, outlining strategies they had used and giving reasons for their selection of trains.

As each of the 20 subjects was assigned four trip-segments, data were collected on a total of 80 trip-segments. According to criteria established by the experimenters, the subjects' trip-segment solutions were categorized in three ways. Of the 80 trip-segments, 37 were direct solutions (the shortest and simplest routes), 10 were indirect solutions (adequate but roundabout), and 33 were mistaken solutions. Mistaken solutions were those which failed to take the subjects to their destinations in the manner they had planned. At least 26 of the mistaken solutions were related to unreliable information provided by the subway map. The other seven mistaken solutions were related to incorrect assumptions about the system based on the subjects' past experience with the system or on the subjects' inability to find necessary graphics for locating trains.

When the subjects were questioned about their selection of indirect solutions, most said that they believed their search of the map for routes had produced the optimal solution. However, some of these solutions did contain trains and stations with which the subjects were already familiar, and therefore he had less chance of getting lost.

When asked to describe their trips, the subjects frequently revealed feelings of insecurity and hostility that were related to the difficulty they had in finding their way. Frequently there were inadequate graphics in the system for locating and identifying trains. As a result, subjects were often reduced to wandering around stations trying to find their desired trains. These feelings were augmented by the frequent inability of the subjects to figure out easily why trip-segments planned from the map did not work. One subject who planned an operationally impossible transfer between trains based on the map and tried to perform it twice drew an analogy between his subway experiences and those of the main character in Kafka's book, *The Castle*.

In this experiment, the subjects by the nature of the task were asked to view the subway system both as a real external environment and as a setting for action. They were told to go to a series of publicly identifiable places in the system, were given a guide that modeled the system, and were asked to reconstruct the events of their trip. Correspondingly, their ability to orient themselves within the system was analyzed in terms of the nature and kind of information in the system that they were able to find and use. At times the subway guide provided them with unreliable or invalid information about the environmental contingencies within the system. At other times the system lacked categories of information necessary for acting out correctly learned environmental contingencies.

Naturalistic Study of Newcomers to the City

A longitudinal exploratory study of two groups of newcomers presents an opportunity to examine the process through which a person experiences a relatively novel environment (Franck, Unseld, and Wentworth, 1974). Through the use of in-depth interviews, diaries, and map tasks, the experiences of graduate students who had recently moved to New York City and to a town in rural New York State were studied over an eight-month period. Due to the limitations of space and the illustrative power of the urban situation, the 45 newcomers to the New York will be the focus of the following discussion.

The experiences of these newcomers reveal an essential characteristic of environmental experience: that it is an active creative process. Rather than adapting to or habituating himself to environmental properties, the urban newcomer actively chooses and utilizes certain opportunities from the range which he perceives. It is through these decisions and through his actions that the individual creates his experience of the new environment. The experiences he has will affect, in turn, his subsequent decisions and actions as well as his perception of what opportunities are available.

The urban newcomers reported that before they moved, they had deliberately weighed the advantages and the disadvantages of attending graduate school in New York; they arrived at a definite decision concerning not only their choice of graduate school but also their choice of environment. Upon arrival an active searching and a testing of environmental contingencies were reflected in their efforts to learn their way around the new setting. The amount of exploring that was done, as measured by the number of particular places a newcomer had visited, was clearly associated with his sense of how well he knew his way around. Those newcomers who reported a relatively low degree of such knowledge had visited significantly fewer places than those who had reported a higher degree of environmental knowledge. Newcomers described conscious strategies they had used in order to increase this knowledge. These strategies illustrate the active, searching quality of gaining knowledge of a new environment: asking questions; casually walking around; sightseeing or deliberate exploring; studying maps and trying to master transportation routes; purposely trying to become familiar with new areas in which they happened to be. These actions that were undertaken to learn one's way around led to a new way of experiencing the environment; that is, the need to actively orient oneself was no longer the focus of activity, and the newcomer's feelings toward the environment changed. After gaining greater knowledge, newcomers reported increased feelings of confidence.

More than half of the urban group reported that they experienced more tension living in New York than living in other places. Pollution, noise, the sight of poverty and the rushed, cold behavior of people on the street were frequently cited as sources of stress. However, the newcomer to the city did not habituate himself passively to the tension and stress he experienced. Instead, he dealt with these experiences in a more active and deliberate manner through the use of strategies that included: increased vigilance and safety precautions, the attempt to repress the negative qualities of life in the city and to concentrate on the positive ones, and trying to be friendly. As this last strategy suggests, the newcomers directed time and energy into establishing friendships. Urban newcomers perceived a difficulty in meeting people and establishing close relationships in the city, and there is some indication that they attempted to compensate for this difficulty. For example, one-fifth of the newcomers reported becoming more outgoing or friendly in order to meet people, and one-fourth of the group invited friends to their homes and visited friends in turn on a weekly basis. As the year progressed, they spent more time with friends and less time studying. In terms of orienting himself, dealing with tension, and making friends, the urban newcomer was actively constructing an existence that would allow him to fulfill future goals.

Newcomers' expectations about people and life in the city were an integral part of their experience in the new environment. More than half of the urban newcomers reported that they had held negative expectations about the people in New York, and about one-quarter of them reported negative expectations about living in the city. The expectations were often vivid and sometimes extreme: "I was scared as hell"; "I thought it would be exciting and grim"; "I expected to die the first day." Such expectations did have an emotional impact on the newcomer's experience and also set constraints on his actions; several newcomers reported being quite nervous during the first few days, waiting anxiously for their expectations to be fulfilled, and a few did not leave their immediate surroundings during that period.

However, the expectations often were not fulfilled. More than half of the group reported that people in New York were not as unpleasant as they had expected, and more than one-fourth of them found that living in the city was not as bad as they had expected. The contradiction between a negative expectation and a positive experience often increased the positive affect of that experience. For example, one respondent wrote in his diary:

> The most pleasant and unexpected thing was three of the other couples on this floor introduced themselves and invited us to coffee. Really hadn't expected that.

Discovering parks or patches of grass and trees was also pleasurable, partly because it contradicted the expectation of a dreary, asphalt city. We would also hypothesize that this type of contradiction would lead to new guidelines for action since the perception of environmental contingencies has changed. However, such a direct consequence is not easily demonstrated; one newcomer did change his guidelines based not on a new perception of contingencies but rather on the intolerableness of his existence. He wrote:

> I am now willing to go out after dark. I have no rational justification for this idiocy, but I cannot live eternally within a fortress.

A few weeks later he wrote:

> To an extent the tension has decreased, but you can't stay on panic alert all the time. I do expect to die in the city . . . but you can't run like a rabbit all the time, so you just wait for it to happen and you become fatalistic.

The dramatic fulfillment of a negative expectation seemed to intensify the negative affect of that experience. One respondent wrote:

> In the hotel the guy there fit my stereotype of what a New Yorker would be like perfectly. He talked very fast, seemed to be doing five things at once and snapped at me.

Similarly, a professor's murder by three teenagers was a shock partly because it epitomized the newcomers' expectations about the imminence of crime and death in New York. One might question how such experiences would influence later decisions and actions; there is some indication that newcomers did become more distrustful and cynical. The point is that expectations are constantly being fulfilled and contradicted, so that affect as well as guidelines for action will be in a corresponding state of change. Expectations, affect, perception of environmental contingencies, and guidelines for action are woven into environmental experience in complex and changing ways.

Another mode of experiencing a new environment is the sense of being at home in it. About half of the newcomers began to consider their apartments "home" during the first week after arrival. The reasons they gave for this feeling include: having personalized it; identifying with it or feeling a sense of ownership; and having met people. The relationship between the sense of home and other modes of environmental experience presents an interesting area are further investigation. It may be that those people who gained this sense soon after arrival were more able to explore the larger environment and to deal with the tension and the stresses they encountered.

The process of experiencing and dealing actively with the new environment seemed to alter the newcomer's sense of himself. More than three-quarters of the groups felt differently about themselves after living in New York for eight months, and almost all of them felt they had grown personally from the experience. Some of the other changes they reported were: increased independence and self-reliance; a broadening of perspective; becoming more cynical and fatalistic; and becoming more defensive or distrustful.

It may be that the newcomer's experience of the urban environment involves a greater degree of deliberate activity and choice and also a greater amount of affect and personal change than does the experience of a less urban setting. Our results comparing experiences in the two settings do indicate such a difference, although the difference is only in degree, for the nonurban newcomers' experiences also reflected the active and affective characteristics discussed here. The novelty of an environment may also increase the degree and salience of these characteristics. Thus, the intensity or salience of the affect which is part of environmental experience and the extent of personal change which is generated may be influenced by the relative novelty of that environment and be the perceived nature of it. Clearly, the nature of the actions undertaken would be similarly influenced.

CHARACTERISTICS OF ENVIRONMENTAL EXPERIENCE

The results of these and other environmental studies show a number of common characteristics that suggest a direction for the understanding of environmental experience. The first and most salient is that environmental experience is an active process in which the individual utilizes his resources in order to create a situation in which he can carry out his activities with a maximum of satisfaction. Within this overall process, however, several distinct characteristics concurrently can be observed. It is our hypothesis that any specific instance of environmental experience can be analyzed in terms of these four characteristics. Indeed, people in their daily experiences use these levels of analysis to understand their own experience. Thus, these characteristics reflect the subject's theorizing as well as the investigator's.

Orientation

The establishment of orientation within the environment is an important characteristic of all environmental experience. Orientation is the process of establishing a locus in the world, of finding a basis for one's relationship to the world. The clearest example is orientation in space, which means finding a place or set of places in the physical environment from which one's activities can be directed. The identification of escape routes is perhaps the most primitive form of orientation in space and becomes more elaborate in the development of complex cognitive maps. The field experiment of orientation in subways is one empirical example of orientation in physical space. However, orientation also occurs with respect to other people and with respect to one's emotional attachment to places and things. This is illustrated by the experiences of the newcomers, by their exploration of the environment, by the development of friendships, and by their attachment to particular places in the city.

Categories for Analysis

Another characteristic of environmental experience is the development of a taxonomy for the environment that, in a sense, is never completed by the individual. The categories an individual develops are not imposed by the external situation but are largely governed by goals, predispositions, and generalized expectations; they always relate to the individual's own pattern of needs and activities and become progressively more differentiated over time. In the novel environment laboratory, what was initially perceived as a mass of stimulation was gradually separated into distinct classes by the subjects—the most global classes being lights, mirrors, colors, and sounds. Then a subject may have divided the environment further into certain types of sounds and certain types of lights. In the field experiment as well as in the naturalistic study, the development of categories of trains was very important for understanding and using the subway system. In the naturalistic study, several newcomers were surprised to discover the difference between local and express trains; the differentiation between different lines would constitute another set of categories. Again, it should be clear that categories are not limited to a taxonomy of the physical environment; we also use categories for understanding other people, their actions and emotions and our own.

Analysis of Environmental Contingencies

Predictable sequences of events are identified and separated from random or unique occurrences. Casual connections are postulated and verified. The complex set of interrelationships between aspects of the environment and between the individual and the environment are gradually brought into order and harmony. Like the development of categories, this is a never-ending process since any environmental situation potentially provides an almost unlimited set of contingencies. The individual develops and seeks out those that are related to his own goals and activities.

In the novel environment laboratory, some subjects realized that their actions triggered off the vibrations of the mirrors; in this sense they had learned a set of environmental contingencies. The urban newcomer developed many sets of contingencies, such as: "If I become more friendly and outgoing, I will make more friends" and "If I take certain precautions such as not going out at night, I will not be mugged." In this way one's analysis of environmental contingencies leads to the development of guidelines for action in the environment.

Purposeful Action

The individual is never passive in his experience of the environment; he acts within and is part of the situation as he tries to achieve his particular goals. The pattern of orientation, categories, and contingencies he develops will affect the kinds of action he undertakes. These actions, in turn, will alter other characteristics in a continuing process through which the individual actively creates the situation within which he has his experience.

MODES OF EXPERIENCING THE ENVIRONMENT

Characteristics, as we have outlined them, are analytic categories for understanding the ongoing process of environmental experience. Modes provide another approach to environmental experience; they are an attempt to clarify the more phenomenological nature of that experience. Modes are descriptions of the experience itself. The difference, then, is that characteristics are ways of analyzing experiences and modes are ways of experiencing the environment. The determinants of a particular mode are not yet clear, but they probably include the goals one sets for oneself and the actions undertaken to reach these goals. Following is a preliminary suggestion of possible primary modes.[3]

Environment as an External Physical Place

The developmental psychologists tell us that the infant initially does not make the distinction between himself and his surroundings. As a matter of fact, the differentiation of self from environment is an accomplishment of some magnitude in the earlier stages of our personal development, and if we can take the developmental psychologists' word for it, it is an essential requirement for effective functioning in the world. They tell us that one must have a sense of an autonomous self which is separate from a surrounding environment or one cannot function in the world. To experience the environment as an external place thus conforms to the individual developmental pattern all of us have gone through, as well as to the cultural pattern of preconceptions we described earlier and which undoubtedly was shared by all our subjects.

To a certain extent, all of the subjects experienced the environment as something out there, detached from themselves and existing independently of

[3] This system of categories is derived from the work of D. Geoffrey Hayward (Hayward, 1975).

them. For some, however, this was the salient and dominant mode of experiencing the environment. Those people who gave structural descriptions of the novel environment laboratory seemed to have experienced that environment primarily in terms of its physical properties, the lights, the sounds, and the reflected images. These people also became more aware of the consequences of their own actions upon the sequence of changing properties than those who seemed to experience the environment in terms of their own feelings. Relatedly, in order to learn their way around the city, newcomers in the naturalistic study focused on the relationships between streets and transportation routes, on the physical location of buildings and services. Subjects in the field experiment also focused on the environment as a physical system in order to complete the task of reaching a given destination.

It may well be that this mode of experience facilitates or is necessary for the development of a sense of orientation in space and for an understanding of some environmental contingencies. Once a newcomer or a subject in the laboratory has gained a sense of orientation and has grasped, to some extent, the relationships between physical elements, this mode may become less salient. There is some indication in the newcomer study that physical properties of the environment did become less salient over time.

The physical scientist is one investigator who takes the process of developing categories and analyzing environmental contingencies to a high level of abstraction. Certainly, in taking on those tasks and in applying the necessary instruments, he is defining and experiencing the environment as external, physical place. The scientific tradition, as well as the tasks and experience of every scientist, epitomizes the mode of environment as physical place.

Environment as Self

The experience of the environment most distant from that of the traditional scientist is that of the mystic in which a total merging of self and environment is accomplished, in which the strict boundary vanishes, and environment becomes self, and self, environment. Although such an extreme form of this mode is uncommon in Western experience, people often experience the environment as an important part of themselves, as an integral component of self-identity. In this mode the environment ceases to be something detachable from the person, since the very act of detaching it changes the person into something else. A change in the environment is experienced as a change in the self. To a certain extent this is a familiar mode to most of us. If a cherished object, for example, is lost or stolen, we sense that some part of ourselves is gone. Newcomers reported that certain possessions which they brought with them such as books, furnishings, and mementos made their apartments personal for them. Such possessions, as well as a personalized space, may be important sources of support and familiarity in a new environment; in this sense they function as ways of orienting oneself in an emotional sense.

However, the mode of experiencing the environment as self is not only identification with physical objects or with physical properties of the world. It is also the deep sense of identification with other people in the environment, with one's experience of the environment and with one's actions in and upon it. This identification with the total environment in which one is living can be so deep and sustaining that separation from it brings severe grief and self-doubt as in Fried's study of people who were forced to move from the West End (1973).

When one chooses to move to a new environment, as in the case of the newcomers to New York, the sense of identification with one's experiences and actions in the new environment may lead to changes in one's self-identity. In New York, after dealing with various sources of stress, newcomers described changes in themselves such as becoming more cynical and more fatalistic.

The developmental psychologists, in emphasizing the development of barriers between the self and the environment as an important and necessary part of the development of the infant, have perhaps stopped too soon in their analysis.[4] There may indeed be a further developmental step involving a reintregration with the surroundings, a sense no longer of autonomy from but a sense of belonging to and being part of the environment. The mature adult, having made the distinction between self and environment, now regains a sense of identity with the world around him and breaks down the barriers he so painfully constructed. This is a process that some people undoubtedly go through and that may indeed represent a further developmental step. It is the work of the mature adult, as opposed to the work of the developing infant, and is suggested as a way of explaining one mode of environmental experience.

Environment as Social System

For some people the environment seems to be experienced neither as an external physical entity nor as part of the self, but rather as a separately existing, autonomous social system or cultural network. For them the physical setting drops almost completely out of awareness, and the social interrelationships form the salient and perhaps only element of environmental experience. An individual may describe his life situation primarily in terms of the people he knows, the people he works with and his relationships with his family; his environment would seem to be other people. The social scientist frequently

[4] This line of thought is adapted from the work of Natalia Krawetz.

defines the environment as a social system in much the same way that the physical scientist defines it as an external, physical system.

A particular situation may lead a person to experience the environment primarily in terms of his relationships with other people. Being in a new environment is one example; newcomers to New York were highly concerned with establishing satisfying relationships. During times of personal crisis such as death or divorce, one's relationships with others may also become the dominant mode of experience.

Environment as Emotional Territory

The direct emotional impact of a situation is probably part of all environmental experience, but sometimes affect becomes the dominant mode of experience so that a certain environment is experienced solely in terms of the emotions and associations that one feels. It is the experiences of the poet and the artist that reflect the environment as emotional territory; for them this mode of environment as emotion is not only a theme but also an inspiration.

Most of us have particular familiar environments for which the principal experiential mode is emotional. Returning to a childhood home as an adult brings back vivid associations; each room possesses myriad clues to forgotten events, and the smells alone seem to bring back entire years of experience. Environments can thus become deeply associated with particular events; being in that environment may rekindle the emotions that were part of the original experience of the event.

A novel environment as well as a long-forgotten one may be experienced in affective terms. The newcomers experienced considerable affect in the dramatic fulfillment or contradiction of their expectations. We can hypothesize that there are some people for whom the environment takes on the form of an emotional territory on a continuing basis. Those subjects who described the novel environment laboratory in terms of their own feelings and moods may also experience other environments primarily in the context of their emotions.

Environment as Setting for Action

We have emphasized the importance of action in relation to environmental experience and that experience and purposeful action cannot be separated. However, this can become dominant, and the environment is then experienced exclusively or primarily as a setting within which action takes place. In this mode the environment is analogous to a stage that has significance only because it makes it possible for the actors to carry out their roles. This mode of seeing the environment only as a setting for action is exemplified by the activities of laymen and professionals who create and evaluate environments in terms of how those environments will enable participants to carry out certain actions or meet certain goals. Buildings are designed and cities are planned with respect to experience, with the emphasis only on the completion of actions and the reaching of goals and without consideration of the individual's experience in carrying out those actions.

It is through action that people experience environments. Indeed, action and experience are inseparable; current experience will influence future actions, and consequently, future experience in a never-ending process. One's goals and the particular actions undertaken to reach them are probably important in determining which mode of experience occurs. Hence, when the action to be undertaken is clearly defined for a person, as in the case of research where the investigator assigns a task to the subject, the mode that is experienced will be partly determined by the task. It is essential for researchers to be aware of the variety of modes of environmental experience and to assign tasks that are compatible with the modes under investigation.

The three studies discussed here enable us to illustrate how different research objectives affect the task that is defined for the subject and consequently the kind of modes he experiences. The aim of the laboratory study and the newcomer study was to understand the dynamics of all possible modes of environmental experience. Therefore, the researchers avoided any task requirements that would restrict the range of experiential modes. They attempted to elicit the full range of environmental experiences of the subjects by assigning the subjects the task of reporting on all their experiences. In the controlled field experiment, the objective was to understand individuals' experiences of spatial orientation within a public transportation system. The task—to reach certain destinations in the shortest possible time—was based on the assumption and the expectation that the subjects would view the task as an orientation problem in a real, external setting-for-action. Experiences and actions were interpreted in terms of this task-defined environment. The aims of research and the task requirements will affect both the modes of environmental experience and the interpretation of the data.

SUMMARY

We have suggested a methodology that, first, tries to make explicit our commonly shared presuppositions about the nature of environment so that these presuppositions will not necessarily color and determine the conclusions of our study, and that, secondly, emphasizes a different set of assumptions. We have also suggested a series of studies in a variety of simulations with emphasis on the study of novel situations in order to bring to the fore the salient elements of environmental experience. We have briefly described three studies: a laboratory investigation of a novel situation, a field experiment, and a naturalistic study of newcomers to the city. From the results of these and other studies, we suggest characteristics of environmental experience and specific modes of experiencing the environment. While all of the details remain open for modification in the course of future study, we believe that one conclusion is inescapable: Environmental experience is the continuing product of an active endeavor by the individual to create for himself a situation within which he can optimally function and achieve his own particular pattern of satisfaction. We believe it is particularly important for us as scientists not to accept any particular mode of environmental experience as representing a true picture of the environment, but rather to emulate the individual and to develop a view of the environment that will optimally enable us to carry out our goals both as students and as concerned human beings.

ACKNOWLEDGMENTS

This work was supported in part by the following grants: Faculty Research Award Program of City University of New York, Grant #1098, 1383; National Institute of Mental Health, Grant #MH12441; National Institute of Mental Health, Grant #MH24795; and National Science Foundation, Grant #GZ-2606.

REFERENCES

Bronzaft, A., Dobrow, S., and O'Hanlon, T. Spatial orientation in a subway system. *Environment and Behavior,* 1975. In press.

Franck, K. A., Unseld, C. T., and Wentworth, W. R. Adaptation of the newcomer: A process of construction. Unpublished manuscript, Environmental Psychology Program, City University of New York, 1974.

Fried, M. Grieving for a lost home. In L. J. Duhl (Ed.), *The urban condition.* New York: Basic Books, 1973.

Hayward, D. G. Individual concepts of home. Unpublished manuscript, Environmental Psychology Program, City University of New York, 1975.

Ittelson, W. H., and Krawetz, N. Further research in the novel environment laboratory. Unpublished manuscript, Environmental Psychology Program, City University of New York, 1975.

Libassi, P. Another part of the forest. *The Sciences,* 1975, *15,* 6–10.

Medwar, P. What's human about man is his technology. *The Smithsonian,* 1973, *4,* 22–29.

Nahemow, L. Research in a novel environment. *Environment and Behavior,* 1971, *3,* 81–102.

Schiff, A. *Fire and water.* Cambridge, Massachusetts: Harvard University Press, 1962.

X

Exploratory Applications of the Organismic–Developmental Approach to Transactions of Men-in-Environments

BERNARD KAPLAN, SEYMOUR WAPNER, and
SAUL B. COHEN[1]

Abstract: A variety of techniques issuing from the organismic–developmental approach to transactions of men-in-environments are described and critically evaluated in this paper. The major paradigm characterizing all of the studies deals with entrance and adaptation to new environments. The *single-frame analysis* is illustrated by several studies with subjects varying in age and race, and with environments ranging in scale from a room to a large institutional setting. The *frame-sequence analysis* is illustrated by two cases of temporary migrants to a new country in two environmental settings. *Group debriefing* is illustrated by a constructed case history of a brief professional task-oriented migration. From one technique to the next, the boundaries between subject and experimenter are progressively blurred. The roles of subjects range from being passive respondents to participants and finally to participant-experimenters. The role of investigators range from preparing the instruments for "others to use" to cooperating with participants in determining the character and significance of the transactional experience.

[1] With the collaboration of William Clark, Patricia Dandonoli, Eric Edelman, Ogretta McNeil, Dorothy Pemstein, Amram Pruginin, Jill Rierdan, and Liza Wofsey.

BERNARD KAPLAN, SEYMOUR WAPNER, and SAUL B. COHEN • Clark University, Worcester, Massachusetts.

In our first paper (Wapner, Kaplan, and Cohen, 1973), we sketched a general perspective and introduced a number of procedural guidelines, in terms of which we intended to explore problems of man–environment transactions; we also outlined several paradigms of inquiry. On that occasion, we were still operating under the "onlooker" conception of the scientist, in which the investigator is a value-free observer of what takes place in nature. Since that time, we have reflected on this kind of posture, and decided that we were not solely concerned with finding out about things. We wanted to be explicit about certain ulterior goals, which we all shared, and which we wished to insinuate into our program of research. This decision has really come to us in the process of examining and questioning the studies we have undertaken during this past year, in the process of asking "why" we have undertaken each of these studies.

In these processes of reflection, we have recognized that we are not simply interested in value-free research in the social and human sciences. We are concerned with knowing about the nature of men–environment transactions in order to enable individuals to improve the quality of such transactions and to liberate themselves from various kinds of bondage, to enable them to enrich their experiences of their surroundings, and where necessary to act to change environments that hamper their lives.

In other words, there is, ingredient in our perspective, an intertwining of policy considerations and empirical research. As will be seen, in our discussion of the studies to be reported, these policy considerations play a significant role in the critique of some of our own work that was in process before these considerations were articulated.

In these studies, all undertaken during the past 18 months or so, we adopted traditional techniques and tried to develop new ones. They were all intended to yield adequate characterizations of the ways in which individuals construe their environments in the process of transactions with such environments. These techniques, and the kinds of tasks involved in their application, differed in the range, scope, and depth of activities and responsibilities allowed to the participants. In techniques where our focus was on the comparability of responses from the various subjects, we emphasized the use of a circumscribed and relatively fixed set of tasks and materials that demanded of the subjects responses that had to fall within our *a priori* categories of analysis. On the other hand, in techniques where our focus was on the complex transactions, construals and experiences of individuals, the tasks were more open-ended, allowing for a variety of personal expressions. It follows from the employment of these different kinds of techniques that the participants sometimes functioned merely as the typical subject in the typical psychological experiment; and at other times functioned in the role of a co-experimenter. Finally, some techniques allowed only for a cross-sectional spotlighting of one or more abstract features of transactions, whereas others permitted the reconstruction of changing and evolving transactions and construals.

SINGLE-FRAME ANALYSIS

In the first set of studies, we explored the relationships between certain general variables (e.g., agent status, nature of the audience, etc.) and punctiform construals of environments. We here put into operation some of the paradigms discussed in our earlier paper, selecting one or two of the procedural principles to determine their isolated "effect." Let us now discuss some inquiries reflecting this approach.

Edelman, Rierdan, and Wapner (1973)

The chief issue in the studies carried out by Edelman *et al.* was the effect of different kinds of audiences on the representation of environmental transactions. How does a direction to communicate one's experience of a global milieu to different "receivers" affect the structure and content of the communications? Specifically, they were concerned with the differences in verbal representations of environments when these representations were addressed to: (a) one's self; (b) a relatively intimate other person; (c) a nonintimate other.

The subjects were college students. They were requested to write a brief (10–15 lines) characterization of their university environment for: (a) themselves; (b) an intimate other; and (c) a nonintimate other. The protocols of the subjects were analyzed in terms of certain categories, partly derived from earlier investigations (Werner and Kaplan, 1963), partly derived from a scrutiny of the responses. The representations for the different audiences differed significantly in the first study and in the replication along the following dimensions of interest to us in the present context.

1. Egocentricity–exocentricity (with regard to reference): focusing on one's needs, reactions, and desires in relation to aspects of the environment as opposed to focusing on the environment as an entity existing apart from one's self.
2. Idiomaticity–conventionality (with regard to expression): using personal idiosyncratic terms to characterize persons and places as opposed to using conventional, communal expressions.
3. Associative–informative (with regard to mode of thinking): going from

the objects to one's feelings, ideas, and associations to the objects as opposed to relating the objects to each other in terms of spatial relations, functional relations, etc.

4. Involved–detached (with regard to affectivity): going from the expression of strong, intense feelings—e.g., excitement, agitation, despair, etc.—as opposed to the absence of such affective expressions.

5. Ambivalence–univalence (with regard to attitude): going from an oscillation between positive and negative feelings concerning the environment to the unequivocal expression of one or another attitude.

Characteristically, representations for the self were more egocentric, idiomatic, associative, involved, and ambivalent than representations for nonintimate-others. The representations for intimate-others were typically in between.

There are several points we would like to make about this study. First, it was undertaken prior to our recognition and formulation of our goals in inquiry. It was a kind of "let's see what happens" study. We were trying to find out how individuals construe their transactions with environments in multiple ways, and to suggest that these different ways ("multiple worlds") become manifest only with respect to different "priming" audiences or interlocutors. Reflection on this study and our analysis of it has suggested to us a clarification of the concept of "construal of the environment." It is not possible to obtain an unmediated construal of an environment, even for one's self. Such construals are always mediated through some medium of representation or are always evoked by some auditor (tacit or otherwise). One could assume, of course, a single construal that is variably expressed. We prefer to maintain a conception of multiple construals, including in the concept of construal the mode of mediation and the nature of the auditor.

This suggests that an environment for an individual is not in any way a simple matter. An environment—let us give a provisional formulation—is constituted by the individual's needs, internalized constraints and taboos, tasks either self-assigned or assigned by others, conventional prescriptions and proscriptions as to action in a particular milieu, present companions, and internalized alter egos. These factors, among others, we believe, affect not only how one represents the environment but how one perceives it and acts within it. Changes in these factors ensue in "multiple worlds."

McNeil and Wapner (1974)

The first of a series of studies carried out by McNeil and Wapner (1974) was directed toward understanding how "outsiders" and "insiders," with respect to the membership within a particular milieu, construe this environment for varied kinds of addressees. In addition, this study asked not only for verbal representations or construals, but also for pictorial representations. This is, of course, a much more complicated situation than that involved in the Edelman *et al.* inquiries. The protocols are now in the process of being analyzed.

The subjects in this study were black and white female college students, residents in an institution that until recently had not only solely white students, but solely male students. Both samples were therefore, to some degree, "outsiders," but the black group was distinctly more remote from the center than the white group. As in the studies by Edelman *et al.* (1973) the subjects were asked to represent their environments for self, intimate other, and nonintimate other; this was to be done both verbally and pictorially. The experimenter in this study was a black female professor.

In the analysis, we expect to follow, as far as possible, the dimensions considered in the Edelman *et al.* studies. Do the black and white students differ, under the various audience conditions and between audience conditions in the salient features to which they refer? Do they differ in the mode of expression? Do they differ in mode of thinking (associative versus informative)? Do they differ in degree of involvement–detachment? Do they differ in terms of homogeneity of attitude toward the environment?

Irrespective of these categories of analysis, and the findings that may be derived from their application, there were very striking differences between the two groups in the pictorial representations of their environments. In Figures 1 and 2, we present a typical "sequence" of the drawings of white students and black students for (a) self, (b) intimate other, and (c) nonintimate other.

As one can see, one white student, for self, represents a two-person positive interaction as characterizing the environment; for an intimate other, she depicts her personal "home on campus," again revealing positive social interaction as well as a clear articulation of her immediate ambiance: The room she shares is well laid out and the various parts are marked off and related to each other; for the distant other, there is presented an aerial view of the campus that captures the spatial relationships of the various buildings on the campus. There is an increasing "distancing" in these depictions, personal reactions and emotions progressively excluded.

In the case of a black student, the representation for the self focuses on the isolation of the individual, the environment as a "prison," the felt desperation of the person; the representation by another student for an intimate other, reveals the experience of the environment as one consisting of uniformly contented others, hostile to one's self; the only aspect of the environment represented is "social-emotional." Finally, in representing the environment for a distant other, one black student depicted leaves and snow ("a cold environment" expressed in objective correlative terms) without any indication of the

A. For Self

B. For Intimate Other

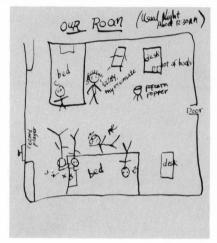

C. For Nonintimate Other

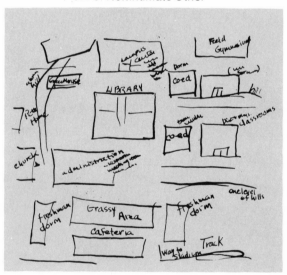

Figure 1. Drawings by white students.

A. For Self

B. For Intimate Other

C. For Nonintimate Other

Figure 2. Drawings by black students.

objective characteristics of that environment, viz., no buildings, no relations among places, etc.

This study, like the first one, was also a "let's see what happens" inquiry. Irrespective of the findings that may emerge on completion of the analysis, we now recognize that they can be of only limited significance with respect to the goals of our program. It is not now our concern to show merely that blacks differ from whites in their construals of a predominantly white-centered environment. It is not now our concern to demonstrate differences in the two groups in relation to varying audiences. If we find a "poor fit" between individuals and their environments, we want to know why there is this maladaptation and what is necessary to transform the situation to meliorate the lack of fittingness. In order to approach this goal, we must know more about the factors that enter into the different construals—the historical–biographical factors, attitudes toward self, stereotypes, expectations, fears, etc. We must know more about the real as contrasted with imagined constraints of the environment, the overt rules, and covert patterns of expectations that have come to constitute the environment over a period of years. These and other factors we did not take into account in our study. We have become aware that it is only with this kind of information that it becomes possible to interpret what is going on in transactions, what underlies the construals. Only then would it be possible to determine, at least in part, to what extent the construals are grounded in the reality of the situation; to what extent in the biographically based characteristics and attitudes of the agent, etc. Only then would it be possible to have some inkling of the changes that must be instituted in agent and/or environment to optimize the fit between the two in a way that will increase the enjoyment and self-determination of the individual and facilitate movement toward personal, intellectual and social maturity.

Wofsey, Rierdan, and Wapner (1974)

There is no question that individuals differ, in everyday life, in the extent to which they formulate their plans to leave a home environment for a novel milieu. The issue addressed in this set of studies by Wofsey *et al.* (1974) was whether this variation in explicit formulation of plans affects how one construes the base environment in which one is still located. Does an imaginative projection of activities, etc., in a new environment do something to the saliency of the features of the current milieu? Does it change the affective relationships the individual has to the base environment?

In one study, eight subjects who had spent seven or eight consecutive semesters at the same university, already had clearly articulated plans and goals as to what they would be doing and where they would be following graduation. Another group of eight subjects, comparable with respect to length and continuity of stay in the university, had no such formulated plans. They did not know what they were going to do subsequent to departure. Members of both groups, as well as two independent groups of eight subjects each in a replication study were asked to represent their university environment (home environment) both verbally and pictorially.

There was a consonance between the verbal representations and the drawings. In both cases, the individual with plans tended to represent the university in a more impersonal, more "objective," more psychologically distant manner. This is reflected in the findings for the drawings, which are summarized in Figure 3. Illustrations are given of drawings made by: a subject lacking articulated plans (A, upper left); a subject having articulated plans (B, upper right); a subject possessing semi-articulated plans (C, lower left); and a subject with highly articulated plans (D, lower right). Drawing A exemplifies behavioral indices indicative of lesser self–world distancing (e.g., the subject waves to friends he is leaving behind; three-dimensional perspective employed); drawing B exemplifies the categories indicative of greater self–world distancing (e.g., maplike, aerial view); drawing C exemplifies elements from both categories of self–world relations (e.g., maplike, aerial view yet containing three-dimensional perspective); finally, drawing D, from a subject with highly articulated plans shows an extreme of self–world distancing (e.g., the university is characterized as a dot located on the Western Hemisphere, as if viewed remotely from the moon). The following verbal representation by "planless" subjects reveals the lack of distance of such subjects from the home environment: "The university is my refuge." "The university is my second home." "I must prepare myself vocationally for the cold cruel *terra firma* out there." "The university is a place where one can develop lasting friendships." "The university is part of me."

Of considerable interest in this study were the subjects from the first study who moved from a "planless" to a "planful" future in the course of the inquiry. In such instances, there was a clear-cut movement with respect to the home environment from immersion to distance in both drawings and verbal representations. There was also one individual who had certain formulated projects that fell through in the course of the inquiry. He reverted from more distant representations to less distant ones.

Through an examination of the verbal protocols and our interpretation of the pictorial representations, we have tried to reconstruct an idealized picture of stages in transition from one environment to a new one.

In Stage 1, an individual inhabits an environment and has no plans to leave this environment. The orientation of the individual *vis-à-vis* this environment is assumed to involve a relative lack of self–world distancing; this orientation is assumed to mediate an experience of the environment as familiar and meaningful, and an experience of the self as embedded in the environment.

A. **S** lacking articulated plans

B. **S** with articulated plans

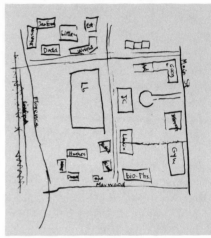

C. **S** with semiarticulated plans

D. **S** with highly articulated plans

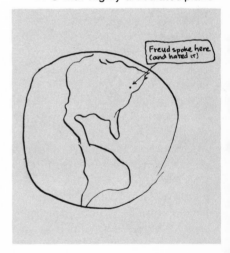

Figure 3. Drawings by students with future plans varying in degree of articulation.

In Stage 2, an individual inhabits an environment but is planning and anticipating a move to a new locale. The individual is, so to speak, on the threshold of transition. The individual's orientation *vis-à-vis* the currently inhabited environment is assumed to involve some degree of self–world distancing and is assumed to mediate an experience of the environment as relatively apart from the self, and as relatively lacking in meaning and significance.

In Stage 3, an individual inhabits a new environment and has plans to remain in this new environment. The individual, however, is in what Schutz (1971) calls "a crisis of transition": The individual is an estranged outsider who must orient to and interpret the cultural pattern of the new social group, thereby structuring the new environment; such an individual seems to correspond to what Park (1928) and Stonequist (1935) call a "marginal man." Physically removed and psychologically distanced from the old environment, and physically located in but not yet integrated in the new environment, the attitude of the "marginal man" is assumed to be one of distance and detachment; the "self-world" orientation is assumed to mediate construal of the new environment as ". . . a thing apart from themselves" (Nahemow, 1971).

In Stage 4, an individual inhabits a new environment, is integrated within this environment, and has no plans to move. It is assumed that the individual's orientation *vis-a-vis* the environment involves a relative lack of self–world distancing (as in Stage 1) that mediates construal of the "new," currently inhabited environment as familiar, meaningful, manageable, and secure.

In our reflections on this and the other studies, where we have dealt with the transition from a base environment to a new one, we have spoken of a process of distancing from the (old) environment. Earlier we have suggested that the concept of a personal environment requires considerable clarification, and cannot be identified with the geographic–physical–sociological "environment" as specified by detached investigators. A personal environment is a constellation of "meanings," some of them exemplified in actual objects, places, and persons; of expectancies, of internalized constraints and possibilities of movement all reflected for the individual in the objects, persons, and places surrounding him/her.

In this context, distancing involves the detachment of de-cathexis of persons, places, and things. In other words, our work suggests to us that the next step in articulating the concept of distancing and in giving it some depth will take us into the problems partly treated by analysts. It also suggests to us that we must develop concepts to deal with the construal of environment in what Werner and Kaplan (1963) have designated as "physiognomic properties"—repulsion, attraction, heaviness, enticing.

The studies we have discussed thus far were analyzed primarily in terms of a concept of "distancing." Tentatively, it seems to us that transactions with environments are construed more impersonally, more "distantly," more neutrally, where the audience for a representation is nonintimate, where the agent is relatively secure in his/her environment, where the agent is relatively secure concerning his/her plans in leaving the environment. There is no question for us that the global concept of "distancing" requires considerable articulation and clarification. It is now a general cover term for what we believe to be a variety of different processes.

A. Photograph of miniature model of experimental room and objects

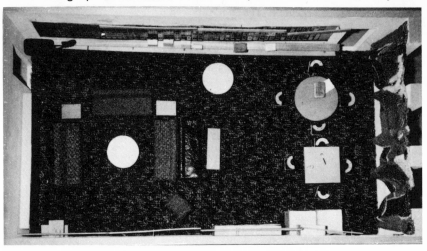

B. Classification Task

Child   Adult

C. Memory Reconstruction Task

Child   Adult

Figure 4. Age differences in construal of a multifunctional room.

Dandonoli, Clark, and Wapner (1974)

In this study, we were primarily concerned with the determination of qualitative differences in the construal of environments by individuals of different ages (specifically children versus adults). The experimental environment we set for these two groups was a "multifunctional" room in the Psychology Department at Clark University (Figure 4A). The subjects entered and explored this room for a limited time. They were then taken outside the room and asked: (a) verbally to recall the room—"Please tell me everything about the room that you can remember"; (b) to group miniature object replicas of the items in the room into "groups which belong together"; and (c) to regroup the miniature object replicas into an alternate grouping. Following these steps, they were asked: (d) to arrange the miniature object replicas in the model of the room to duplicate the arrangement of the room to which they had been exposed; and (e) to state whether a number of individual or group behaviors were appropriate for the room.

In the process of writing up the findings for this inquiry, we became aware of a number of flaws in the study. We shall resume the findings and then discuss the flaws, hopefully setting the stage for a more adequate inquiry.

One finding elicited by the request to recall the room was that adults recalled significantly more objects in the room than did the children. This is scarcely a surprising finding. A second finding was that the recall of items was in terms of kinds of objects for children, e.g., three tables, two sofas; for adults, the recall was in terms of functional grouping. The grouping of miniature object replicas revealed the same pattern: The children (six to eight) tended to group the miniature objects in terms of specific perceptual characteristics—a group of round tables, a group of square tables, a group of blue sofas, etc. (Figure 4B). In contrast, the adults typically grouped the miniature objects into socially functional unitary wholes; e.g., chair, table, sofa, and other objects as a setting for social interaction (Figure 4B).

In the memory task, in which the experienced room was to be duplicated in the miniature room, the findings were similar (Figure 4C). The children reconstructed the original room by clumping together similar objects, while the adults reconstructed the room in terms of functional wholes. It is important to note here—something we did not take into account at the beginning—that the room was already established within the department in terms of functional units; e.g., a conversation setting, a kitchen setting, etc.

With regard to the issue of appropriate and inappropriate behaviors in the setting, the children were oriented toward individual activity ("what I can do or want to do"); the adults were more oriented than the children to what can be done socially, even though they also could look at the room in terms of personal activity.

As we have already noted, we did not take cognizance of the fact that the experimental room was already biased in an adult-centric way. The room was organized in terms of functional wholes and thus fit in with adult modes of organization. Obviously, one of the things we have to do is to present a room that has no principle of functional organization, or present a child's room to both groups.

The "grouping tests" were also quite limited. There was no attempt really to assess the limits of alternative groupings either with children or adults. Would adults, if pushed, provide the kinds of groupings that children manifested? In the alternate grouping task it was interesting to note that the adults in the study had difficulty breaking down their functional groupings, but this may have been due to the tendency of the experimenter not to push for such groupings. The larger environment in which the experiment took place— viz., a school environment—may also have set certain unrecognized limits on what was done by both groups. There was in all cases a teacherlike authority (experimenter), not known to the participants, for whom they had to construe the environment.

FRAME-SEQUENCE ANALYSIS

The studies thus far, undertaken in terms of single-frame analysis (an atemporal relationship between abstracted variables), do not permit a reconstruction of the changing transactions of individuals with environments. In our attempt to provide a fuller and deeper representation of the transactions an individual participates in when entering and engaging a new environment, we thought it necessary to obtain some indices of the ostensibly changing relationships to such an environment from point of entry to point of exit. A traditional technique here is that of "time-sampling," viz., eliciting responses to a relatively fixed set of tasks at different time slices. We hoped that such a procedure would allow us, to a certain extent, to reconstruct experiential vicissitudes in the *process of adaptation* to a novel setting.

Cohen, Wapner, Pruginin, and Dandonoli (1974)

Our use of this technique will be exemplified here by two individual "cases," one from each of the two different groups of college students who were "temporary migrants." The members of one group spent a typical year abroad at Hebrew University, living in student dormitories or apartments near the institution, studying in a special program; within normal university constraints they could do whatever they wanted to do. The members of the second group were a sub-set of an American student aggregate who had enrolled in a work–university program, based at a kibbutz; they were required to live together in one dorm, to work thirty hours a week, and to adjust themselves to a fixed university regimen.

In attempting to reconstruct the processes of adaptation of the members of these two groups, we used the following instruments: (1) preliminary forms covering expectations; (2) personal comments forms, covering expectations prior to departure, experiences of different aspects of the environment at different times, etc.; (3) psychological distance maps, in which the participants were asked to represent their feelings of psychological closeness to places that constitute their psychological environments; (4) topographic maps of their new environments (Jerusalem, kibbutz); (5) activity logs, in which the participants were asked to note and characterize salient events at different times in their sojurn; (6) landscape impression checklists, to assess the changing saliencies of different environmental features; and (7) communication inventory (letters, telephone calls) to members of old and new environments. These different instruments were to be used by the participants at stipulated times.

The returns from this study are admittedly disappointing. Responses were often sketchy. Participants reported some disgruntlement, some grudging acquiescence, etc. Nevertheless, two participants provided us with sufficient material and sufficiently different kinds of material to exemplify the method, to suggest the strengths and weaknesses of this kind of approach, and to stimulate our concept formation.

The responses of the participants to the varied instruments were utilized to reconstruct different aspects of the person's changing relationships to both old and new environments in the process of coming to terms with the new environment. The aspects we were concerned with are reflected in the following questions: (1) Was there a change over time with regard to the operation of internalized constraints and expectations emanating from the old environment? To what extent did the old environment intrude into the new in the course of the person's stay in Israel? (2) Was there a change over time in the membership-feeling of the individual with respect to the old environment? To what extent did the individual feel now an outsider, now a member and participant at different phases of the stay? (3) Was there a change in the conception of the self during the process of coming to terms with the new environment? (4) Was there a change over time with regard to the diversity, range, and depth of the new environment to which the person was exposed? (5) Were there any effects on the ways in which the individual coped with the new environment over time as a consequence of presence or absence of discrepancy between expectations and experiences? It was these questions—partly emerging from the initial examination of the protocols—that guided our analysis of the responses and productions of the participants.[2]

Here now is our reconstruction of the two cases mentioned above.

Case X (Female Student in Kibbutz Program)

1. In the process of adapting to the new environment, X's relationship to the home environment, which had remained strong throughout, underwent a qualitative change; from a sense of bondage, she began to experience her home environment in a more benign way—an environment to which she could now relate positively and independently. This reconstruction was drawn chiefly from her responses to two instruments: (a) personal comments, and (b) psychological distance maps. In the middle of her stay, she recounts her feelings upon receiving an audio-tape and special letter from her father; it was, for her "a dramatic event." It led to her reflections on her past and present and culminated in the change of attitude mentioned before. At this point, her psychological distance maps undergo a change. The relation of home to herself becomes markedly closer.

2. With an increasing number of transactions with persons and places in the new environment, the sense of membership in the new environment progressively increased. The evidence here is drawn from all of the instruments. In the personal comments, there is specific reference to her desire to integrate, her strategies to achieve integration, her achievements in those goals. She describes in detail the development of the relationship with the "adopted" (kibbutz) family, which becomes closer, more sincere and meaningful with time. Her integration within the kibbutz is viewed by her as an expression of her integration with Israeli society in general. "Walls started to fall between me and my adopted family." On one occasion late in her stay after returning to the kibbutz, she states: "They (kibbutz people) were happy to see me back." "I feel like I really belong here, actually part of the goings on. The people really matter." "Now (June 8) I am looking from the eyes of one who is part of the kibbutz. If able to stay this feeling will grow . . . because of the Hebrew, I am taking part in more activities." In the psychological distance map, there is a dramatic decrease in distance between the circle that represents "me" on the map and the circle that represents the kibbutz; at the end of her stay the involvement is sharply represented by an overlapping of the "me" and "kibbutz" circles. In the topographic maps, there is a greater saliency of members' residences, children's homes. In the activity logs, there is a shift from early

---

[2] It may be noted that the instruments were chosen intuitively, and were not directly grounded in the questions we were later to address to the protocols. Our experience with this material will now enable us in subsequent studies to modify some of the instruments, develop others, etc., and thus be able to obtain less equivocal evidence from the protocols of subjects. This does not gainsay the need for open-ended items that allow for unexpected issues to emerge and lead to the formulation of new questions.

references to being watched closely by kitchen supervisors (she is the "outsider") to later references in which the people with whom she works treat her as an equal, act friendly, etc. In landscape impressions, she views the kibbutz principally in terms of place of joint communal activity rather than impersonal objects.

3. Throughout her stay at the kibbutz, X expressed her concern with her status as an adult person. Her sense of bondage to her family (noted above) was initially coupled with her resentment at being treated as a child. On the kibbutz, she experienced a transition from being regarded as "one of the American students" to being looked at as a co-worker expected to operate as an adult. In other words, there was in increasing sense of self-determination and independence. This was revealed principally in her personal comments; at the end of her stay, she remarked, "I feel so much my own person." There was also a somewhat ambiguous indication of her increasing sense of independence in her landscape impressions. The dormitory in which she lived with the other American students was first assimilated to "home"; later on, it is viewed as a place of noise and absence of privacy; finally, it is just another building in the kibbutz.

4. The main change that appears to take place in her experience of the environment pertains to the social-human features of the environment. The evidence relevant to this reconstruction has been presented above. Her landscape impressions indicate little change in the diversity, range, and significance of the nonhuman environment, or of the larger cultural network in which the kibbutz is set. There is, to be sure, in her topographic maps, evidence that she is organizing her immediate environment in a more integrated fashion: She connects functionally places on her maps.

5. X went to the kibbutz with the expectation that she and the other Americans would have to work hard in order to be accepted by the Israelis. She therefore set herself to work hard, and this activity—whether it was a realistic demand or not—facilitated her adaptation to the new environment and her sense of acceptance in the new environment. The expectations emerged from the preliminary form. The sense that her adaptation was facilitated emerged from her personal comments and activity logs: The acceptance by others often was experienced by her as having something to do with her accomplishments on the kibbutz. There was also some indication of the relation of work to adaptation in the topographic maps; the office of the kibbutz, in which work is assigned, is entered on the maps at earlier points in the representations of the life space.

Case Y (Male Student, University Program)

1. Y had a definite mission in mind in going to Israel: He wanted to enrich himself in terms of his studies, learn to improve his Hebrew, increase his

self-sufficiency, learn to adapt to a new environment away from home. From a superficial point of view—we had no instruments to assess depth—Y appears to be an extremely self-sufficient person. As far as could be determined from his protocols, his real home environment, although it might impinge on him externally, did not seem to intrude on his relations to the new context. From his personal comments and his activity logs, there is evidence that his family did come to visit him while he was in Israel, but he notes this contact did not alter his routine operations and observations. On the psychological distance maps, his home is represented only twice, in the initial map and the final map before returning home. The general picture that emerges is that he cut off the home base once he arrived, and resurrected it only when he was ready to leave.

It is important to point out that Y had relatives and friends in Israel. It may well be that the presence of such people in Israel constituted a vicarious home away from home, and dispensed with the necessity for any deep contacts with the home environment. On the psychological distance maps, friends and relatives are represented as close, especially at the beginning and end of the sojourn. Their places are also represented on the topographic maps.

2. Despite Y's desire to attain membership in the new environment, he experienced himself as failing to achieve such membership, identification, or participation. This striving and sense of "failure" is revealed in the personal comments and the psychological distance maps. In the personal comments, the opposition between "me and the public" runs throughout. Even the October War ordeal did not facilitate his integration into the community. He felt segregated from Israeli students and Israeli society. Most of his time was spent with other students or Americans who had settled in Israel. At the end, he stated, "I gave up the attempts to integrate." He blamed himself for that failure, defining himself as "marginal" and an "onlooker." The psychological distance maps reveal that throughout his stay, the closest thing to him is the dorm that he shares with other American students.

3. Throughout his stay, there was a concern with himself and his status. He experienced the external environments as challenges to himself, and reports frequently on experiences of triumph and self-esteem in overcoming environmental obstacles: He manages to convey information to a Russian family even in the absence of a common language; he makes his way into a mayor's office despite the bureaucratic barriers, etc. His self-esteem does not come from his membership in the environment, but rather from overcoming the barriers the environment places in the way of his doing what he wants to do. This information comes primarily from personal comments.

4. In his appreciation and comprehension of the new environment, Y shows a split. He shows an increasing sensitivity to the physical environment, a considerable range of exploration of the more distant areas away from the university, a recognition of interdependencies between people and things. On

the other hand, his relations to other people (Israelis) is essentially that of a detached onlooker. This material comes from landscape impressions, topographic maps, and personal comments.

5. Here there seemed to be a self-fulfilling prophecy operative. He expected—perhaps due to a basic attitude—to confront a frustrating, obstacle-filled environment. He expected diversity in the behaviors of people and diversity in the landscape. He also expected that he would have to alter his life-style somewhat in order to adapt. Throughout his stay, he seemed to be trying to confirm these expectations. The environment was found to be filled with obstacles and showed the diversity he expected. His learning to cope with the environment in large measure seems to stem from challenges to be overcome, challenges that demand greater knowledge of what is going on. The material relevant to this question comes from personal comments, psychological distance maps, and topographic maps. In the personal comments, he notes that his triumph over bureaucracy was one of the most significant achievements for him during his stay. Despite his frustrations, he could leave Israel with a sense of accomplishment in terms of the contributions of his varied experiences to his academic education. In the psychological distance maps, his identification with the "learning experience" as top priority is reflected in the centrality of the Hebrew University campus and dormitories. This is reinforced in the topographic maps; the university is the center from which all other places radiate.

From the reconstruction of these two cases, it seems to us that the instruments used were adequate for uncovering differences in the experiences and construals of environments where the individuals involved migrated with basically different attitudes. We also were able, to some degree, to link reconstructions with indices from the various instruments, although we recognize considerable ambiguity in this respect. Perhaps the major thing we have learned from this reconstruction derives from our struggle to link responses and productions of participants to general questions. We have recognized that it is extremely important in subsequent studies to refine our instruments in such a way as to elicit material that can more unequivocally answer the questions we address to the protocols.

Among other things, we recognized that in order to understand the nature of the transactions and environmental construals of individuals ("migrants") we must know much more about their life histories and attitudes than we had here anticipated. We must know more about their relationships with the members of the home base. We must know more about their habitual ways of coping with stress and novelty. We must know more about their below-the-surface expectations concerning the new environment. We must know more about their ties and aversions to others at home. We must know more about the complex of motives which lead them to "migrate."

These issues have led us to recognize the importance of developing new instruments (and modifying old ones) that will enable us to answer these kinds of questions. We need some kind of *self-status* inventory that will enable us to assess the changing conceptions of the self as a consequence of vicissitudes of transactions in the new environment. We need some kind of *attitude* survey that will enable us to determine whether the individuals are yea-sayers or nay-sayers in their approach to life. We need a more explicit *motivation* inventory, to ascertain the variety of reasons the individual has for migrating (or remaining at home). We need an instrument to determine habitual modes of *coping with stress*; e.g., flight, introversion, fantasy, increased activity, etc. (mechanisms of defense). Finally, we see the need for an inventory of *experience-curtailing and experience-facilitating* transactions: transactions with the environment that forestall other kinds of transactions, limit the range of exploration, turn the individual away from any tendencies toward full participation in the novel environment, as against transactions that allow for a sudden burst of exploratory activity in the new environment with regard to persons, places, and things.

DEBRIEFING ANALYSIS

Thus far, the studies we have presented have been carried out using more or less traditional techniques and dealing with relatively circumscribed aspects of men-in-environment transactions. There is one inquiry we have undertaken that exploits a technique developed in a military context for exploring what takes place on a temporary migration. We refer to the technique of "debriefing" following a mission: In this technique those who have remained at home (the experimenters) ask probing questions of the "migrant" to provoke the recollection of different kinds of experiences. In this process, the questions, comments, and reflections of a variety of "probers" tend to bring out diverse aspects of transactions, many of which may never come to light except in such a group debriefing context. In this process, the experimenters and participants play different roles during different phases. Prior to the "mission" (migration), the experimenters informed the participants of their general lines of interest: They were "pure experimenters." The instructions to the participant were open-ended: Keep a diary of your experiences with persons, places, and things in the process of leaving your home environment, in the process of transition to the new environment, while you are in the new environment, during the process of return, etc. Because of the open-ended character of the instructions, the participant, from the start, assumes responsibilities for direction of orientation, for selection of the transactions to encode and report, etc.: He or she is thus, from the beginning, a participant-experimenter. Once the mission is completed, and the debriefing begins, the experimenters become vicarious participants—many of their probing questions stemming from their theoretical interests, from their experiences as temporary migrants, and from their empathy with the participant in the mission. Concurrently, the participant in the debriefing session becomes more of an experimenter in the sense that he/she asks herself questions about his/her experience from a more detached point of view. There is thus for the participant a transition from participant-experimenter to experimenter-participant.

In selecting individuals for such "missions," several factors must be taken into account. The person who is involved must have certain intellectual capacities; e.g., the capacity to see a potential generality in a particular transaction, a capacity for reflection, etc. The persons must also be able to "read their bodies"; i.e., be alert to their feelings, emotions, inner tensions, etc., in their ongoing transactions with different features of the environment. Finally, there must a twofold motivation: The particular "migration" must be something in which the participant is deeply involved, even if ambivalently; the participant must also have an experimentalist's attitude, wanting to transform experiences into knowledge for himself/herself.

Kaplan, Pemstein, Cohen, and Wapner (1974)

In discussing the debriefing technique here, we are obliged to present an artificial, constructed case that, nevertheless, captures issues we believe are important in the processes of temporary migration. We do not discuss a particular case because material in such a case is characteristically too personal; we do not as yet have a sufficient number of cases so that the identity of any one participant can be obscured. What we have done here, therefore, is to construct a case on the basis of the various experiences of temporary migration by all the investigators.

With regard to the use of a debriefing technique in migration, the following should be considered: background variables concerning the participant; the nature of the instructions prior to mission; the use of debriefing after re-entry.

As to the migration proper, one can provisionally divide it into a series of chronological stages:[3] (1) pre-departure experiences of the base environment and expectations (realistic or otherwise) concerning the projected new environment; (2) transition from base to new environment; (3) initial entry into new environment; (4) processes of adaptation while in the new environment; (5) preparations to return to the base environment; (6) transition from the "new" environment to base; (7) re-entry.

[3] For other examples of analysis of stages of transition in the context of a sojourn see: Coelho (1962), Gullahorn and Gullahorn (1963), Jacobson (1963), Selltiz and Cook (1962), Schild (1962), Smith (1956).

Case A

In understanding the nature of the transactions uncovered in the debriefing with regard to each of the phases of a "migration," it is essential to know something about the status, background, and personal history of the potential migrant. In the case of A, he was an academic, middle-class, an associate professor of humanities. He was married, in his mid-thirties, with one retarded child. His wife was aspiring to a new professional career, which might require that he spend more time at home. He experienced a marked ambivalence about his home environment and considerable irritation with the institution at which he worked. He was very much concerned about his public visibility and the likelihood of advancement in his professional life. Recently, he had thought a great deal about leaving his present environment and undertaking a new direction in his life.

The temporary migration he planned had come about through the request of acquaintances he knew at a university in the British West Indies. He was one of a number of people who were being invited for a two-week professional conference. Ingredient in the invitation, at least for him, was the possibility that if he performed outstandingly, he might be offered an advanced position in the academic setting there, a position that would (at least in his imagination) provide considerably more income and allow him sufficient time for scholarly activities and sufficient occasion for "roaming the beaches."

Predeparture Transactions. In the week or so before departure, the imminence of the temporary migration suddenly struck A. Whereas earlier he had looked forward to the trip, he now began to experience a variety of conflicts. Could he leave his family for that period of time? Wasn't he shifting too much responsibility to his wife? Was this too much of a self-indulgence? Concurrently, there was the emergence of some anxiety concerning how he would be received in the new environment. Would others at the conference be more intelligent, better equipped, more personable? How about his presentation? Would he be a flop with the consequence that the possibility of changing his environment would disappear? As he oscillated, he found himself trying to detach himself from both environments. In order to forestall fear of rejection by the new environment, he found himself diminishing the value of the new place. At the same time, he found himself increasingly irritated with those in his home environment (both his family and his academic colleagues). As the day of departure came closer, he tended to automatize his behavior, arranging for the departure in an almost robotlike fashion. He bought his wife a gift—something she had wanted for a long time—partly to overcome his guilt, partly to establish his presence (the gift was an "objectification of himself") during the period he would be away.

Although he was not usually obsessive about what he wore, he became concerned with how he would present himself to the people in the new environment. He was not certain whether they expected formal or informal dress, whether he would be unfavorably regarded if he brought along a tennis racket, whether or not he should bring with him esoteric books or mystery stories. He finally packed everything.

Transitional Period Transactions.   Even in the transitional period from the base to the new environment, there was a tension between the two worlds: He reminded himself that he had to bring back with him for his family some items from the new world; at the same time, he found himself on the plane looking at a picture of his wife. Concurrently, there was also some sense of liberation. In the old environment, he had characteristically listened to music that he felt was consonant with his position. On the plane, he selected music from his playful college days, popular forms in which the lyrics emphasized a carefree mode of life. During the plane ride, there was little thought of the new environment. The transition mainly enabled an increasing distancing from the base.

The awareness of the incipient new environment came only when the announcement was made that the plane would land shortly. He was suddenly in another world. He had emerged from the zone of transition and most of his thoughts were now directed to what was to come.

Initial Entry Transactions.   The major concern during this period was that of "sizing up the environment." He found himself projecting expectations and constraints on to other members of the group. The physical differences between the old and new environment were noticed, but only marginally at first. He was more interested in locating himself *vis-à-vis* the human environment. His first contact was with someone more or less formally dressed. Immediately, on a *pars pro toto* basis, he projectively construed the new environment as one that would be highly formal, and one in which he would feel out of place. He was aware of an increasing self-consciousness, a concern with behaving in ways that would not make him conspicuous, in any negative way. He wanted very much to be able to relax and orient himself. This came about to some extent when he was finally located in a room of his own, where he could just take cognizance of himself and where he was at. Within this context he no longer felt himself as a passive respondent to others, but experienced some degree of control and self-determination. Here, again, he was less concerned with the physical aspects and trappings of the room. It was more a place where he could shut out the world if he wished or go out into the world if he wished.

From this anchor point (room as a secure new home), he felt himself able to begin to establish social relationships and to explore the physical environment. He felt that if things got too heavy he could always return to his room. As he was introduced to more and more of the conferees, he found himself dividing his human world into those people with whom he felt comfortable and able to relax, as against those with whom he felt he had to maintain a posture of a sophisticated humanist. He found himself gravitating toward a few of the conferees, with regard to whom he felt there was a kind of mutual respect. He now had a "social anchor point" as well as the *physical* anchor point of his room. He no longer felt alone. He had established sufficient analogies to his base environment to feel relatively comfortable, spontaneous, and casual.

In this process of adapting to the new environment, establishing physical and social anchor points, there were some intrusions in his thoughts pertaining to the base environment. As he became more comfortable in the new context and began to enjoy himself, there were fleeting concerns about how his wife and child were getting along without him. This prompted him to call them. He also wondered whether or not he was being missed at his institution. He didn't like the idea that his absence might not even be noticed. On one occasion, the intrusion was manifested in the following way: He found himself showing pictures of his wife and his child to his newly found friends, thus magically bridging the two worlds.

Midprocess Adaptational Transactions. With the establishment of a personal space and a social anchor point or "we group," there emerged tendencies to explore contacts with other conferees and to go farther and farther into the outside environment. He began to take walks by himself or with members of the social anchor group. There was an increasing awareness of features of the physical environment. With the sense of security provided by the anchor points, he found that he was able to expose more facets of himself to the wider range of conferees. He could take risks; he was no longer on the defensive. He could disagree with the views of others without concern about fears of rejection.

Once there had been the establishment of a sense of place in the new environment, he found himself more and more concerned with the primary mission. He was to present a paper to the conference, and his focus shifted to the presentation of that paper. He began to imagine different scenarios for the presentation. He now found himself almost exclusively occupied with the new environment with few intrusions from the old.

Preparing to Return Transactions. About two or three days prior to return to the base environment, there was an increasing psychological intrusion from that environment. He called home several times. He called the departmental secretary. At the same time, as he was preparing to rejoin the base environment, he wanted very much to hold on to the new environment. He talked about the possibility of another visit soon. He wrote down the addresses of conferees and promised to get in touch with them very soon. He discussed exchange visits to different institutions. There was even a discussion among some of the conferees about another meeting in a year, a magical device to perpetuate the new environment even as it dissolves.

As the old environment intruded, there was the beginning of attempts to distance himself from the new environment. He wasn't certain how well he had been received. He found himself, in a way, preparing for rejection and loss by devaluing the whole conference or dwelling on certain negative experiences in the conference. In going back, he wanted to bridge the two environments by bringing home some gifts that would be unexpected, that would reflect aspects of himself that he had experienced in the new context.

Transactions of Returning Transition.   In this context, he found himself on the plane with considerable ambivalence, wanting both to stay and to return. As the plane got closer to home, he found that the base environment dominated his thinking, with only fragments from his visit entering his thoughts.

Reentry.   His wife and child met him at the airport. He spent most of the time returning to his home talking about his trip and his experiences with them. He also wanted to get the sense that they missed him in his absence and were overjoyed at his return. He also wanted very much to relocate himself—as if he had not left—in his base environment, and tried to find out all the news that had taken place during his absence. He also called a few colleagues to determine whether the university was still standing and to catch up with the gossip.

What have we learned from this kind of study? Through the debriefing technique, we have become much more aware of the importance of the kinds of issues we raised at the conclusion of our discussion of the case studies using frame-sequence analysis. There is no question now that the manner in which an individual construes a new environment and engages in transactions with such an environment depends on very basic attitudes, past-history experiences, basic motivations, habitual ways of coping with stress, fundamental cognitive-affective, connotative styles, etc. On the other hand, we believe that it is necessary in the debriefing inquiry to sensitize the participant-experimenter to the variety of aspects of environmental transactions in which we are interested. This would enable us to determine the significance of the absence or presence of certain material in the protocols.

CONCLUDING REMARKS

The research we have conducted thus far has been exploratory. Guided by underlying principles and assumptions of our "organismic–developmental" approach we have adapted and constructed a variety of techniques to extend this approach to human-environment transactions. Of the three techniques discussed here (single-frame analysis, frame-sequence analysis, and debriefing analysis), we have learned that no single one suffices for the task of presenting an adequate and general characterization of the complexities of living transactions between human beings and their environments. On the other hand, we believe that the three techniques, used in interlocking fashion, can be used to complement each other and thus provide insights and questions for the generation of meaningful hypotheses, hypotheses adequate to the level of the analysis at which we wish to examine man–environment transactions.

We do not wish to suggest that there is any rationale for the sequential use of the different techniques. We believe that one can start with any one of the techniques and then go to the others. The important point here for us has been that insights and categories involved in the scrutiny of phenomena using any one technique can be applied to the examination of phenomena using the other techniques. Our understanding of the implications of the data in one set of studies was continually enriched by what we learned in analyzing the data using the other techniques.

Obviously, certain kinds of issues can be better studied through one of the techniques, if only because of issues of timing, cost, availability of collaborators, subjects, and participant experimenters, etc. It is our firm belief, however, that the complementarity of techniques is most suited to an approach that searches for both universality and comprehensiveness in dealing with the transactions of human beings and their environments.

Our future plans call, then, not for a single study of one issue or multiple studies of the same kind of issue, but for a program of studies using interrelated issues that will permit us to apply the most appropriate of the three (and probably other) techniques. Such a program will allow for transferring the benefits gained from insights coming from large-scale data collection with many subjects to cross-validation by repeatedly collecting data from a number of individuals over a long period of time; and beyond that, to the study of the complex transactions of a single individual. We see these techniques as an interconnected circle. What matters is not the technique with which one begins, but one's flexibility in transferring the insights gained from the use of one technique to the search for insights into phenomena uncovered by other techniques.

Perhaps the most important learning experience we have had this year comes from the use of these different techniques to increase our own sensitivity to the range of issues that must be taken into account, if one is to understand in any depth the factors that underly the ways in which human beings construe their environments in the process of transactions with such environments.

ACKNOWLEDGMENTS

This study was supported, in part, by Research Grant MH-00348 from the National Institute of Mental Health; and, in part, by the National Science

Foundation/Departmental Science Development Grant to the Psychology Department, Clark University, GU 03173. In addition, we wish to acknowledge the efforts of the following who helped in bringing this paper to its final form: Merrill D. Griff, Shinji Ishii, and Emelia Thamel.

REFERENCES

Coelho, G. V. Personal growth and educational development through working and studying abroad. *The Journal of Social Issues*, 1962, *18*, 55–67.

Cohen, S. B., Wapner, S., Pruginin, A., and Dandonoli, P. *The process of adaptation to a new environment: Israel*. Working notes, 1974.

Dandonoli, P., Clark, W., and Wapner, S. *Age differences in construal of a multifunctional, built environment*. Manuscript in preparation, 1974.

Edelman, E., Rierdan, J., and Wapner, S. *Differences in the linguistic representation of a macro-environment under three communication conditions. Environment and Behavior*, in press.

Gullahorn, J. T., and Gullahorn, J. E. An extension of the U-curve hypothesis. *Journal of Social Issues*, 1963, *19*, 33–47.

Jacobson, E. H. Sojourn research: a definition of the field. *Journal of Social Issues*, 1963, *19*, 123–129.

Kaplan, B., Pemstein, D., Cohen, S. B., and Wapner, S. *A new methodology for studying the processes underlying the experience of a new environment: Self-observation and group debriefing*. Working notes, 1974.

McNeil, O., and Wapner, S. *Differences in representations by black and white students of a predominately white college environment*. Manuscript in preparation, 1974.

Nahemow, L. Research in a novel environment. *Environment and Behavior*, 1971, *3*, 81–102, 72.

Park, R. E. Migration and the marginal man. *American Journal of Sociology*, 1928, *33*, 881–893.

Schild, E. O. The foreign student, as stranger, learning the norms of the host-culture. *Journal of Social Issues*, 1962, *18*, 41–54.

Schutz, A. *Collected papers*. The Hague, Netherlands: Martinus Nijhoff, 1971.

Selltiz, C., and Cook, S. W. Factors influencing attitudes of foreign students toward the host country. *The Journal of Social Issues*, 1962, *18*, 7–23.

Smith, M. B. Cross-cultural education as a research area. *Journal of Social Issues*, 1956, *7*, 3–8.

Stonequist, E. V. The problem of the marginal man. *American Journal of Sociology*, 1935, *41*, 1–12.

Wapner, S., Kaplan, B., and Cohen, S. B. An organismic-developmental perspective for understanding transactions of men in environments. *Environment and Behavior*, 1973, *5*, 255–289.

Werner, H., and Kaplan, B. *Symbol formation*. New York: Wiley, 1963.

Wofsey, L., Rierdan, J., and Wapner, S. Changes in representation of the currently inhabited environment as a function of planning to move to a new environment. *Environment and Behavior*. In press.

XI

Afterword

In this book, there is no record of the amicably sharp discussions that took place around each of the papers. Some of the questions and issues raised in these discussions are to some degree reflected in many of the papers, either in slight revisions of text or in epilogues. Nevertheless, there is no point in the preceding text where a summary is presented of the major points of controversy and consensus among the various participants. We thought that, in these closing comments, we would take it upon ourselves to state briefly our perception of the issues that united and divided those who attended the conference.

One major issue had to do with the *definition of the environment* in the study of men-in-environment relationships. Some of the participants were inclined, at least for purposes of their inquiries, to conceive of the environment in terms of independent or quasi-independent physical features—objective properties of phenomena that impinge on and affect human experience and behavior. On the other side, there were those who insisted that environments could not be characterized independent of either human perception or human action, individual and collective; this latter group appeared to reject the notion that one could speak of a determinate environment outside of human needs, interests, and characteristics. At certain points, there seemed to be some consensus that environments could be characterized on several different levels: in terms of properties (physical, chemical) articulated by natural scientists; in terms of socio-cultural categories pertaining to groups rather than individuals (socially defined features of the world); and in terms of idiosyncratic individual characterizations of what there is.

Correlative to these different conceptions of the environment, another issue pertained to the image of man underlying the different perspectives. On one side, there seemed to be the tacit conception of human beings as reagents and respondents to environmental stimuli, an image of man rooted in the classical empiricist doctrine. On the other side, there were those who stressed a view of human beings as active, striving agents, capable of construing their worlds in various ways and acting in terms of their definitions of situations.

An issue related both to the conception of the environment and to the image of man is that of the *preferred units of analysis* and *modes of analysis.*

235

Some of the participants seemed inclined toward an atomistic, elementaristic orientation, in which both environments and human beings were conceived as bundles of distinct variables; the search here was for functional relations between variables. Others were more holistic in their orientation, more or less rejecting the value of partitive analysis, of presupposing fixed dimensions of environments or of individuals. It was generally recognized that the elementaristic orientation was more in keeping with established psychological methodology, while the holistic perspective still requires more precise formulation and development. The issue here may be summarized in the question, not easily answered, whether it is preferable to have precision at the expense of validity or validity at the expense of precision.

All of the participants, despite their specific orientations, seemed to agree on the *value of diversity* of approach in this emerging field, rather than the establishment of a monolithic orientation or of canonical methods. There also was general consensus that the long-term test of any of the approaches was *applicability in everyday life* to the complex environmental transactions of human beings. Finally, most of the participants seemed to be committed, either tacitly or explicitly to the study of men-in-environment relationships in order to *improve the quality* of such relationships. This is not to say that the research reported incorporated techniques for bettering human transactions with their environments. In almost all instances, research has been directed toward discovery and not toward policy.

There were, of course, many more issues on which there was agreement and disagreement. The reader will surely have discovered these in the course of comparing the different papers. It seems to us that there is now need not only for more research in the field, but for a closer scrutiny of the hidden presuppositions and consequences of various approaches, for a more rigorous analysis and criticism of the conceptual bases underlying the different perspectives. Only if theory and method are clearly formulated and rationalized will the goal of adequate praxis be attained.

The Editors

Author Index*

* Boldface type indicates page numbers of entries on reference lists at the ends of chapters.

Subject Index